Mobile Sensors and Context-Aware Computing

Mobile Sensors and Context-Aware Computing

Manish J. Gajjar

MORGAN KAUFMANN PUBLISHERS

AN IMPRINT OF ELSEVIER

Morgan Kaufmann is an imprint of Elsevier
50 Hampshire Street, 5th Floor, Cambridge, MA 02139, United States

British Library Cataloguing-in-Publication Data
A catalogue record for this book is available from the British Library

Library of Congress Cataloging-in-Publication Data
A catalog record for this book is available from the Library of Congress

ISBN: 978-0-12-801660-2

For Information on all Morgan Kaufmann publications
visit our website at https://www.elsevier.com/books-and-journals

Working together
to grow libraries in
developing countries

www.elsevier.com • www.bookaid.org

Publisher: Jonathan Simpson
Acquisition Editor: Jonathan Simpson
Editorial Project Manager: Lindsay Lawrence
Production Project Manager: Punithavathy Govindaradjane
Cover Designer: Alan Studholme

Typeset by MPS Limited, Chennai, India

Dedicated to my parents Jayantkumar and Indiraben
Inspiration to Aryan and Amani

Contents

Preface

Today, technology is fast growing in fields such as virtual reality, merged reality, drones, automated driving, artificial intelligence, gaming, and so on. For all of these applications, sensors and sensor technologies play a key role that radically enriches user experience and allows the user to be the focus of all actions or applications. For example, with a combination of advanced drones, cameras, and computer technology, virtual reality has the potential to save lives during search and rescue missions, or it can ensure safer workplaces by allowing employees to conduct dangerous inspections from a safe distance, or it can enable a global engineering team of an auto company to simultaneously walk around the engine they are developing as if they were in the same room.

I had an opportunity to work in the exciting field of sensors during my 20-year career at Intel spanning hardware development, validation, and prototyping. The industry today has various implementation architectures for sensors-related technology. As I tried to understand these concepts and technologies, I found that there is a need to document the basic and fundamental concepts of this field in order for me to drive product planning, architecture, development, prototyping, and validation.

This book is an attempt to introduce the audience to the basics of the fast and growing field of mobile computing and sensor ecosystems. It includes aspects of the field such as sensors and sensor usages, sensor platforms, converged hardware—software architecture, prototyping architectures, and product life cycle, which enhance user experiences.

With any new technology transition, hardware is typically first in the market before the rest of the ecosystem needed to drive the new technology mainstream. The book highlights the importance of hardware—software codesign and the use of prototyping platforms to enable covalidation in an effort to reduce the overall cost and time to market.

As a faculty member during my tenure at California State University, I have realized the importance of comprehensive reference books and hence this text is developed for use in university-level graduate or elective undergraduate course offerings. It is also intended for use by researchers, and computing professionals interested in research and development activities and would like a reference presentation put together from various, different experiences in the field of smart sensor technology, and context-aware computing.

Acknowledgments

Thank you God for giving me the strength, opportunity, and for being with me at every moment of my life.

I am dedicating this book to my parents whose determination, sacrifice, and struggle to provide me with the best possible environment throughout my life is the reason behind everything that I am today. My Father, a retired professor of physics and electronics, has always been my guiding light, a friend, and a role model. My mother is my first teacher and a powerful source of my lifelong inspiration and motivation. I bow down to them with love and respect and wish that they be my parents every time I am born. I also want to thank my lovely sister Jigisha who along with my parents worked hard to remove every obstacle in my life and paved a path of success for me.

I am grateful to Dr. Suresh Vadhva (Professor, Computer Architecture & Software Engineering, California State University, Sacramento) and Dr. S.K. Ramesh (Dean, College of Engineering and Computer Science, California State University, Northridge) who selflessly nurtured me at the universities, and guided me through my career. They empowered me to contribute at Intel and as a faculty/industry advisor at the California universities. I am also obliged to all my school teachers and professors.

I want to thank all reviewers, mentors, industry technologists, and my managers at Intel whose collective contributions have made it possible for me to present the content in this book.

Special thanks to Dr. Tushar Toprani, my friend and a blessing in my life, without whom it would have been impossible to manage through the struggles of life. I also want to thank all my friends for supporting me at crucial moments.

Through this book, I want to acknowledge God's grace which has given me my wonderful family with wife Neeta, son Aryan and daughter Amani.

Introduction

INFORMATION IN THIS CHAPTER:

- Definition of Mobile Computing
- Constraints and the Challenges Faced by Mobile Computing System
- Historical Perspectives and the Influences of Market
- Market Trends and Growth Areas

DEFINITION OF MOBILE COMPUTING

Mobile computing refers to the computing that happens when the user interacts while the computer or parts of the computer are in motion during the use. Hardware components (like computing silicon, various sensors, and input/output devices), software components (like programs that communicates with underlying hardware, device drivers, applications, and software stacks to support communication protocols), and communication protocols like Wi-Fi protocols and hypertext transfer protocol (HTTP) are some of the main components of mobile computing. Through these components user-to-computer or computer-to-computer communications/computing happens.

The following are the three main classes of mobile computing:

- *Mobile phones*: Mobile phones are primarily used for voice calls and voice communication but with the advent of smartphones these devices are now used for computing applications, games, and data access over Wi-Fi or other wireless networks. These devices are increasingly adding to computational capabilities.
- *Portable computers*: Portable computers are devices with only essential computing components and input/output devices. These are lighter in weight than desktops, and weight reduction is achieved through removal of nonessential input/output devices like disc drives, use of compact hard drives, and so on. Extra connecting ports like USB and Firewire are used to connect external I/O drives or other devices if needed. These compact, lightweight computers have full-character-set keyboards and host software like Windows, Android, and Mac OS. Examples are laptops, notebooks, tablets, notepads, and so on.

Mobile Sensors and Context-Aware Computing. DOI: http://dx.doi.org/10.1016/B978-0-12-801660-2.00001-X

- *Wearable computers*: These are mobile computing devices that have the technology that users may want to put on their body with the dual purpose of fashion plus computation/connection to the external world through wireless or communication protocols. These devices are capable of sensing, computing, running applications/software, reporting, and connecting. Examples are watches, wristbands, necklaces, keyless implants, and so on, which can take voice commands, or sense various environmental or health parameters and communicate either with mobile phones, portable computers, or the Internet.

Let us evaluate the differences of mobile computing devices versus other computing devices, as shown in Table 1.1.

Table 1.1 Quick Comparison Between Different Forms of Mobile Computing Devices

	Mobile Phones and Smartphones	Tablets	Laptop	Wearables
Primary use	Phone/voice communication; text messages	Surf web, video chatting, social networking	Computing, cannot make phone calls (need to use VOIP/software to make calls)	Fashion + sensing environment/ health parameters
Features	Virtual keyboard on screen	Virtual keyboard on screen	Full keyboard (including virtual keyboard), better multimedia experience, bigger screen	Sensors, no keyboard, no multimedia, extremely small screen if any
Connectivity	Wi-Fi, 3G/4G, etc.	Wi-Fi, 3G/4G, etc. (sometimes with additional cost)	Has Wi-Fi but 3G/4G, etc. connectivity comes with additional costs	Wi-Fi, Voice networks (3G/4G, etc.)
Usage	Make calls, surf net, take pictures, shoot videos, chat live with friends, social networking	Connectivity and basic computing, watching videos, social networking	Basic computing functions, watching videos and listening to MP3 songs on the Internet, take picture/videos, social networking, play a CD or DVD	Sensing, computing, reporting user health or environment parameters surrounding the user

(Continued)

Table 1.1 Quick Comparison Between Different Forms of Mobile Computing Devices *Continued*

	Mobile Phones and Smartphones	Tablets	Laptop	Wearables
Form factor	Very portable, able to carry in pocket	Heavier than phones but lighter and smaller than laptops	It is heavier, has bigger screens, additional I/O devices like CD or DVD drivers	Designer form factor that user can wear
Software/ applications	Apple iOS, Android and Win OS. Additional custom applications downloaded as needed	Apple iOS, Android, Win OS, Linux. Custom Applications downloaded as needed	Can run almost all desktop software and operating system	Custom OS and applications to collect, compute, and report sensing data

CONSTRAINTS AND THE CHALLENGES FACED BY MOBILE COMPUTING SYSTEMS

Mobile computing devices have a smaller form factor than traditional desktops. There is need to impose constraints on space, weight, and form factors of these devices since their users are on the move while computing or connecting. These constraints in turn impose various technological and design restrictions on the devices. Let us briefly look at those restrictions:

RESOURCE POOR

A computer system requires various components to process, compute, or connect. Hence any device in the computer system or connected to the computer system is a *resource* or *system resource*. These resources can be physical or virtual component. Example of such resources include the CPU, RAM, hard disks, storage devices, various input/output devices like printers, and connectivity components like Wi-Fi or modem. Mobile computing devices are resource limited. For example, their screens and keyboards are small, they have reduced I/O connections, reduced RAM, power storage, and so forth. This makes them challenging to use, program, and operate.

Resource restrictions can be mitigated with the use of alternate methods for input, storage, processing, and so on. For example, alternate input methods of speech or handwriting recognition can be used instead of keyboards, alternate storage methods such as cloud storage can be used instead of hard disks, and cloud computing can be used for certain processing instead of more power hungry on device CPU. These methods however require training of the devices and efficient communication capabilities.

LESS SECURED/RELIABLE

All compute devices have important resources and store valuable data and/or programs. It is important to protect access to all of these compute resources and data through user recognition and user authentication. Appropriate gatekeeper procedures and mechanisms should be deployed to protect the underlying data, programs, and applications while enforcing appropriate privacy guidelines and protocols. Since mobile devices are mostly in transit, their security becomes increasingly more challenging since these devices may use wireless channels, public resources, or networks that can provide easy access to these mobile systems.

With the explosion in smartphone usage, a lot of personal information is now saved and stored on smartphones. Users employ smartphones for communication, planning, organizing, and accessing and processing financial transactions.

Hence smartphones and information systems supporting them carry increasingly more sensitive data, thereby introducing new security risks while posing serious privacy access and processing complexities.

Some of the sources of security risks are

- Through messaging systems like SMS, MMS
- Through connection channels like Wi-Fi networks, GSM
- Through software/OS vulnerabilities to external attacks
- Through malicious software and user ignorance about it.

Some of the mitigation options are

- Use of encryption methods (Wired Equivalent Privacy: WEP, Wi-Fi Protected Access: WPA/WPA2) encryption
- Using VPN or HTTPS to access Wi-Fi/Internet
- Allow only known MAC addresses to join or connect to known MAC addresses only.

INTERMITTENT CONNECTIVITY [1]

Mobile computing devices may be away from various communication infrastructures like Wi-Fi or the Internet for considerable periods of time. However to access required data and programs stored at remote locations, they need to be connected even if possible only intermittently. Such intermittent connectivity needs a different kind of data transfer mechanism that can handle power management issues, package loss issues, and the like.

Mobile devices need data to be buffered in the case where only intermittent connections to the network are possible. To prevent any data loss, the data transfer mechanisms in mobile devices need to handle cases when data is generated or received more frequently than the available connectivity. There could also be interruptions, interference, downtime, and so on that cause interruptions in communication links. Power scarcity can also cause a device to throttle communication or a connection. In such cases mobile devices and their data transfer mechanisms should be able to effectively and efficiently manage all available resources and connection time while avoiding user noticeable data loss.

Mobile devices should also be able to handle and deploy additional mechanisms to support interoperability (rate, routing, and addressing methodology) among communication protocols because it may dynamically move from one protocol to another during device transit.

ENERGY CONSTRAINED [2]

The lack of a readily available power source, smaller and compact size and resources for power storage and complex data management, security requirements, and connectivity requirements make energy availability and battery life a key constraint for mobile devices.

In addition, mobile devices use power-hungry sensing, storage, and communication capabilities but have some very stringent power and thermal budgets. These devices are without fans, are often in close skin contact with the user, and have restricted surface area; hence they are limited by peak power consumption since the user experience is affected by the temperature of the device. This further underscores why power management and battery life are key design parameters and constraints for mobile devices.

A mitigation plan for these challenges includes power management with an emphasis on platform power optimization and user experience:

- Platform power and optimization: the power management policy should be inclusive of available hardware resources of the mobile platform and manage their operation for energy efficiency.
- User experience: the usage of mobile devices extends from CPU- or graphics-intensive usage to sensor-heavy usage. Various location-based services and applications would require sensors like accelerometers, gyrometers, and cameras. Applications using touch capabilities would require quick exit from power-managed states and gaming applications would require higher throughput with brighter display. Thus power management system should consider these use cases, and corresponding system responsiveness requirements.

Thus mobile devices need hardware resources that provide various low-power states along with energy-aware operating systems and applications. Both hardware and software should be intelligent to incorporate user interaction, sensor inputs, and computational and protocol optimizations and their dynamic behavior/loads.

HISTORICAL PERSPECTIVES AND THE INFLUENCES OF MARKET

The following are some of the key factors influencing the move to mobile computing. Some of these factors also influence the form factors within mobile computing options.

ENHANCED USER EXPERIENCE

Mobile computing changes our approach to connectivity: in how we connect to different geographical locations, different people, cultures, and processes. It changes the way we gather, interact with, and process the information based on various sensing applications and location-based services. It enhances our perception of the digital world and merges that digital world with our physical world. It increases our computing power over our traditional standalone and stationary computers while enabling us to carry this enhanced computing experiences to carry it around wherever we desire.

Improved applications have been developed to harness hardware resources: various leading providers (such as Apple and Google) are offering many applications that extend the range of functionality of smartphones and other mobile devices, such as application to measure the heart rate using the rear camera of a smartphone. Such applications use hardware for functions other than their primary functions thereby extending the capabilities of mobile devices beyond traditional usage.

IMPROVED TECHNOLOGY

With improved technology, mobile devices now have improved battery life, faster processors, user-friendly and lightweight manufacturing materials, power-efficient flexible displays, and high-bandwidth networks. The devices also have numerous sensors like biometric sensors, temperature and pressure sensors, pollution sensors, and location sensors. There are also infrared keyboards, gesture and retina tracking sensors, enhanced artificial intelligence, and new context-aware user interfaces. All these features increase the clarity of videos, images, text, and the like while generating new use cases and applications, making it possible to manufacture mobile devices in various shapes, forms, and designs.

NEW FORM FACTORS

The way the user interacts with and uses mobile devices will change with advancements in the underlying technology. For example, a user has to reach his/her pocket many times a day (typically 150 times a day) to access a smartphone, but as the proliferation of wearables increases over time, much of this access will become hands-free. The amount of data and content uploaded from mobile devices is also increasing at an amazing growth rate. The uploaded content includes images, video, music, and so forth, but with increasing use of wearable devices (such as Nike Fuel and Google Glass), more personal data related to fitness, financial information, location services, and so on would be uploaded.

INCREASED CONNECTIVITY/COMPUTING OPTIONS

There is now an abundance of wireless connectivity through various means like cellular mobile networks, wireless LAN, Bluetooth, ZigBee, ultra-wideband networks, Wi-Fi, and satellite networks. Additionally, with the birth of cloud computing, users are now also offered shared resources along with connectivity. The user is no longer tied to a particular location or device to upload, access, or share data. Availability of such a wide variety of connectivity and "shared computing" options has enabled both personal and business users to add more mobile devices/computing on such networks to improve their mobility and reduce infrastructure costs for business/personal data sharing.

MARKET TRENDS AND GROWTH AREAS

There are three fundamental driving factors for the growth of mobile computing devices: new sensor technology and products, sensor fusion, and new application areas.

NEW SENSOR TECHNOLOGY AND PRODUCTS [3–5]

Sensors are fundamental to the growth in mobile device functionality. Technological progress and enhanced functionalities of mobile MEMS (micro-electronics-mechanical systems) sensors like microphones, cameras, accelerometers, gyroscopes, and magnetometers have enabled services like navigation, context awareness, location-based services, and augmented reality in the mobile computing devices.

Cameras and display technologies are showing considerable innovation with touch sensors, flexible and energy-efficient displays that brings reality to images, videos, and even 3D perception. For example, multiple cameras are being used to track user eye movements to highlight only relevant sections of the display while masking the "not needed" text or images on other parts of the display.

There is also an emergence of wearable technology, particularly related to health and fitness, which rely heavily on sensors that measures temperature, pressure, humidity, physical activity, and other key aspects of the body.

The worldwide wearable computing device market [6] (wearables) is expected to reach 126.1 million units by year 2019, with higher volumes expected to be driven by increasing end-user acceptance of wearables and increasing number of vendors entering the market with more device variations.

The key takeaways from the current market analysis are:

- Basic wearables that do not run third party applications will reach 52.3 million units in 2019.
- Smart wearables which run third party applications on them will grow at a faster rate than the basic wearables and is expected to reach 73.8 million units in 2019.
- Wrist worn wearables will account for 80% of all wearable shipments by 2019.
- The worldwide wearables market revenue opportunity is expected to reach 27.9 billion by 2019.

The market analysis could be impacted by the following potential scenarios over the next 5 years:

- The mobile market plateaus and the PC regains traction, thereby cooling off the MEMS market. This might seem unlikely but 5 years ago no one would have predicted that the PC market would stall in the way that it has.
- Wearables take off in a big way, with Google Glass leading to Kindle Glass and iGlass, giving MEMS sensors an even bigger boost.
- New classes of devices emerge, fueling even greater demand for MEMS.

Fig. 1.1 shows the worldwide wearables shipment for basic and smart wearables.

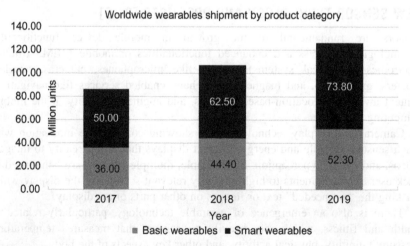

FIGURE 1.1

Worldwide wearables shipments by product category, 2017–19 [7].

Fig. 1.2 shows the worldwide wearables average selling price for basic and smart wearables.

Fig. 1.3 shows the worldwide wearables revenue for basic and smart wearables.

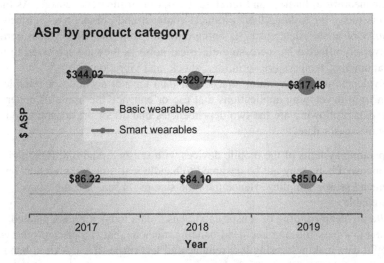

FIGURE 1.2

Worldwide wearable technology ASP by product category, 2017–19 [7].

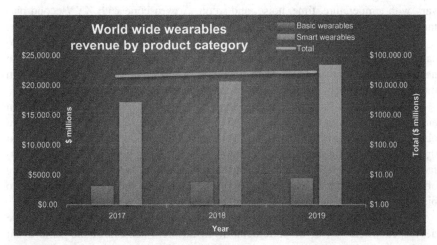

FIGURE 1.3

Worldwide wearables revenue by product category, 2017–19 [7].

SENSOR FUSION

Sensor fusion [7] is the process of merging data from different sensors such that final output data conveys more information than each of the individual sensors whose data was merged.

Today's smartphones and tablets are not exactly ideal sensing platforms, due to their inability to harness and redefine the power of inherent sensors. As manufacturers today try to keep their products compact and competitively priced, the reliability of underlying sensors is compromised, while the sensor measurements are adversely affected by increasing electrical noise as they are subjected to magnetic anomalies, temperature variations, shock, and vibrations.

Developers today may think that sensor data are not accurate or reliable and refrain from developing applications that use or enhance the usage of underlying sensor data. Following are the two dependencies that affect the accuracy and reliability the sensor data:

- Operating systems of the mobile devices with sensors: Android, IOS, and Windows Phone may not be designed to handle real-time tasks such as on-demand sensor sampling. Hence the time stamps on sensor samples are unreliable.
- Filtering/dead-banding of sensor data: Sensor data today are manipulated using low-pass filtering and dead-banding methods that can discard otherwise useful data making sensing less reliable and less responsive. (A dead band is a band where no actions occur.)

For example, a gyroscope will have numerous error sources. One of the error sources is gyroscope bias. Bias is the signal output when the gyro is not experiencing any rotation. It represents a rotational velocity. This bias error will vary with temperature, time, noise, and so on. A gyroscope with $XY°$/second bias may appear to be spinning when the device is at rest (Fig. 1.4).

A magnetometer measures Earth's magnetic field and its readings are used to calculate the heading of the rigid body. But it also suffers from errors resulting in heading errors (such as those from magnetic materials in the sensor, noise from magnetic components inside the sensor, or from nearby ferrous objects).

Accelerometers measure proper/g-force acceleration. This is the acceleration an object experiences relative to freefall and is the acceleration felt by people and objects. But it also suffers from bias. This bias is the difference between the ideal $0g$ output and the $0g$ output reported by the sensor. On a perfectly horizontal surface, if there were no bias error, then the sensor output would read the ideal $0g$ offset voltage on the x- and y-axis, $+1g$ output voltage on the z-axis but due to bias error, it would show values other than ideal values.

So each of the individual sensors have biases and errors. An algorithm can be developed where sensor measurements from different sensors of the same event can be processed to separate out the real data and noise/sensor errors. This process is known as *sensor fusion*. With appropriate implementation of such

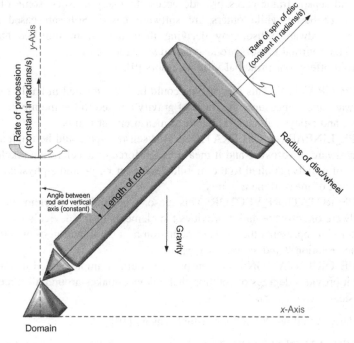

Rate of spin of disc
(constant in radians/s)

Rate of precession
(constant in radians/s)   y-Axis

Radius of disc/wheel

Angle between
rod and vertical
axis (constant)

Length of rod

Gravity

x-Axis

Domain

FIGURE 1.4

Gyroscope basics [8].

algorithms, the perception of ideal responsiveness can be maintained while offsetting errors and shortcomings of individual sensors, thereby providing useful and reliable results.

For example, if a gyroscope is used along with an accelerometer and magnetometer to determine the device's absolute orientation (the 3D rotation angle), then the sensor fusion process can be used to generate an interpreted event by collecting data from the three different sensors, performing mathematical calculations to remove individual sensor biases and errors, converting resultant data into format suitable to the developer and representing it in the same form of "interpreted events." Such interpreted events can be considered as output of "virtual sensors" and be represented in the same form as original sensor events. These virtual sensors provide a solution and measurements that cannot be obtained from any single sensor. Measurements from virtual sensors are in between what can actually be measured on real sensors and the ideal measurement desired by the developers. Sensor fusion algorithms can reside in low-level code, in the sensor itself, or as part of application, and they can remove the biases and errors, thus providing designers with greater flexibility in selecting and combining sensor components.

Android sensor frameworks provide access to many sensors, some of which are hardware based while others are software based. Software-based sensors mimic the hardware sensors by deriving their data from multiple hardware sensors. These virtual sensors are also called *synthetic sensors.*

Android offers four principal virtual sensors [9]:

I. TYPE_GRAVITY: This sensor type could be implemented in hardware or software and it measures the force of gravity applied to the mobile device on x-, y-, and z-physical axes. The unit of measurement is m/s^2.

II. TYPE_LINEAR_ACCELERATION: This sensor type could be implemented in hardware or software and it measures the force of acceleration (excluding force of gravity) applied to the mobile device on x-, y-, and z-physical axes. The unit of measurement is m/s^2.

III. TYPE_ROTATION_VECTOR: This sensor type could be implemented in hardware or software and it provides the elements of the device's rotation vector that represents the device orientation as a combination of an angle of device rotation θ and an axis $<x, y, z>$.

IV. TYPE_ORIENTATION: This sensor type could be implemented in software and it provides degrees of rotation that a device makes around all three physical axes (x, y, z).

Similarly, Windows 8 has four virtual sensors [10]:

I. ORIENTATION SENSOR: This sensor provides information regarding the device rotation in three dimensions. It is similar to Android TYPE_ROTATION_VECTOR sensor rather than Android TYPE_ORIENTATION.

II. INCLINOMETER: This sensor provides information on the Euler angles (yaw, pitch, roll) values corresponding to the rotational angles around the device's x-, y-, and z-axes, respectively.

III. TILT-COMPENSATED COMPASS: This sensor provides information on the device's heading (device's direction [11]) with respect to true north or even magnetic north based on sensor capability in the plane perpendicular to gravity.

IV. SHAKE: This sensor reports the event when the device is shaken (in any direction).

The mentioned android and windows virtual sensors are implemented using sensor fusion. They provide information related to user context and hence help in developing context-aware applications.

Fig. 1.5 shows example of fusion sensor compass generated from basic sensors [11].

Fig. 1.6 shows example of fusion sensor for device orientation generated from basic sensors.

Fig. 1.7 shows example of fusion sensor inclinometer generated from basic sensors.

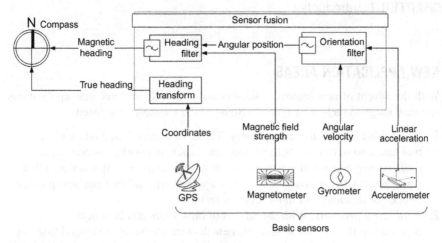

FIGURE 1.5

Sensor fusion via combining output from multiple sensors (compass).

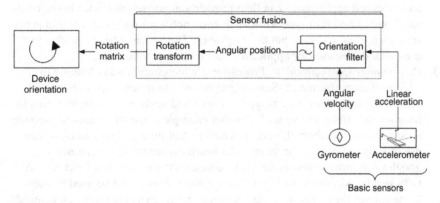

FIGURE 1.6

Sensor fusion via combining output from multiple sensors (device orientation).

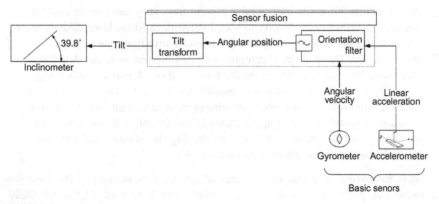

FIGURE 1.7

Sensor fusion via combining output from multiple sensors (inclinometer).

NEW APPLICATION AREAS

With the advent of new improved sensors and sensor algorithms, new applications and new usage models are expected. Some of the examples are listed:

1. *Companion devices for smartphones*: These are sensor-based add-on devices that can send notifications to smartphones, such as jewelry connecting to users' smartphones and alerting them of notifications or a fitness watch that can connect to four smartphone fitness applications and that can also provide phone notifications and music control features.
2. *Healthcare products*: With the advent of biosensors and healthcare applications that use these sensors, new devices are being developed that can measure various biodata like pressure, glucose, and heart rate, and upload to a dedicated cloud service so that the data can then be shared with family, and doctors. For example, a sun intensity sensor can measure total daily exposure. Its associated applications can then provide sun protection advice based on the user's habits and skin type while delivering notifications about when to apply sunscreen, wear a hat, or put on sunglasses. The personal health market that uses such devices/sensor applications is growing at a fast rate.
3. *Professional sports products*: Professional athletes are always looking to analyze their performance. Sensors can be used to measure gyroscopic and vibrational data of a tennis player's racquet and applications can offer tips to improve the stroke and control. Another example is use of sensors to measure a user's swing in baseball, golf, or tennis in real time and professionals can use this data to perfect the swing. The heartbeat sensor in a swimmer's googles can provide instant visual feedback on the swimmer's heart rate. A GPS watch and fitness tracker with low-power sensors can be used to track the user over the course of fitness training. Such devices/sensors can demand premium price in the professional sports and coaching market.
4. *Life-logging devices*: Life-logging devices and applications help users to pass the content directly to social networking sites. These devices, e.g., have Wi-Fi, Bluetooth, LTE, and cellular capabilities. They can stream content through cloud services directly to social networking sites. Users like extreme sports enthusiasts can feed their social streams with real-time content.
5. *Nanosensors*: These are new categories of flexible sensor under development that could be used in clothing, on the body, and on objects to track things like strain, pressure, human touch, and bioelectronic signals. These sensors will kick-start innovations in embedded sensors in objects such as clothing and could have a wide range of applications in sport (athlete fitness tracking), healthcare (precise patient monitoring), gaming (immersive and accurate controls), and entertainment (gesture controls).

It is forecasted [12] that the number of applications developed for wearable devices will grow at a compounded annual growth rate of 81.5% till 2020. Applications for Smartwatch, and eyewear for gaming and enterprise use cases would be enabled by augmented reality and will drive upward growth.

A significant growth is also expected in the area of artificial intelligence and machine learning applications which is crucial for user experience in wearables, automotive and home environments.

REFERENCES

[1] Ho M, Fall K. Delay tolerant networking for sensor networks, poster.

[2] Umit Y, Ayoub RZ, Kadjo D. Managing mobile power, Publication: ICCAD 2013.

[3] Kingsley-Hughes A. for Hardware 2.0 | May 29, 2013 | Topic: Mobility. Mobile micro sensors estimated to generate almost $8 billion by 2018: report, online report/news.

[4] Juniper research report.

[5] Llamas RT. U.S. wearable computing device 2014–2018 forecast and analysis, IDC: Market Analysis.

[6] Llamas RT. Worldwide wearables 2015–2019 forecast, IDC: Market Analysis.

[7] Steele J, Sensor Platforms. Electronic design: understanding virtual sensors: from sensor fusion to context-aware applications, July 10, 2012.

[8] Gyroscope Physics, online reference from Real World Physics problems.

[9] Sensors Overview: Android, <http://developer.android.com/guide/topics/sensors/sensors_overview.html>, online Android reference.

[10] Gael H (Intel), Added September 4, 2013. Intel: Ultrabook™ and Tablet Windows* 8 Sensors development guide.

[11] Course (navigation). <https://en.wikipedia.org/wiki/Course_(navigation)>.

[12] Jackson J, Llamas RT. Worldwide wearable applications forecast update, 2016–2020, Market Forecast.

Context-aware computing

2

INFORMATION IN THIS CHAPTER:

- Context-Aware Computing
- Context
- Location Awareness
- Location Sources in Mobile Phones
- Localization Algorithms
- Navigation
- Other Approaches to Localization

CONTEXT-AWARE COMPUTING

Let us start by exploring what content means. Context means user's preferences, likings, dislikes, location, and general awareness of the surrounding environment in which the user is operating, located, or situated. Examples of awareness of the surrounding environment could be information related to weather, climate, traffic, the time of the day, or physical location of the user. It could also be information related to user's computing device like battery level, available network bandwidth, available Wi-Fi infrastructure, and so on.

Now we shall expand this basic definition of context to context computing. Context-aware computing is the computing environment that is aware of the context of the computing device, computing infrastructure, or the user. A computing device could be any of various devices including smartphones, tablets, wearables, or traditional devices like laptops and desktops. Computing infrastructure can include hardware, software, applications, network bandwidth, Wi-Fi bandwidth and protocols, and battery information.

A smartphone, e.g., is a computing device that is aware of the surrounding context. The computing infrastructure, such as its operating system, acquires this context, stores it, processes it, and then responds to the context by either changing or adapting its functionality or behavior. It will also make certain context-aware

Mobile Sensors and Context-Aware Computing. DOI: http://dx.doi.org/10.1016/B978-0-12-801660-2.00002-1

decisions. The computing infrastructure could process and respond to the context with minimal or no inputs from its user. Some of the examples of how context-aware infrastructure do and will respond are as follows:

- A smartphone could detect that it is in a crowded place like an airport, railway station, or mall and automatically change the device behavior to implement noise cancellation algorithms. This would enable the device to respond better to a user's voice commands.
- Smartphones could detect the location of the user and alter its functionality, such as, e.g., by automatically increasing or decreasing speaker volume, or changing to silent mode if the user is in the meeting, change ringtones based on whether the user is at home, at the office, or traveling by car.
- Smartphones could automatically respond to certain calls with messages if the user were in the office or driving. It could even block some calls based on the user's location context.
- Wearables could use environmental context and automatically compensate its calculations for calories burned.
- A smart watch could automatically adjust daylight savings or time zone based on the location context.
- Traditional or contemporary smart devices can use location-based services to suggest dining locations, entertainment centers in the area, or even emergency services like hospitals and urgent care centers.

A context-aware device can acquire context data through various mechanisms like generic or specific sensors, through the Internet, via GPS, or through a history of logs, past decisions, locations, or actions. Today sensor types and availability have increased and become more sophisticated. This enables a large number of context-aware use cases on devices like tablets, wearables, smartphones, and even on traditional laptops and desktops. Even basic gyroscopes, accelerometers, and magnetometers can acquire direction and orientation data, resulting in use cases like shutting down when an accidental fall is detected or suggest upcoming dinning place or gas station based on the current user location.

Thus context awareness is now becoming a necessity for various computing devices and infrastructure, including applications, in order to make smart decisions, predict user actions, and alter device functionality in order to reduce the need for users to manually input context-related information (Fig. 2.1).

LEVELS OF INTERACTIONS FOR CONTEXT-AWARE INFRASTRUCTURE

There are three level of interactivity for context-aware computing, infrastructure, or applications:

1. Personalization: Here users specify their own settings/environment that controls how the context-aware infrastructure (hardware, software, applications, and so on) should behave or respond in a given situation.

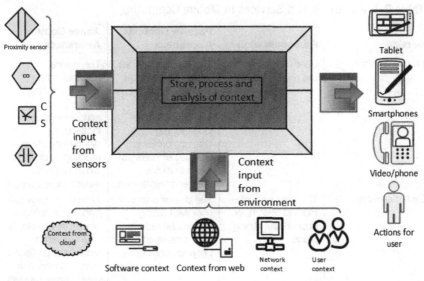

FIGURE 2.1

Concept of context-aware computing.

2. **Passive context awareness:** In this case the context-aware infrastructure provides the user with information from the sensors or changes that occurred in the previous context; however the infrastructure does not act or change behavior based on this. The user decides on the course of action based on the updated context information.

3. **Active context awareness:** In this case the context-aware infrastructure collects, processes, and takes all required actions based on the sensor or context information. It offloads the work from the user by taking active decisions.

Table 2.1 lists some categories of context-aware applications and services based on the level of interaction with the user [1].

UBIQUITOUS COMPUTING

The word *ubiquitous* means omnipresent, universal, global, or ever-present. Ubiquitous computing means a computing environment that appears to be present everywhere, anywhere, and anytime. Unlike a traditional unconnected desktop computer, which is stationary and can only be accessed while sitting in front of it, the concept of ubiquitous computing points to availability of a computing power through use of any device or infrastructure, in any location, in any format, and at any given time.

Table 2.1 Context-Based Services in Mobile Computing

Service	Personalization	Passive Context Awareness	Active Context Awareness
Ringing profiles	User manually sets the ringing profiles	The device provides options to the user to change ringing profile based on sensor data on location, e.g., different profile in meeting or class vs when in movie theater or restaurant	The device automatically changes ringing profile based on sensor data on location, e.g., different profile in meeting or class vs when in movie theater or restaurant
Dining services	The user performs manual search for appropriate dining place	The device prompts user with dining options based on user's preference or previous choices	The device provides options of dining places when user is near preferred location at preferred time and matches user criteria (reviews, cost, menu choices, etc.)
Document search	The user performs manual search for appropriate documents on the device	Based on user preference, the device provides options to load/ download or bring up the document	The device automatically load/ downloads or brings up the document based on user's location, preferences, and time
Location-based services (such as identifying friends in vicinity, changing device profiles, display backgrounds, sounds, and content)	The user performs manual search/ changes in preferred services User sets the device to display user's situation/ location. User can manually set other preferences/ services based on location	The device provides the user with options to perform search/changes in preferred services based on user location The device can prompt user to display user's status, location, etc. to potential callers, or options to block calls	The device automatically performs search/ changes in preferred services based on user location The device automatically displays user's status, location, etc. to potential callers, or even blocks certain calls based on user location or alerts users of known persons or friends in the vicinity

A user today interacts with the computing environment through a number of different devices like laptops, smartphones, tablets, phablets, and even connected home appliances like microwaves or refrigerators. With the availability of wearables like smart watches and Google Glass, the access to the underlying computing environment has become really ubiquitous.

There are many essential components of compute infrastructure that enable the concept of ubiquitous computing. Some of these components are: the Internet, wireless or network protocols, operating systems supporting ubiquitous behavior, middleware or firmware, sensors and context-aware devices, microprocessors, and other computer hardware.

Ubiquitous computing can provide users with two crucial user-experience enhancing qualities: "invisibility" and "proactivity." For example, imagine a completely context-aware shopping experience where user does not have to wait at traditional checkout lines but instead can automatically scan the basket for all goods, scan the user's device/identity, and charge the relevant credit card based on the user's preferences. In this case the individual serial process of checkout is completely invisible to the user and the system can be proactive in identifying the user and payment method, thereby enhancing the user's shopping experience in terms of time and ease of use.

In ubiquitous computing, computers are no longer tied to physical space like in a computer room or laboratory, but can be deployed and accessed at arbitrary locations throughout the world. Due to this phenomenon, the following changes have occurred in computing devices:

1. Form factor changes: These simple form factor changes in display size, hardware sizes, and so on supported the physical movement of computers outside of the traditional room. However, such computers lacked sensitivity to any attributes of the surrounding environment.
2. Context-sensitive changes: Changes needed to be made to overcome the drawback of insensitivity to the surrounding environment. Initially the sensitivity was limited to detecting other compute devices nearby but later it expanded into parameters like time and light intensity of the day/night, light level, amount of nearby cell-phone traffic at the current physical location, identity or role of the person using the computer, roles of other persons near the computer, vibration, and so on.

In general, context-aware computing attempts to use *When (time)*, *Where (location)*, *Who (identity)*, *What (activity)*, and *Why (usage)* as part of its decision-making algorithms.

Examples: In an exercise room, context-aware computing will sense when to infer the possible tastes of the user to control the type of music and control the sound system accordingly. Or in some other use case, an algorithm can use various other environmental parameters like sound or light level to infer whether a particular message can be sent to the user or not.

CHALLENGES OF UBIQUITOUS COMPUTING

The key issue [2] of the sensors and their network, however, is that since sensors are inaccurate, they make the computing environment uncertain and probabilistic. The following are the few examples of uncertainties:

Where uncertainty: Location sensors reports location probability of "true" location on X, Y, and Z space.

Who uncertainty: Face recognition sensor returns the probability that it has just seen a particular person through probability distribution.

What uncertainty: A camera sensor trying to recognize an object will send a set of estimates as to the object seen (again a probability distribution).

Let us now also explore the system level challenges of ubiquitous computing.

Power management: Ubiquitous computing requires ubiquitous power. There are three main components or sources of power consumption in ubiquitous computing devices: processing, storage, and communication.

Processing for ubiquitous computing platforms is highly variable since it can vary from simple applications to computationally intensive tasks. There are many controls available for controlling power consumption in a single processing unit, such as power-gating certain units or blocks inside the processor when not in use or lowering operating voltages to slow down energy consumption. The platform can also use multiple task-specific processing units or processors to perform specific tasks, thereby gating power to other blocks when not needed for that specific task. For example, one could have a minute processor for addressing and handling sensor interrupts/data while utilizing a high-performing processor for full function computations and a network processor for processing network data. The software in the case of multiple processing components needs to be able to dynamically control and gate power to certain blocks, while running required processing components at full voltage or reduced voltage depending on the requirement of a particular task.

Just like processing units, the wireless interface and protocol used affects the power requirements and policy of a ubiquitous computing platform. For example, Wi-Fi, Bluetooth, ZigBee, and ultra-wide band are some of the standards with varying capabilities and characteristics. Each of the protocol has defined power and performance settings (like transmit strength and duty cycle) that can be effectively used to manage power in the platform. Multiple protocols can be used in the platform depending on the targeted use cases. For example, Wi-Fi is used for home networks and Internet, while Bluetooth is used for hands-free or voice communication on mobile phones. The operating software on a ubiquitous platform needs to transparently provide the user with services that consider different power-performance characteristics of these protocols like energy consumption per bit, standby power, and so forth.

The third component that affects the power profile of a ubiquitous system is the storage media, such as SRAM, DRAM, flash, and disc drives. Each of these storage types has a different power profile (idle power, active power, leakage power, and so on). For example, SRAM can be lower power than DRAM, while FLASH has a better idle power profile. The software will need to deploy various schemes to manage power consumption and access to these various storage options on the platform.

Limitations of wireless discovery

The world has moved from era of one person, one computer to one person, multiple computing devices. Today an individual has multiple devices: a desktop computer, notebook, tablets, smartphones, and other such portable computing devices that share the same/surrounding space at home or office. With multiple computing devices being associated with each individual, the physical and virtual management of these devices becomes challenging. In the future, we could also have embedded processors in numerous household and office products trying to identify or associate with an individual. This further complicates the management of computing devices associated with each person in that space.

Such a collection of small devices needs to be found in the surroundings (home/office), identified by each by its type (phone, notebook, tablet, or the like) and functionality, and then each device needs to be associated with a particular user/system. Today there is some kind of unique name/IP/MAC address to identify these devices but such identification may not be always available as in the case of embedded systems. It is also possible that ubiquitous and/or pervasive devices may not be plugged into a wired network. Such ubiquitous devices that are coexisting in the same space will not only have to be identified appropriately by the managing software but will also need to be connected with other available devices based on their functionality, user preference, and authenticity.

User interface adaptation

Ubiquitous computing refers to different types of devices ranging from small sensors to tablets to notebooks and desktops to complex computing devices. Each one of these will have varying display types and sizes. An application that runs on a smaller display of a smartphone should work as effectively on larger screens of desktop computers. The physical difference of displays should not matter to the user experience across these different devices. The user should be able to manipulate the touch controls and tiny menu on smartphones as easily as on larger displays of notebooks or desktops. So an application designed for a smartphone with a smaller display should be able to adapt easily to a larger display size when that display size is available and vice versa, where server applications designed for a larger display should adapt to smaller smartphone display size. A pragmatic approach would be to generate user interface components based on underlying basic user definition plus knowledge of target display capabilities on the go. To build such applications, four main components are needed:

1. A user interface specification language,
2. A control protocol that provides an abstracted communication channel between the application and user interface,
3. Appliance adaptors, allowing the control protocol to be translated into the primitives available on the target device, and
4. The graphic user interface generator.

Since a user interface is visible to the customer, it is important to maintain its usability across multiple display targets. But user interface designers would not know how their application would appear on various different screen sizes used by customers. In ubiquitous computing environments, the range of target screen sizes is much greater than what is found in traditional desktop or notebooks. Hence, significant software engineering hurdles still remain in creating standards and the basic mechanisms to generate and display content to the user.

Location-aware computing

Ubiquitous computing uses location of the device to enhance user experience and its most important feature is to customize services that are made available to the user, such as automatically locating other devices nearby, remembering them, and then offering services/data to the user after appropriate user authentication.

The location context is not just limited to knowledge of where a user is but also includes knowledge of who the user is and who else is near that user. Such context can also include historical usage of the user and thereby determine applications that the user might want to access based on history, such as a scenario where a ubiquitous system supporting location context automatically controls device volume or notification alerts based on whether the user is in a crowded place like a shopping mall or in a quiet place like a library. Another scenario would be to determine whether there are people around and whether the user is likely to be in some meeting with them. It can also control the display brightness based on time and location of the user.

There are many location-based services that can be offered by applications, such as finding nearby restaurants, cheap gas stations, localizing Internet searches, and so on.

Traditional location-context–based systems have the limitation of "uncertainty of location estimates" where it is not possible for the system to know the exact location of the device/user and hence cannot describe the range of possible locations. To resolve this, a fusion of several sources of location information can be used to improve accuracy of location and allow users/applications to understand and compensate for the error distribution of the estimated location.

CONTEXT

Context means the idea of "situated cognition." For mobile computing, context can be defined as an environment or situation surrounding a user or a device. Context can be categorized based on the location of the user or the device, identity of the user, activity performed by the user or the device, and time of the task, application or the process. Context can be used to authenticate the identity of the user or the device, to perform authorization of location, function or data and to provide services.

COMPUTING CONTEXT

A computing context is information about a situation, location, environment, identity, time, or location, regarding the user, people, place, or things. This information is then used by context-aware computing devices to anticipate user requirements and predictably offer enriched, situation-aware and usable content, functions, and experiences.

Fig. 2.2 shows examples of context environment that are applicable to context-aware computing. These can be categorized into three main areas:

- Physical context—lighting, noise levels, traffic conditions, and temperature.
- User context—user's profile, biometric information, location, people nearby, current social situation.
- Time context—time of a day, week, month, and season of the year.

PASSIVE VERSUS ACTIVE CONTEXT

An active context awareness refers to processing that changes its content on its own based on the measured sensor data. An example would be how time and location change in smartphones based on where the user is (provided the "auto-update" is selected for these features in user settings). Active context is also considered proactive context.

A passive context awareness refers to processing where an updated context (based on sensor data) is presented to the user and user then has to decide if, how, and when the application should change. For example, when the user is in a different time zone or location and "auto-update" is turned off in the user settings for these features, then the smartphone will not automatically update time and

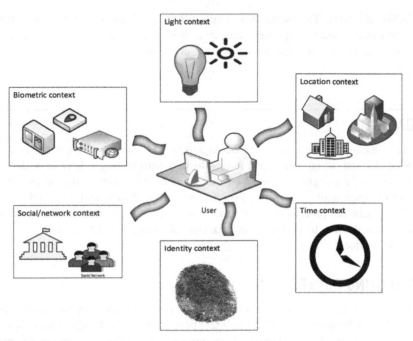

FIGURE 2.2

Example of context environment.

Table 2.2 Passive Context and Active Context Response to Inputs

Service/Sensor Inputs	Device Action in Passive Context	Device Actions in Active Context
Location based: change in time/ location	Offer user to change time/ location; offers nearby restaurants for dinner/lunch User then takes action or ignores	Automatically changes time/ location or selects the restaurant based on historical preference and automatically plots route in GPS. No user inputs/decisions needed
Position based: display position or orientation	Prompts user if it wants to power down or change display orientation, etc.	Automatically changes screen orientation or enters power down state, etc.
Acoustic environment	Prompts user to adjust for volume, notifications, and alerts	Automatically adjusts for volume, notifications, and alerts
Biosensor data	Prompts user do calorie estimation of user activities	Automatically does calorie estimation of user activities

location but instead will prompt the user with all required information and let the user decide on subsequent action.

Table 2.2 shows device actions to inputs based on passive and active context.

CONTEXT-AWARE APPLICATIONS

Context information can be used in software applications [3] to enhance user experience and facilitate effective hardware and software resource usage. It can be used to personalize user interface, add or remove drivers, applications, and software modules, present context-based information to user queries, and perform context-driven actions. Following are some examples of applications that uses context information.

- Proximate selection: Proximate selections refer to the user interface that highlights the objects or information which are in proximity of the user at a particular instance of query. Such user interface can use user's current location as default and can offer the user to connect or user nearby input—output devices such as printers, audio speakers, display screens, and so on. It can also offer to connect to or share information with other users within the preset proximity and it can also provide information about nearby attractions and locations that the user might be interested to visit/explore, such as restaurants, gas stations, sports stadium, and so on.
- Automatic contextual reconfiguration: The process of adding or removing software components, or changing the interaction between these components is referred to as automatic contextual reconfiguration. For example, device drivers can be loaded based on user profile. The context information can thus be used to support personalized system configurations.
- Contextual information and commands: By using context information such as location or user preferences, the software can present the user with commands that are filtered or personalized with context (e.g., send file command will send it to the nearby connected device by default), or it can change present user with certain execution options based on current location such as offer to silent the mobile device while in library.
- Context-triggered actions: The software or applications can automatically invoke certain actions based on if-then condition-action rules. For example, applications can offer automatic reminders to checkout certain reading materials or it can automatically put the mobile device in silent mode when user is detected around library. Such automatic actions however require higher degree of context information accuracy.

LOCATION AWARENESS

Location awareness refers to the capability of a device to actively or passively determine its location in terms of coordinates with respect to a point of reference. Various sensors or navigational tools can be used to determine the location. Some of the application of location awareness can be:

1. Emergency response, navigation, asset tracking, ground surveying
2. Symbolic location is a proxy for activity (e.g., being in grocery store implies shopping)

3. Social roles and interactions can be learned by collation
4. Coordinate change can imply activity and mode of transportation (i.e., running, driving).

LOCATION SOURCES IN MOBILE PHONES

There are many location technologies and sensor types that can be used in the devices with location context awareness. Some of the technologies and sensors are listed:

GNSS [4] (Global Navigation Satellite System)

This system is made up of a network of satellites that transmits signals used for positioning and navigation around the globe. Examples include GPS, GLONASS, and GALILEO systems. Each one of these systems consists of three main segments: (1) Space segment: This segment refers to satellites or network of satellites; (2) Control segment: This segment refers to system of tracking stations located around the world that controls functions like satellite orbit determination, synchronization, and so on; (3) User segment: This segment refers to satellite receivers and users with different capabilities.

GNSS is suitable for outdoor location context, has good coverage and accuracy across the globe (Fig. 2.3).

Wireless Geo

Wireless Geo refers to wireless mechanisms used to identify actual location of the device. In this method, actual physical location rather than geographic coordination is provided by the underlying wireless locating engines. An example would

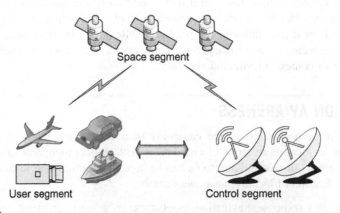

FIGURE 2.3

Key segments of GNSS.

be Cell ID (CID), which is a unique number used to identify each mobile/smart-phone. The CID-based mechanism uses cell tower, CID, and location area code to identify the mobile phone.

Sensors

Sensors can be used to enhance the accuracy of determining the location of a device. For example, in dead reckoning, sensors can be used to determine relative motion from a reference point, such as to detect whether the system moves outside of a 3-m radius, or to determine relative positioning of devices, such as the case of bumping two devices up against each other to establish common reference and then they can track their relative positions. Sensors can also be used stand-alone when other methods are not available. First let us understand what dead reckoning is. Dead reckoning (deduced reckoning) is the process of calculating current position by using previously determined reference position and advancing that position based upon known or estimated speeds over elapsed time and course. Although it provides good information on position, this method is prone to errors due to factors like inaccuracy in speed or direction estimations. Errors will also be cumulative since new estimated value would have its own errors and it will also be based on previous position which had errors, thus resulting in cumulative errors. Some of the sensors used are accelerometers and gyroscopes for acceleration/velocity integration for dead reckoning, accelerometers for bump events, pressure for elevation, and so on.

LOCALIZATION ALGORITHMS

The discovery of the position can be realized utilizing range measurements including received signal strength (RSS), time of arrival (TOA), time difference of arrival (TDOA), and angle of arrival.

ANGLE OF ARRIVAL

Angle of arrival [5] is the angle between a reference direction and the direction of propagation of an incident ray. The reference direction is called orientation and is fixed. The angle of arrival is measured in degrees and in clockwise direction from the north as shown in Fig. 2.4. The angle of arrival is called absolute if it is pointing in the north direction (angle of arrival $\theta = 0$ degree). Fig. 2.4 shows sensors/nodes A and B aware of their positions at θ_a and θ_b, respectively. Geometric relationships can be used to estimate the location of the unknown user/sensor from the intersection of the lines from two or more sensors/nodes/users which are aware of their respective positions. Example in Fig. 2.4 determines the orientation of unknown user/sensor at an angle of 59 degrees from the north. Other methods can be used if the orientation of the unknown sensor/node is not known.

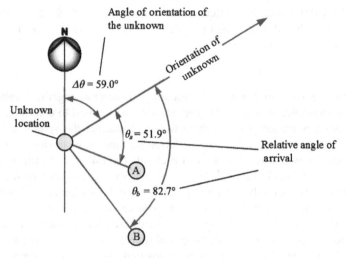

FIGURE 2.4

Localization (with orientation information).

TIME OF ARRIVAL

TOA [6−8] utilizes the information of time to travel (time of flight) between the source sensor and the receiver sensor to measure the distance between them. The transmitted signal is time-stamped and exact TOA is measured at the receiver. The travel time for the signal is direct measure of the travel distance. The source and the receiver sensors in this case should be synchronized to avoid errors due to clock offsets, and hardware/circuit delays. Such synchronization would not be needed if roundtrip TOA is calculated. The distance is obtained from the TOA by multiplying it with speed.

$$\Delta \text{Distance} = \Delta \text{Time}(t_r - t) \times \text{Velocity}$$

Δ Distance = distance between the source sensor and the receiver sensor
Δ Time = difference between the arrival time at receiver (t_r) and the source time t
Velocity is the speed of light.

Using Pythagoras theorem, for three-dimension the distance between a receiver location at coordinates (x_r, y_r, z_r) and the source location (x, y, z) is given by

$$\text{Velocity} \times (t_r - t) = \sqrt{(x_r - x)^2 + (y_r - y)^2 + (z_r - z)^2}$$

For two-dimension the equation can be written as

$$\text{Velocity} \times (t_r - t) = \sqrt{(x_r - x)^2 + (y_r - y)^2}$$

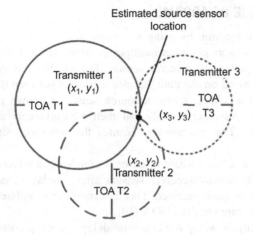

FIGURE 2.5

Time of arrival positioning system: trilateration.

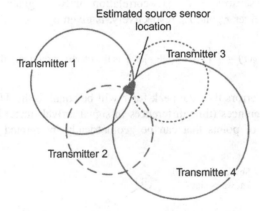

FIGURE 2.6

Time of arrival positioning system: multilateration.

When multiple receivers at known locations receives the same signal at different times (due to different distance traveled by the signal), the measured TOA represents a circle (circle for two-dimension and sphere for three-dimension) with receiver at its center and the source at a location on the circumference in a two-dimensional space. Using trilateration and multilateration, a distinct intersection point of circles can be determined. This intersection point is the location of the source sensor as shown in Figs. 2.5 and 2.6.

The mathematical measurement model [9] for TOA-based Source Localization Algorithm is given by the equation

Measurement vector r = Nonlinear function of source sensor position x

+ Zero mean noise vector

TIME DIFFERENCE OF ARRIVAL

TDOA identifies a location by using the difference in travel times of the same signal received at sensors placed at multiple locations versus using absolute travel time from source sensor to receiver sensor. The localization systems based on TDOA does not depend on absolute distance estimates between the sensor pairs.

Fig. 2.7 shows a scheme where a source sensor at known position (anchor) sends out multiple reference signals and then measurements are taken by the receiving sensor R. The synchronizer ensures that reference signal sources are synchronized.

Fig. 2.8 shows a scheme where a sensor R broadcasts a reference signal which is then received by several receiver sensors after a delay τ_r depending on the distance of source to each receiver. This τ_r cannot be calculated. The receivers estimate TOA and compute the TDOA [10].

Correlation analysis will provide a time delay $\tau_{rA} - \tau_{rB}$ corresponding to the difference in path of reference signal to receivers r_A and r_B. A simple method of estimating that time difference is to cross-correlate [11] the signals arriving at a pair of receiving sensors. The cross-correlation of two signals $r_A(t)$ and $r_B(t)$, received from receiver r_A and r_B, respectively, is given by

$$R_{A,B}(\tau) = \frac{1}{T}\int_0^T r_A(t)r_B(t+\tau)dt; \text{T is the observation interval}$$

If there are no errors then the peak for τ will be equal to the TDOA.

The range-differences (time-differences in signal arrival times) from two receivers provides set of points that can be geometrically interpreted as a hyperbola

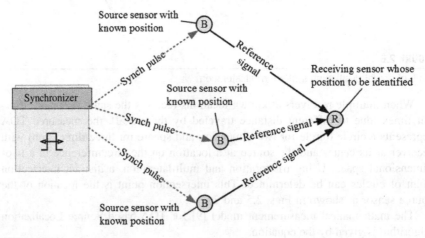

FIGURE 2.7

Time difference of arrival scheme.

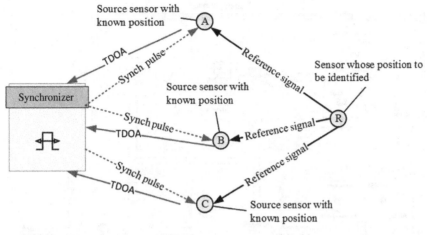

FIGURE 2.8

Time difference of arrival scheme: broadcast.

(in two-dimension). Several hyperbolic functions can be computed which intersect in one unique point. This unique intersection point provides the location of the source sensor.

RECEIVED SIGNAL STRENGTH

RSS [12,13] at a particular location is the average of the signals received through multiple paths. RSS indicator indicates the power of the received signal and is a function of distance between the transmitter and receiving device that gets impacted due to various in-path interferences.

Fig. 2.9 shows an example of indoor positioning system [14] using RSS which consists of a training phase and a positioning phase. In training phase RSS readings from available wireless local area network access points at known locations referred to as reference points are collected by pointing the mobile devices in different orientations (all four directions). Affinity propagation algorithm is then used on the raw RSS time samples to identify and adjust or remove outliers. The references points are then divided into different clusters (independent clusters for each orientation) and radio map (set of RSS measurements) stored as fingerprints.

In positioning phase, real-time RSS is collected by the mobile device in arbitrary orientations from the access points at unknown locations (referred to as test points) to form RSS measurement vector. Coarse localization algorithms can be used to compare the collected RSS to each of the reference point RSS vector to identify the cluster to which the test point RSS measurement belongs to. Thus it helps to narrow the area of interest. The final location of the mobile device can then be estimated using fine localization.

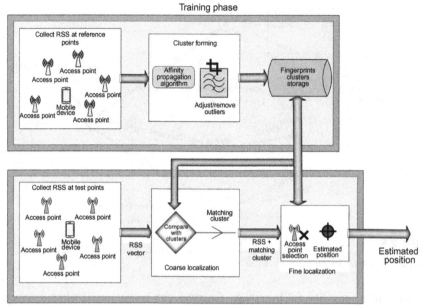

FIGURE 2.9

Restricted signal strength-based indoor positioning system.

There are four possible schemes that can be used during coarse localization to find the similarity between the test point RSS and the different clusters and to recognize the matching cluster with the highest similarity for that test point:

1. Use Euclidean distance between a RSS measurement vector of test point and each RSS in the reference point clusters to match the test point to a particular cluster.
2. Use Euclidean distance between a RSS measurement vector of test point and the average of all the RSS readings in the cluster (instead of each RSS reading) to match the test point to a cluster.
3. Use Euclidean distance between a RSS measurement vector of test point and weighted average for the reference points (instead of simple average as in Scheme 2) to give higher weightage for reference points with higher stability.
4. Find similarity of test point to the cluster using any of the above three schemes considering only the highest strength RSS readings.

Next step is to estimate the fine location using fine localization. Following steps describe fine localization algorithm in its basic form.

1. There may be more access points than what is required to estimate the position of the mobile device. There could also be access points which can be unreliable with high RSS variance that can affect the stability of positioning

system. To eliminate redundant and unreliable access points only those access points (and readings from them) are considered that have highest RSS readings or satisfies Fisher criterion.

2. The RSS vector of test points is then compared with RSS vector of each cluster members of the cluster that was identified during the coarse localization stage, and Euclidean distance is computed.

3. The reference point that has the minimum Euclidean distance with the RSS vector of test point is then selected as the estimate of mobile device position.

REFERENCES

[1] Barkhuus L, Dey A, Is Context-Aware Computing Taking Control Away from the User?, Three Levels of Interactivity Examined, IRB-TR-03-008, May, 2003, Proceedings of the Fifth Annual Conference on Ubiquitous Computing (UBICOMP 2003), IRB-TR-03-008; May 2003.

[2] Want R, Pering T. System challenges for ubiquitous & pervasive computing, Intel Research.

[3] Stefanidis K, Pitoura E. Related work on context-aware systems, p. 1–2.

[4] Kornhauser AL. Global Navigation Satellite System (GNSS). Princeton University.

[5] Peng R, Sichitiu ML. Angle of arrival localization for wireless sensor networks, Angle of Arrival.

[6] Dobbins R. Software defined radio localization using 802.11-style communications. Project report submitted to the Faculty of Worcester Polytechnic Institute Electrical and Computer Engineering.

[7] Cheung KW, So HC, Ma W-K, Chan YT. Least squares algorithms for time-of-arrival-based mobile location.

[8] Rison B. Time of arrival location technique. New Mexico Tech.

[9] Ravindra S, Jagadeesha SN. Time of arrival based localization in wireless sensor networks: a linear approach.

[10] Gustafsson F, Gunnarsson F. Positioning using time-difference of arrival measurements.

[11] Caceres Duran MA, D'Amico AA, Dardari D, Rydström M, Sottile F, Ström EG, et al. Terrestrial network-based positioning and navigation.

[12] Chapre Y, Mohapatra P, Jha S, Seneviratne A. Received signal strength indicator and its analysis, in a typical WLAN system (short paper).

[13] Polson J, Fette BA. Cognitive techniques: position awareness.

[14] Feng C, Anthea Au WS, Valaee S, Tan Z. Received-signal-strength-based indoor, positioning using compressive sensing, indoor positioning.

Sensors and actuators

INFORMATION IN THIS CHAPTER:

- Terminology Overview
- Sensors Ecosystem
- Accelerometers
- Gyroscopes
- Magnetic Field Sensors
- Light Sensor
- Proximity Sensor
- Temperature Sensor, Pressure Sensor, Biosensors

TERMINOLOGY OVERVIEW

Sensors, transducers, and actuators forms the base of a sensor ecosystem. This section covers their basic definition.

A *sensor* is a device that converts physical activity or changes into an electrical signal. It is the interface between the physical or real world and electrical system and components of the computing device. In the simplest form a sensor responds to some kind of physical change or stimulus and outputs some form of electrical signal or data. Sensors are required to produce data that the computing system can process. For example, opening a washing machine stops the washing cycle. Opening of a house door results in activation of a house alarm. Without the sensing of these physical activities there would be no change in washing cycle or triggering of the house alarm.

A *transducer* is the device that takes one form of input (energy or signal) and changes into another form, as shown in Fig. 3.1. A transducer can be part of our earlier defined sensors. Many times the terms sensor and transducer are used interchangeably, but we can differentiate them by saying that sensors measure the change in physical environment and produce electrical signals using a transducer, where the transducer takes the measured change in the physical environment and transforms it into a different form of energy (such as an electrical signal) as shown in Fig. 3.2.

Mobile Sensors and Context-Aware Computing. DOI: http://dx.doi.org/10.1016/B978-0-12-801660-2.00003-3

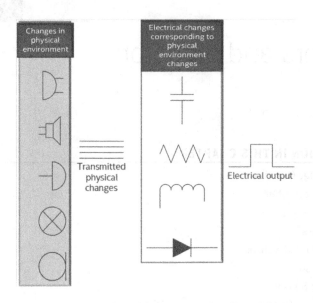

FIGURE 3.1

Basic concept of transducers.

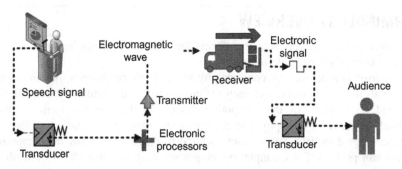

FIGURE 3.2

Example of sensor with transducer.

A *combination transducer* performs detection of one energy form and can create an energy output. For example, an antenna can receive (detect) radio signals and also transmit (create) radio signals.

The performance of a transducer can be measured in terms of its accuracy, sensitivity, resolution, and range.

An *actuator* is a transducer that takes one form of energy as input and produces some form of motion, movement, or action. Thus it converts some form of energy into kinetic energy. For example, an electrical motor in an elevator converts electrical energy into the vertical movement of going from one floor to another floor of the building. The following are the main category of actuators:

1. Pneumatic: These actuators convert energy from compressed air (at high pressure) to either linear or rotary motion. Examples include valve controls of liquid or gas pipes.
2. Electric: These actuators convert electrical energy to mechanical energy. An example would be an electric water pump pumping water out of well.
3. Mechanical: These actuators convert mechanical energy into some form of motion. An example would be a simple pulley used to pull weights.

The performance of actuators can be measured in terms of force, speed, and durability.

SENSOR ECOSYSTEM OVERVIEW

The sensor ecosystem is complex with many significant components, players, and segments of enabling technologies (such as sensor types and wireless protocols), manufacturers, developers, markets, and consumers. One of the components of this ecosystem is the set of enabling technologies. Let us look at some of the sensor types such as location based sensors, proximity sensors, touch sensors, and biosensors.

LOCATION-BASED SENSORS

Location sensors can help enable use cases such as ones mentioned in Table 3.1.

Table 3.1 Location Sensor Use Cases

Sensor Algorithms	Experiences
Determine whether user is in the proximity of a known Wi-Fi hotspot	The user can identify and label (home, work, school, etc.) and therefore can tailor the device to those locations
Determine absolute location, no matter whether the user is indoors or outdoors (continuous location)	Users can continuously track their locations, and the device can prompt the user if the location is often used to add as important (i.e., grandparents)
Calculate indoor location using dead reckoning accuracy. Be able to differentiate between store-level accuracy and aisle-level accuracy, with assist for indoor/outdoor switching and GNSS buffering	Once the user has entered a mall, the device can assist the user in getting to the store. The device can alert the user of coupons to the stores they often frequent
Determine whether the user is within 5 m of the phone through multifactor triangulation (voice, location, communications)	In safe areas (home), the authentication requirements can be reduced, and therefore read aloud an incoming email or text

Accelerometer and gyroscopes are location sensors that are described in subsequent sections.

Accelerometer

An accelerometer is a device that measures proper acceleration (g-force). Proper acceleration is not the same as coordinate acceleration (rate of change of velocity) but it is the acceleration the device or object experiences relative to free fall. For example, an accelerometer at rest on the surface of the Earth will measure an acceleration $g = 9.81$ m/s^2 straight upward because any point on the Earth's surface is accelerating upward relative to the local inertial frame (the frame of a freely falling object near the surface). By contrast, accelerometers in free fall orbiting and accelerating due to the gravity of Earth will measure zero because to obtain the acceleration due to motion with respect to the Earth, the "gravity offset" must be subtracted and corrections made for effects caused by the Earth's rotation relative to the inertial frame.

Single- and multiaxis models of accelerometers are available to detect magnitude and direction of the proper acceleration (or g-force), as a vector quantity, and this can be used to sense orientation (because direction of weight changes), coordinate acceleration (so long as it produces g-force or a change in g-force), vibration, shock, and falling in a resistive medium (a case where the proper acceleration changes, since it starts at zero, then increases).

g-Force, axes, coordinate system

g-Force (with g from gravitational) is a measurement of acceleration felt as weight and can be described as weight per unit mass. It is the acceleration experienced by an object due to the vector sum of all nongravitational and nonelectromagnetic forces acting on an object's freedom to move. For example, 1g force on an object placed on the Earth's surface is caused by upward mechanical force exerted by the ground, thereby preventing the object from free fall. The upward contact force from the ground ensures that an object at rest on the Earth's surface is accelerating relative to the free-fall condition. Free fall is the path that the object would follow when falling freely toward the Earth's center and in free fall the objects do not really accelerate.

Unit of measurement

The unit for g-force acceleration is g. This helps in differentiating a simple acceleration (rate of change of velocity) from the g-force acceleration, which is relative to free fall. One g is the acceleration due to gravity at the Earth's surface and is the standard gravity (symbol: g_n), defined as 9.8 m/s^2 or 9.8 N/kg.

Gravity contribution, device behavior resting on a surface and free fall

Let us now describe the effect of an axis on the functioning of an accelerometer. The three axes are as in Fig. 3.3.

Case 1: Stationary car on a flat road In this case there is resistance from the Earth's surface in the upward direction. This resistance is equal and opposite to the

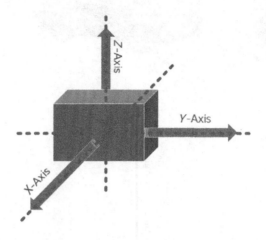

FIGURE 3.3

Three axes of an accelerometer.

gravity. The acceleration that prevents the car from free fall is $1g$ in an upward direction. If a single-axis accelerometer is mounted on this car such that its measuring axis is horizontal, its output will be $0g$, and it will continue to be $0g$ even if the car is traveling at a constant velocity on a level road. If the car stops, then this one-axis/two-axis accelerometer will indicate a positive or negative acceleration. If the single-axis accelerometer is mounted on the car such that its measuring axis is vertical, then its output will be $+1g$ because it would measure the reaction force of the surface it is resting on (it cannot measure the other force, which is the gravitational force). If a three-axis accelerometer is used then this accelerometer will show $+1g$. For a three-axis accelerometer the acceleration is defined as

$$A(\text{overall}) = \sqrt{(a_x^2 + a_y^2 + a_z^2)}$$

$$A(\text{overall}) = \sqrt{(0_x^2 + 0_y^2 + 1_z^2)} = 1g$$

So the acceleration would be in an upward direction (Fig. 3.4).

Case 2: Object in free fall In this case there is no resistance from the Earth's surface in the upward direction. The object will have coordinate acceleration (a change in velocity) and no weight (weightlessness). Hence the acceleration in upward direction is $0g$. The accelerometer in this case will show $0g$ in all directions (Fig. 3.5). For a three-axis accelerometer the acceleration is defined as

$$A(\text{overall}) = \sqrt{(a_x^2 + a_y^2 + a_z^2)} = \sqrt{(0_x^2 + 0_y^2 + 0_z^2)} = 0g$$

Since acceleration in X- and Y-directions is zero in the case of free fall, a two-axis accelerometer cannot capture free fall correctly if it is placed horizontally on the freely falling object, because it cannot differentiate between a stationary

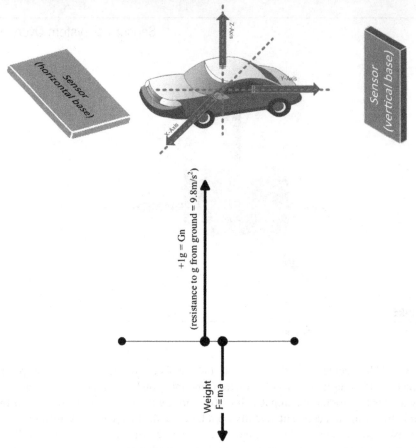

FIGURE 3.4

Accelerometer's horizontal and vertical measuring base with respective *g*-force.

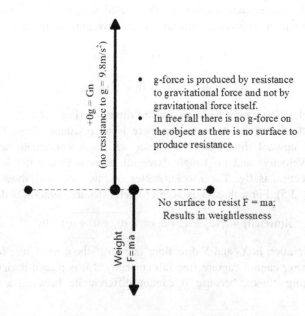

- g-force is produced by resistance to gravitational force and not by gravitational force itself.
- In free fall there is no g-force on the object as there is no surface to produce resistance.

No surface to resist F = ma;
Results in weightlessness

FIGURE 3.5

Object in free fall.

object on Earth and a free falling object (it will show $0g$ even if the body is stationary to Earth as mentioned earlier).

Case 3: Body moving downward Positive g-force in an upward direction produces downward weight on an object. Negative g-force is an acceleration in a downward direction that produces weight force in an upward direction. Consider a person in an elevator accelerating downward. Since the person is also accelerating downward due to gravity, the g-force of $-1g$ is applied to the person (in a downward direction). Hence the weight that is an equal and opposite force is exerted by the elevator floor on the person in an upward direction.

Consider the following parameters:

a = Downward acceleration of the elevator. It is represented as $-a$.
F_d = Downward force due to net acceleration of the elevator = $m \times -a$.
F_e = Net force exerted by the elevator floor on the person in an upward direction.
Gn = g-force on the person (equal to mass $\times g$) = $-1g$. This force causes the equal and opposite force of mg in upward direction.
$F_d = F_e - mg \rightarrow F_e = F_d + mg \rightarrow F_e = F_d + mg \rightarrow F_e = m(-a) + mg \rightarrow F_e = m(-a) + mg$

Therefore $F_e = mg - ma$.

If we divide the equation by g then we get $F_e/g = m - ma/g$, where F_e/g is the weight experienced by the person in an elevator accelerating downward. As seen in the equation, this weight is less than the normal weight of mg.

Tilt sensitivity and accelerometer orientation

Let us now describe different parameters and tilt calculations. Consider Fig. 3.6, where the accelerometer is situated with horizontal measuring base and is measuring $1g$.

In the case of a 15-degree tilt, the net $Gn = G \times \cos \alpha = G \times \cos 15 = 0.97G$ ($\cos \alpha = G/Gn$).

So a 15-degree change causes minor changes in the net G (Fig. 3.7).

Now consider the following situation where the accelerator is in $0g$ position. The accelerometer measuring base is vertical as discussed previously.

In this case $Gn = G \times \sin \alpha = G \times \sin 15 = 0.25G$ ($\sin \alpha = G/Gn$).

So due to a 15-degree tilt, the reading for

Case 1: Accelerometer at $0g$ went from $0G \rightarrow 0.25G$ (a huge percentage change compared to the old value)
Case 2: Accelerometer at $1g$ went from $1G \rightarrow 0.97G$ (a 3% change compared to the old value)

So the percentage change in Case 1 is much more than Case 2, and therefore the tilt sensitivity of an accelerometer with $0g$ orientation is greater than those with $1g$ orientation (Fig. 3.8).

The effect of tilt on accelerometer measurements [1]

Let us first go over the definition of different parameters used for tilt calculations. Consider a smartphone with axes shown as in Fig. 3.9.

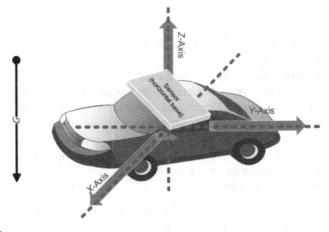

FIGURE 3.6

$1g$ Position with 0-degree tilt.

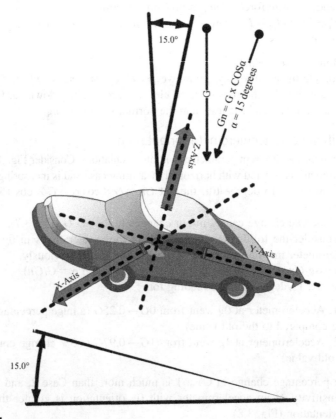

FIGURE 3.7

Net G with 15-degree tilt.

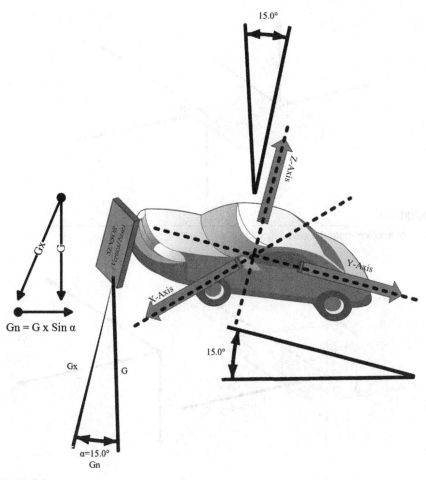

FIGURE 3.8

Tilt sensitivity for accelerometer mounted vertically.

X_s, Y_s, and Z_s are the three axes of the smartphone orientation where X is in forward, Y is sideways (right), and Z is in a downward direction. The three axes of the accelerometer corresponding to the above axes are X_a, Y_a, and Z_a. The accelerometer sensing axis matches the smartphone axis in default position. The sign of Y_a and Z_a is opposite to that of Y_s and Z_s.

Two main important angles in our tilt calculations would be pitch and roll. These angles are with respect to the horizontal plane, which is perpendicular to the direction of Earth's gravity.

Pitch (α) is the angle between the forward axis X_s and the horizontal plane. When the X_s axis moves up or down from the flat level while rotating around the Y_s axis, then the pitch angle changes. If the smartphone moves up from the flat

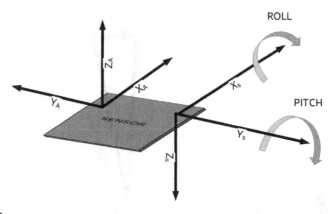

FIGURE 3.9

Axis for accelerometer tilt calculation.

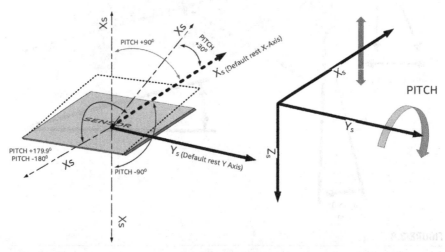

FIGURE 3.10

Pitch angles.

level to end in the vertical position, then the pitch is said to be moving from 0 to +90 degrees. The pitch angle will move from 0 to −180 degrees if the smartphone axis X_s moves downward from the flat level. Fig. 3.10 shows various pitch angles: 0, +30, +90, −90, +179, −180 degrees, and so on.

Roll (β) is the angle between the Y_s-axis and the horizontal plane. When the Y_s-axis moves up or down from the flat level while rotating around the X_s-axis, then roll angle changes. If the smartphone rotates around the X_s-axis and moves upward from the flat level to end up in the vertical position, then the roll angle is said to be moving from 0 to −90 degrees. If it continues further till it is flat again, then the roll angle would be −180 degrees. Assuming angle resolution of 1 degree, the roll angle will move from 0 to +179 degrees if the smartphone axis

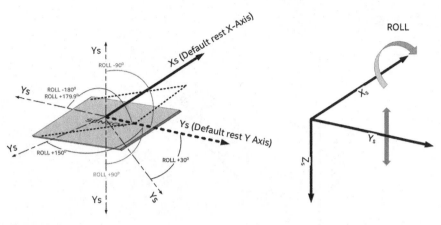

FIGURE 3.11

Roll angles.

Table 3.2 Accelerometer Reading Along Its Three Axes

Smartphone Position	Accelerometer Reading Along Its Three Axes		
	A_x	A_y	A_z
Z_s down	0	0	$1g$
Z_s up	0	0	$-1g$
Y_s down	0	$1g$	0
Y_s up	0	$-1g$	0
X_s down	$1g$	0	0
X_s up	$-1g$	0	0

Y_s moves downward from the flat level. Fig. 3.11 shows various roll angles: 0, +30, +90, −90, +179, −180 degrees, and so on.

Table 3.2 summarizes some of the readings that would help understand accelerometer readings with respect to smartphone stationary position

Now let us see how the tilt can be calculated. This concept was explained briefly in "Tilt sensitivity and accelerometer orientation" section.

Consider Fig. 3.12 with the X- and Y-axes perpendicular to each other, and Y is along the horizontal plane.

Since the accelerometer measures the projection of g gravity vector on its sensing axis, the amplitude A of the sensed acceleration changes as per the following equation:

$$\sin \alpha = A/g \geq A = g \times \sin \alpha$$

or

$$\alpha = \arcsin(A/g)$$

where A = measured acceleration, G is the Earth's gravity vector.

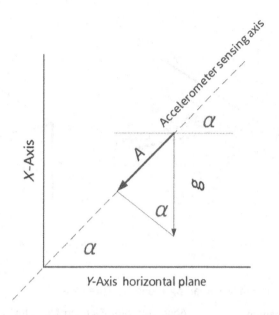

FIGURE 3.12

Operation theory for tilt sensing.

One-axis tilt sensing Let us consider an accelerometer with a sensing axis along the horizontal plane and perpendicular to the force of gravity (Fig. 3.13).

If this accelerometer is tilted as shown in Fig. 3.14 then the corresponding sensed accelerometer reading would be as indicated in Table 3.3.

The graph in Fig. 3.15 indicates that the sensitivity (change in g) measured by the accelerometer is greater when the tilt is closer to the horizontal axis. As direction approaches the direction of gravity, the sensitivity diminishes and becomes 0 at 90 or 270 degrees.

Two-axis tilt sensing Let us consider two different examples in the case of dual-axis accelerometer sensing.

Case 1: Sensor position: Vertical Consider that the accelerometer is rotated counter clockwise around the Z-axis (angle $\beta = \sim30$ degrees in Fig. 3.16), then the sensitivity versus tilt angle for the Z-axis and Y-axis would be as shown in Figs. 3.17–3.19.

The conclusions from the charts in Figs. 3.17–3.19 is shown in Table 3.4.

Case 2: Sensor position: Horizontal In this case (Fig. 3.20), the Y-axis is perpendicular to g and hence the accelerometer measured acceleration $A = g \times \sin$ (tilt angle). But this measured acceleration would be same for two different tilt angles because $\sin(\alpha) = \sin(180 - \alpha)$. Therefore it would not be possible to distinguish whether the tilt angle is α (say 30 degrees) or $180 - \alpha$ (say 150 degrees). This would be a serious drawback of this particular configuration because it inhibits tilt calculation.

Three-axis tilt sensing Combining Z-axis along with X- and Y-axes can help increase accelerometer tilt sensitivity and accuracy.

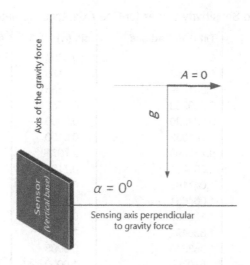

FIGURE 3.13

One-axis accelerometer tilt calculation.

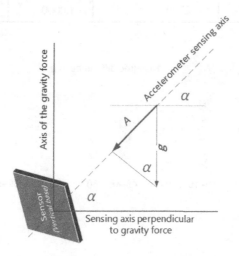

FIGURE 3.14

One-axis accelerometer tilt calculation-tilted accelerometer.

For the X-axis: in Fig. 3.21 this is a horizontal plane. Any tilt is in the same plane and is called the pitch. The acceleration a_x measured by the accelerometer is with respect to force g (and g is in a downward direction).

This measured acceleration $a_x = g \times \sin(\alpha)$

or $\sin(\alpha) = a_x/g$

or $\alpha = \arcsin(a_x/g)$.

Table 3.3 Tilt and Sensitivity Values for One-Axis Accelerometer

Tilt α in Degrees	Tilt α in Radians	sin (α)	$A = 9.8 \times$ sin (α)
0	0	0.0000	0.00000
1	0.017453	0.0175	0.17103
15	0.261799	0.2588	2.53643
16	0.279253	0.2756	2.70125
30	0.523599	0.5000	4.90000
31	0.541052	0.5150	5.04737
45	0.785398	0.7071	6.92965
46	0.802851	0.7193	7.04953
60	1.047198	0.8660	8.48705
61	1.064651	0.8746	8.57127
75	1.308997	0.9659	9.46607
76	1.32645	0.9703	9.50890
89	1.553343	0.9998	9.79851
90	1.570796	1.0000	9.80000
179	3.124139	0.0175	0.17103
180	3.141593	0.0000	0.00000
181	3.159046	−0.0175	−0.17103
270	4.712389	−1.0000	−9.80000

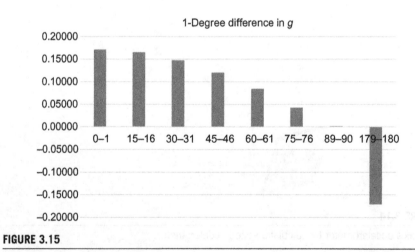

FIGURE 3.15

One-axis accelerometer sensitivity.

For the Y-axis: in Fig. 3.21 this axis is the forward or backward direction of the accelerometer (this axis is also a horizontal plane but perpendicular to another horizontal plane X-axis). Any tilt here is called the roll, which is an angle with

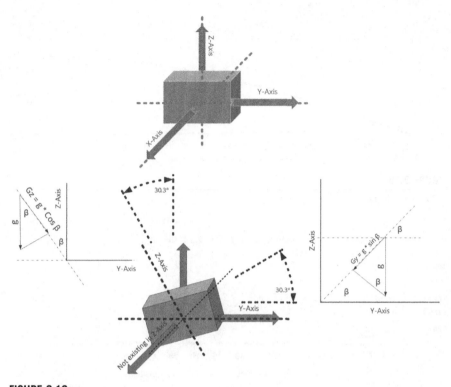

FIGURE 3.16

Dual-axis tilt sensing Case 1.

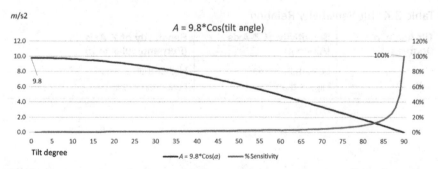

FIGURE 3.17

Z-Axis sensitivity.

respect to the horizontal plane. The acceleration a_y would be measured by the accelerometer with respect to force g (and g is in the downward direction).

This measured acceleration $a_y = g \times \sin(\beta)$

or $\sin(\beta) = a_y/g$

or $\beta = \arcsin(a_y/g)$.

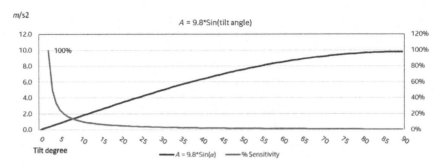

FIGURE 3.18

Y-Axis sensitivity.

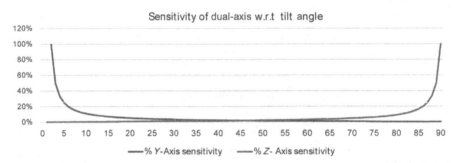

FIGURE 3.19

Sensitivity of dual-axis accelerometer with respect to tilt angles.

Table 3.4 Tilt-Sensitivity Relation

Tilt Angle in Degrees	Sensitivity of Z-Axis (Along *g*)	Sensitivity of Y-Axis (Perpendicular to *g*)
<45	Less than *Y*-axis	Higher than *Z*-axis
>45	Higher than *Y*-axis	Less than *Z*-axis

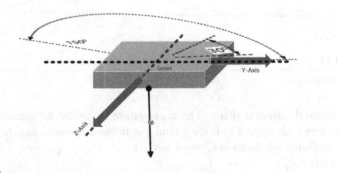

FIGURE 3.20

Dual-axis accelerometer failure (and need for three-axis accelerometer).

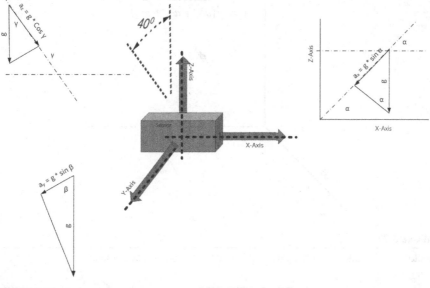

FIGURE 3.21

Three-axis accelerometer and tilts.

For the Z-axis: in Fig. 3.21 this axis is in the upward/downward direction (perpendicular to the horizontal plane and hence perpendicular to both the X-axis and Y-axis). Any tilt here is an angle with respect to force g in a downward direction. The acceleration a_z as measured by the accelerometer is given by the equation $a_z = g \times \cos(\gamma)$

or $\cos(\gamma) = a_z/g$

or $\gamma = \arccos(a_z/g)$.

For a three-axis accelerometer, the overall measured acceleration (Fig. 3.22) is as follows:

$$A = \sqrt{(a_x^2 + a_y^2 + a_z^2)}.$$

Our equation for Pitch is $\sin(\alpha) = a_x/g$.

Based on the vector representation of overall acceleration A (Fig. 3.23), we have $\tan(\alpha) = a_x/I_x$ where

$$I_x = \sqrt{(A - a_x^2)} = \sqrt{(a_x^2 + a_y^2 + a_z^2 - a_x^2)} = \sqrt{a_y^2 + a_z^2}$$

Therefore

$$\tan(\alpha) = \frac{a_x}{I_x} = \frac{a_x}{\sqrt{a_y^2 + a_z^2}}$$

$$\text{Pitch} = \alpha = \arctan\left(\frac{a_x}{\sqrt{a_y^2 + a_z^2}}\right)$$

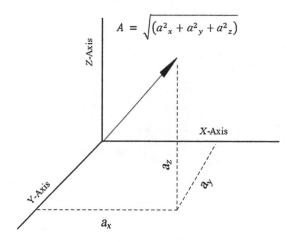

FIGURE 3.22

Vector representation of three-axis accelerometer measured acceleration.

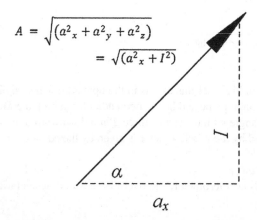

FIGURE 3.23

Measuring roll in terms of measured accelerations along three axes.

Similarly we have $\tan \beta = a_y / I_y$

where

$$I_y = \sqrt{(A^2 - a_y^2)} = \sqrt{(a_x^2 + a_y^2 + a_z^2 - a_y^2)} = \sqrt{a_x^2 + a_z^2}$$

Therefore

$$\tan(\beta) = \frac{a_y}{I_y} = \frac{a_y}{\sqrt{a_x^2 + a_z^2}}$$

$$\text{Roll} = \beta = \arctan\left(\frac{a_y}{\sqrt{a_x^2 + a_z^2}}\right)$$

Gyroscopes

A gyroscope [2,3] is used to determine rotational movement and orientation of a device. There are different types of gyroscopes such as MEMS gyroscope, fiber optic gyroscope, and vibrating structure gyroscope.

Mechanical gyroscopes

A mechanical gyroscope uses the principle of conservation of angular momentum (spin of the system remains constant until it is subjected to external torque). In its basic form, a gyroscope has a freely spinning wheel or disc called rotor mounted on spinning axle. The spinning axle can freely assume any orientation and it defines the spin axis around which the rotor spins. The orientation of the spin axis is unaffected by the motion of the mounting platform according to law of conservation of angular momentum when mounted in a gimbal. The gimbal minimizes external torque.

Components of a gyroscope and axis of freedom

A gyroscope consists of four main components (as shown in Fig. 3.24): the gyroscope frame, the gimbal, the rotor, and the spin axle.

The gyroscope frame is an outer ring that pivots with one degree of rotational freedom about an axis in the plane of the support. The gyroscope frame's axis does not rotate (zero degree of rotational freedom).

Gimbal is the inner ring that pivots about an axis that is perpendicular to the pivotal axis of gyroscope frame. Gimbal has two degrees of rotational freedom.

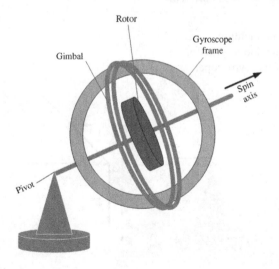

FIGURE 3.24

Gyroscope components.

The axle of the rotor defines the spin axis that is perpendicular to the axis of gimbal. The rotor spins about its axis with three degrees of rotational freedom while its axis has two degrees of rotational freedom. A change in the direction of the spin axis of rotor or the gyroscope is known as gyroscope precession [4].

Gyroscopes precession

Torque is the force which tries to rotate an object around its rotating axis. The magnitude of torque depends on force applied and the distance between the axis and the point where the force is applied

$$\tau = F \times r$$

Consider a gyroscope under the force of gravity (Fig. 3.25). When the wheel/rotor is not spinning, the torque from the weight causes the wheel to rotate downward with an angular velocity [5].

Using the right-hand grip rule (right-hand fingers curled from direction of the lever arm to the direction of force Mg due to gravity), the torque points into the page. The resulting angular velocity also points into the page. The torque due to weight of gyroscope is given by:

$$\tau = F \times r = Mgr$$

As shown in Fig. 3.26, if the rotor is spinning with initial angular momentum L_{init} vector perpendicular to vector of force F due to weight Mg, then the torque τ causes the change in the direction of the angular momentum vector, thereby causing the change in spin axis of the rotor. This change in spin axis or precession will have angular velocity $\omega_{precession}$.

If

L = angular momentum,
τ = the torque due to gravity,
M = mass of the gyroscope,

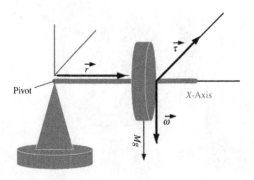

FIGURE 3.25

Gyroscope with nonrotating rotor.

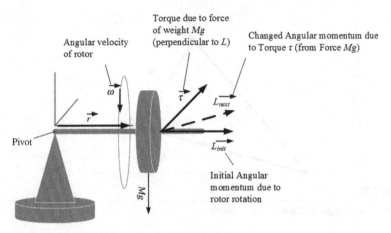

FIGURE 3.26

Gyroscope with rotating rotor.

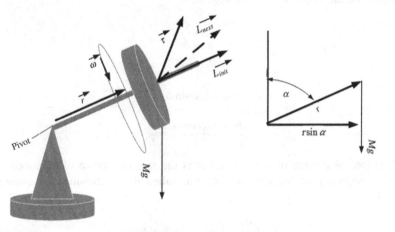

FIGURE 3.27

Gyroscope with rotating rotor (at angle with horizontal plane).

α = angle between the axis of rotation and the vertical down [6] (Fig. 3.27),
g = gravitational acceleration, and
r = torque arm (distance from the axis at which the force gets applied).

$$\tau = F \times r = Mgr\sin \alpha$$

Torque is the rate of change of the angular momentum [7] (dL/dt), so the magnitude of dL/dt is given by

$$\tau = \frac{dL}{dt} = F \times r\sin \alpha = Mgr\sin \alpha$$

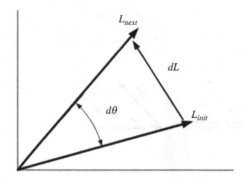

FIGURE 3.28

Incremental change in angular momentum.

In a delta time increment, dt, the angular momentum vector changes from its initial value L_{init} to a new value $L_{next} = L_{init} + dL$ (Fig. 3.28).

Based on the vector triangle in Fig. 3.28:

$$d\theta = \frac{dL}{L}$$

$$dL = L d\theta$$

$$\tau = F \times r \sin \alpha = Mgr \sin \alpha = \frac{dL}{dt} = \frac{L d\theta}{dt}$$

$$\frac{d\theta}{dt} = \frac{Mgr \sin \alpha}{L} = \frac{\tau}{L}$$

The rate of change of angle θ, $d\theta/dt$ is the rate of change of spin axis. The angular frequency of the axis of rotation, called the precessional frequency is given by:

$$\tau = L \frac{d\theta}{dt} = L \omega_{precession} = Mgr \sin \alpha$$

$$\omega_{precession} = \frac{Mgr \sin \alpha}{L}$$

The angular momentum (L) is product of inertia (I) and the angular velocity (ω).

$$L = I\omega$$

$$\omega_{precession} = \frac{Mgr \sin \alpha}{I\omega}$$

If the gyroscope's spin slows down (e.g., due to friction), its angular momentum decreases and hence the rate of precession increases. If the device does not rotate fast enough to support its own weight, then it stops precessing and falls down as in Fig. 3.25.

PROXIMITY SENSOR

A proximity sensor is a device that can detect or sense the approach or presence of nearby objects and for this it does not need physical contact. There are different kinds of proximity sensors. Some of them are listed [8]:

- Inductive: This type of sensor is used to detect nearby metallic objects. The sensor creates an electromagnetic field around itself or on a sensing surface.
- Capacitive: This type of sensor is used for detection of metallic objects and nonmetallic objects.
- Photoelectric: This type of sensor is used to detect objects. A light source and receiver are the main components of such sensors.
- Magnetic: This type of sensor uses an electrical switch that is operated based on the presence of permanent magnets in a sensing area.

Workings of a inductive proximity sensor

An inductive proximity sensor [9,10] mainly consists of a coil, an electronic oscillator, a detection circuit, an output circuit, and an energy source to provide electrical stimulation. This type of proximity sensor works on the principle of inductance and generation of eddy currents. Inductance is defined as the change in current flowing through a conductor that induces a voltage in both the conductor and any nearby conductors. Eddy current is the current induced in the conductor by a changing magnetic field in the conductor. Eddy current creates a magnetic field that opposes the magnetic field that created it (Fig. 3.29).

The oscillator is fed electrical current through a direct current supply. This oscillator generates a changing alternating current (AC). When AC is passed through the induction coil, it generates a changing electromagnetic field. This field creates metal sensing region called an *active surface* in front of the sensor. Fig. 3.30 shows AC and electromagnetic field generation on the sensor side, while the metal object generates a change in impedance due to eddy currents.

When a metallic object comes into the inductive proximity sensor's field of detection, eddy circuits build up in the incoming metallic object. This eddy current reacts to the source of the magnetic field and hence it acts to reduce the inductive sensor's own oscillation field. When the oscillation amplitude decreases

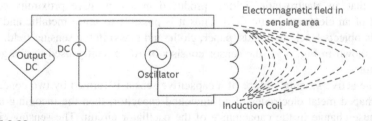

FIGURE 3.29

Inductive proximity sensor components.

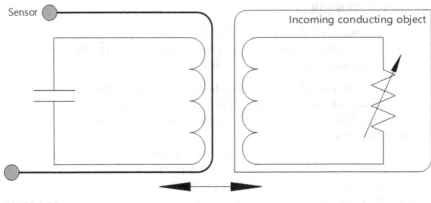

FIGURE 3.30

Proximity sensor operating principle.

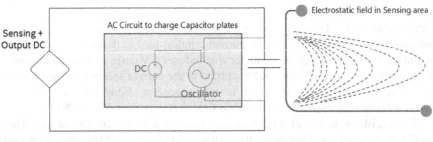

FIGURE 3.31

Capacitive proximity sensor components.

beyond a certain threshold, the sensor's detection circuit triggers an output from the output circuitry [11].

Workings of a capacitive proximity sensor

A capacitive proximity [12,13] sensor is similar to an inductive proximity sensor except that an electrostatic field is produced in a capacitive proximity sensor instead of an electromagnetic field. Thus it is possible to sense metallic and non-metallic objects (such as liquids, paper, cloth, and glass) in the sensing field.

As shown in Fig. 3.31, the sensor consists of AC circuitry used to charge the capacitor.

If the active sensing surface of a capacitive sensor is formed by two concentrically shaped metal electrodes of an unwound capacitor, then the incoming target will cause change in the capacitance of the oscillator circuit. The sensing circuit picks up this change and triggers output change on reaching a threshold value.

If the active sensing surface of a capacitive sensor is formed by only one of the metal electrodes of the capacitor, then the incoming target will behave as the other plate. The presence of the other plate now enables the sensor capacitor plate to take or remove AC, thereby causing a change in the current value that is picked up by the sensing circuit. The output circuitry indicates output change on reaching a threshold value of the AC change of AC circuitry.

The adjustment of the sensor capacitor plate can be used to regulate the operating distance. This helps in use cases of detection of full versus empty containers. The sensor operating distance may require adjustment depending on the dielectric constant of the target material.

The effective sensing distance for the target materials with a larger dielectric constant is more than that for the target materials with a smaller dielectric constant. For example, a capacitive sensor can have an effective sensing distance of 10 mm for alcohol with a dielectric constant of 25, while the same capacitive sensor can have a sensing distance 2 mm for glass with a dielectric constant of 5.

Workings of a photoelectric proximity sensor

A photoelectric proximity [14] sensor is used to detect the distance or presence/absence of a target object. It uses a light transmitter (mostly infrared) and a photoelectric receiver. There are four modes of photoelectric sensors:

- Direct reflection (diffused): In this type (Fig. 3.32) both the light transmitter and receiver are in the sensor and it uses the light deflected directly from the target object for detection. Hence it is crucial that the transmitted light/radiation is reflected off the object and reaches the receiver. The emitter sends out a beam of light (most often a pulsed infrared, visible red, or laser) that diffuses in all directions, filling a detection area. The target then enters

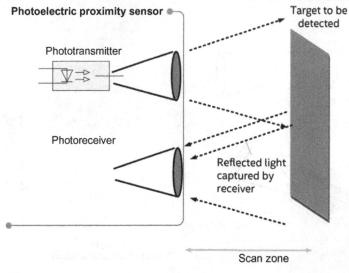

FIGURE 3.32

Diffused mode photoelectric proximity sensor.

the area and deflects part of the beam back to the receiver. Detection occurs and output is turned on or off when sufficient light falls on the receiver. Such sensors are affected by both the color and surface type of the object. If the object is opaque, then lighter color objects can have a greater sensing distance while darker objects will have a reduced sensing distance. If the object is shiny then the operating distance is affected by the type of surface (more than the color of the object).

One of the variation of the diffused mode is a diffused converged beam mode (Fig. 3.33) wherein the transmitter and the receiver are both focused on a same exact point in front of the sensor. This point of focus is called the *sensor focal point.*

The sensor can detect any object at the sensor focal point or within a sensing window around the focal point. Any objects that are outside this sensing window are ignored. Such diffused converged mode sensor enables the sensor to detect low reflective targets better than a simple diffused mode sensor.

Fig. 3.34 shows diffused mode sensor with mechanical background suppression that has two receivers. The first receiver captures reflected light from the target while the second receiver captures reflected light from the background. If the reflected light from the target is of higher intensity than the one captured from the background then the target is detected, otherwise not.

Fig. 3.35 shows diffused mode sensor with electronic background suppression where a position sensitive electronic device acts as a receiver. This receiver

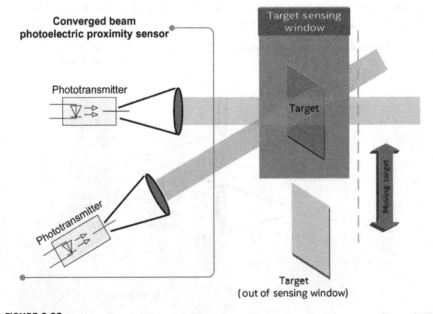

FIGURE 3.33

Diffused converged beam mode photoelectric proximity sensor.

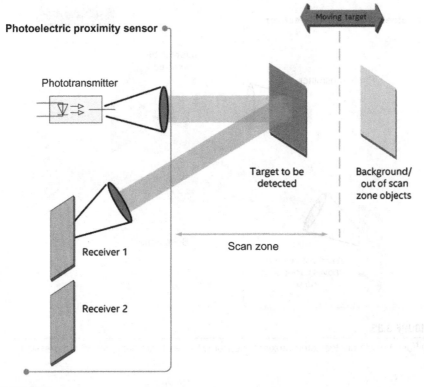

FIGURE 3.34

Diffused mode photoelectric proximity sensor with mechanical background suppression.

compares the received reflected light from the target and from the background with a predetermined value and reports target detection when the reflected light intensity from the target exceeds the predetermined intensity value.

- Retroreflective (reflection with reflector) [15]: In this type of photoelectric sensor the transmitter and the receiver are placed together in the sensor body, but the sensor requires a separate reflector (Fig. 3.36). If an object comes in between the reflector and the receiver in the sensor, then the light beam between them gets interrupted. This allows the sensor to detect the interrupting object. These sensors generally have longer sensing distances due to the increased efficiency of the reflector compared with the reflectivity of most targets. The target color and finish do not affect the sensing range in retroreflective mode as they do with diffused mode.
- Polarized reflection with reflector: This type of sensor is similar to a retroreflective sensor described earlier, but it uses a polarization filter, which only allows light at a certain phase angle back to the receiver (Fig. 3.37). This helps the sensor to see a shiny object as a target and not incorrectly as a reflector because the light reflected from the reflectors shifts the phase of the

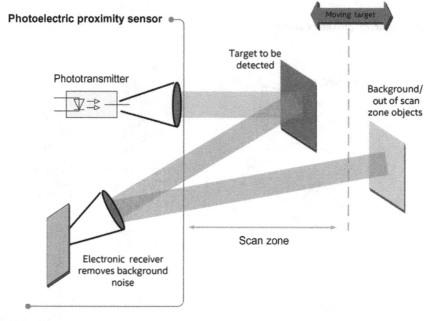

FIGURE 3.35

Diffused mode photoelectric proximity sensor with electronic background suppression.

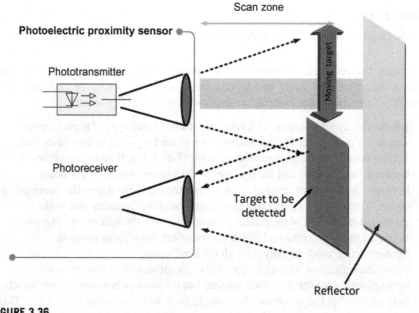

FIGURE 3.36

Retroreflective photoelectric proximity sensor.

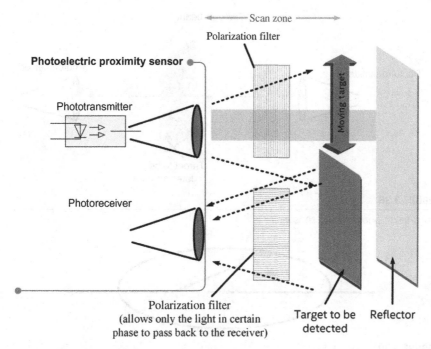

FIGURE 3.37

Polarized photoelectric sensor.

light, whereas light reflected from a shiny target does not. A polarized retroreflective photoelectric sensor must be used with a corner-cube reflector, which is a type of reflector that can accurately return the light energy on a parallel axis back to the receiver. Polarized retroreflective sensors are recommended for use cases with reflective targets.

- Thru-beam: This type of sensor is also known as opposed mode and uses a separate housing for the transmitter and the receiver (Fig. 3.38). The photo beam from a transmitter is pointed at the receiver. When an object comes between the transmitter and the receiver, it interrupts the photo beam between them, thereby causing the sensor output to change. This mode is the most accurate and reliable, and it allows the longest sensing ranges amongst all the modes of photoelectric sensors.

Workings of a magnetic proximity sensor

A magnetic proximity sensor consists of a reed switch. The reed switch is an electrical switch operated by an applied magnetic field. It contains a pair of magnetizable, flexible, metal reeds whose end portions are separated by a small gap when the switch is open (Fig. 3.39). The reeds are hermetically sealed in opposite ends of a tubular glass envelope. The stiffness of the reeds causes them to separate, and

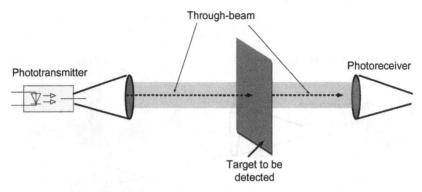

FIGURE 3.38

Thru-beam photoelectric sensor.

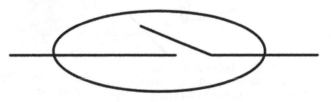

FIGURE 3.39

Magnetic proximity sensor schematic.

open the circuit, when the magnetic field ceases. A magnetic field (from an electro-magnet or a permanent magnet) will cause the reeds to come together and complete an electrical circuit. When the reed switch is turned on, the sensor is turned on.

PRESSURE SENSOR

A pressure sensor is a device that can measure pressure (mainly of liquids and gases) as force/unit area. This sensor, while acting as transducer, generates a signal in response to the pressure applied to the sensor. Following are the different types of pressure sensors:

- Absolute pressure sensor: measures pressure relative to perfect vacuum.
- Gauge pressure sensor: measures pressure relative to atmospheric pressure.
- Vacuum pressure sensor: measures pressure below atmospheric pressure or measures low pressure relative to perfect vacuum.
- Differential pressure sensor: measures difference between two pressures.
- Sealed pressure sensor: measures pressure relative to some fixed pressure.

Pressure sensors can be of the mechanical type (such as a Bourdon tube) or the electronic type (such as a silicon diaphragm or stainless diaphragm). The following are some force collector types electronic pressure sensors: piezoresistive strain gauge, capacitive, electromagnetic, piezoelectric, and optical.

Workings of a pressure sensor [16]

First let us discuss the working principle of piezoresistance, or how the piezoelectric property of certain metals is used in pressure sensors.

In certain materials (conducting and semiconducting), the change in interatomic spacing due to applied pressure or strain results in affecting the energy difference between valence band and the bottom of the conduction band. Such change either helps or makes it difficult for the electrons to jump to a conduction band (depending on the material and applied pressure). Hence the applied pressure results in a change of resistivity of the material.

The equation for the piezoresistive coefficient is:

$$\beta = \frac{\text{(Change in resistivity/Original resistivity)}}{\text{Applied pressure}}$$

Change in resistivity $= \beta \times$ Applied pressure $\times$ Original resistivity R

The resistance of material is given by

$R = \beta \times$ (Length of the conductor)/(Cross-sectional area of the current flow)

In the case of the silicon diaphragm pressure sensor, the strain-sensitive resistor (a semiconductor distortion gauge as in Fig. 3.40) layer is formed on a silicon chip/diaphragm. When pressure is applied on the silicon diaphragm, the resistance value of the strain-sensitive resistor changes. A change in pressure is thereby converted into an electrical signal.

$R = \beta \times$ (Length of the conductor)/(Cross-sectional area of the current flow)

$$\therefore R = \beta \times \frac{L}{A}$$

The change in resistance can be defined in the form of the following equation:

$$dR = \frac{\beta}{A}dL + \frac{L}{A}d\beta + \frac{\beta L}{A^2}dA = \frac{R}{L}dL + \frac{R}{\beta}d\beta + \frac{R}{A}dA$$

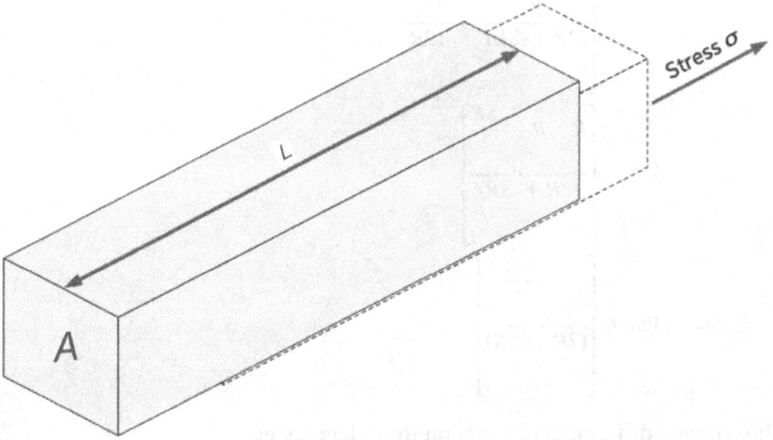

FIGURE 3.40

Physical causes of piezoresistivity.

Dividing the equation by R, we get the following equation:

$$\therefore \frac{dR}{R} = \frac{dL}{L} + \frac{d\rho}{\rho} - \frac{dA}{A}$$

This change in resistance can be transformed into voltage change using a Wheatstone bridge circuit as shown in Fig. 3.41.

At the point of equilibrium, no current flows through the circuit:

$$\frac{R1}{R3} = \frac{R2}{R4} \quad \text{and} \quad V1 = V2; V3 = V4$$

$$Vout = Vin \times \left[\frac{R2}{(R1 + R2)} - \frac{(R4)}{(R3 + R4)} \right]$$

If all R are the same and $R1$ is the pressure sensor demonstrating change in resistivity, then

$$Vout = Vin \times \left[\frac{R}{(R1 + R)} - \frac{(R)}{(R + R)} \right] = Vin \times \left[\frac{R}{(R + \Delta R + R)} - \frac{(R)}{(R + R)} \right]$$

$$= Vin \times \left[\frac{R}{(2R + \Delta R)} - \frac{(R)}{2R} \right]$$

$$= Vin \times \left[\frac{R}{(2R + \Delta R)} - \frac{1}{2} \right] = Vin \times \left[\frac{R}{(2R + \Delta R)} - \frac{\left(R + \frac{\Delta R}{2}\right)}{2\left(R + \frac{\Delta R}{2}\right)} \right]$$

$$= Vin \times \left[\frac{R}{(2R + \Delta R)} - \frac{\left(R + \frac{\Delta R}{2}\right)}{(2R + \Delta R)} \right]$$

$$= Vin \times \left[\frac{R - R - \frac{\Delta R}{2}}{(2R + \Delta R)} \right]$$

$$\therefore Vout = Vin \times \left[\frac{-\frac{\Delta R}{2}}{(2R + \Delta R)} \right]$$

This voltage difference is temperature independent.

Let us now understand working principle of capacitive pressure sensors [17].

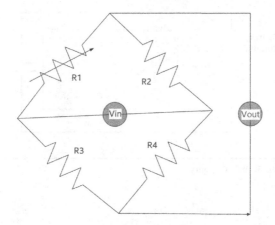

FIGURE 3.41

Wheatstone bridge.

The capacitance of two parallel plates is given by $C = \mu A/d$
where

μ = dielectric constant of the material between the plates,
A = area of the plates, and
d = spacing between the plates.

Capacitive pressure sensors determine the pressure change through a change in capacitance due to:

- Change in dielectric: that is, the change in exposed/porous dielectric
- Change in distance between the plates

Capacitive pressure sensors use a thin diaphragm as one plate of a capacitor. When pressure is applied to the diaphragm, the diaphragm deflects, resulting in the change in spacing between the plates, thereby causing change in capacitance of the sensors.

As discussed "Proximity Sensors" section, this change in capacitance is used to control the frequency of an oscillator or to vary AC signal through a network (Fig. 3.42).

TOUCH SENSORS [18]

Touch is considered one of the five senses of the human body. It is also referred to as tactile perception. The sense of touch can be perceived in several ways, like pressure, skin stretch, vibration, and temperature [19]. Touch includes three main sensory systems:

- Touch/physical stimulus: This is also referred to as a somatosensory system or tactile perception and it consists both of sensory receptors and sensory

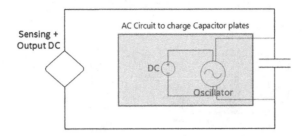

FIGURE 3.42

Capacitive pressure sensor circuitry.

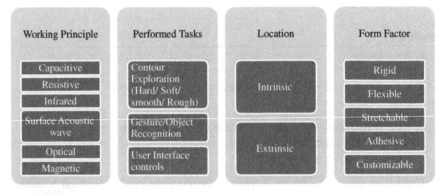

FIGURE 3.43

Classification of touch sensors.

(afferent) neurons in the periphery (skin, muscle, organs) and neurons within the central nervous system.

- Proprioception: This means "movement sense," which refers to the sense of position of different body parts relative to each other and the amount of force involved in the movement.
- Haptic perception [20] refers to the sense/perception obtained through use of or exploration by body parts/sensors. Exploration can be done through motion, pressure, enclosure, or mapping the contours of the object.

Thus the perception of a stimulus can be categorized as cutaneous/tactile perception, proprioception/kinesthetic perception, and haptic perception.

The tactile sensing system consists of various components [21] that help create perception of a touch/contact event. Fig. 3.43 shows the classification [22] of touch sensors based on their different parameters and characteristics.

Touch sensors based on working principles

Touch sensors can be categorized [21] based on their transduction methods. Table 3.5 summarizes some of the main transduction methods.

Table 3.5 Touch Sensor Types Based on Working Principle

Transduction Method	Working Principle	Pros and Cons
Capacitive	Capacitive sensors consist of a plate capacitor in which the distance between plates or the effective area is changed by the applied force by shifting their relative position	✓ Sensitive, just touch no press needed ✗ Severe hysteresis
Resistive	Two conductive sheets separated by insulating material (e.g., air) One of the sheets carries a voltage gradient (reference voltage and ground on its two opposite ends) The second sheet acts like slider in a linear potentiometer when brought in contact with the first by the applied force. A voltage divider is made at the contact point and the voltage of the sheet (slider) can be used to find location of the contact point	✓ Sensitive, inexpensive ✗ Power hungry, need pressure (touch not enough)
Piezoresistive	Made of materials whose resistance changes with force/pressure	✓ Low cost, low noise, good sensitivity ✗ Stiff/frail, nonlinear response, hysteresis, signal drift
Magnetic	Measures the change in flux density caused by applied force on a magnet	✓ High sensitivity, dynamic range, no mechanical hysteresis, physically robust ✗ magnetic interference, bulky, high power
Ultrasound	Useful for detecting surface Noise that occurs at the onset of motion and during slip/surface roughness during movement	✓ Fast dynamic response, good force resolution ✗ Limited utility at low frequency
Piezoelectric	Uses the property of materials that can generate charge/voltage proportional to the applied force/pressure	✓ Dynamic response, high bandwidth ✗ Temperature sensitive
Tunnel	Uses unique capability of material to transform from an insulator to a conductor through quantum tunneling (of electrons) between the material particles when deformed (due to compression, twist or stretch). Stress is converted into light or change in current	✓ Sensitive, physically flexible ✗ Nonlinear response

Ultrasound/surface acoustic wave touch sensors [23]

Consider a bell which produces sound waves through vibrations when struck. The produced sound slowly dampens as the energy generated through vibrations dissipates. If the bell is touched when it is vibrating then the sound dampens more quickly as the touch results in dampening the vibrations. By measuring the change in vibrations, calculating decay rate (which increases with touch), it can be inferred if the bell is being touched or not.

Surface acoustic wave touch sensors have following components:

- Substrates with high quality factor Q. Q factor describes if an oscillator or resonator is underdamped, overdamped, or critically damped. Higher Q indicates that the oscillations die out more slowly (a lower rate of energy loss relative to the stored energy of the resonator).
- The ultrasonic transmitter/transducer launches a small ultrasonic pulse.
- Exposed touch surface.

The surface of high Q substrate (also known as resonator) is contoured to create resonant cavities. These cavities can trap the ultrasound energy and can create miniature islands of vibrations on receiving an ultrasound pulse, which is generated by the accompanying ultrasonic transmitter. On receiving pulses (in the megahertz range) from the transmitter, a wave is created in the resonator as it vibrates. This wave motion propagates through the resonant cavity across the cross section of the substrate with high Q factor. As the pulse wave reaches the exposed touch surface on the other end of substrate, it gets reflected back to the transmitter. The transmitter in this case while acting as receiver captures and measures the strength of received pulse.

Under normal circumstances when there is no touch to the exposed touch surface, the strength of received pulse is within the limits of low-damped waves, meaning it is almost same as the strength of transmitted pulse because the wave energy dies out more slowly in high Q substrates.

However, if the exposed touch surface of the resonator is touched then there is energy loss at the point of contact (e.g., a finger absorbs the energy). This results in faster energy loss than expected in high Q substrate. The transmitter and receiver are in the continuous process of transmitting, listening, and evaluating the signal. When the signal decays faster than the expected normal time to reach threshold decayed value then the receiver senses this higher-than-normal energy loss and reports out in the form of electrical output.

Fig. 3.44 shows how the change in transmit time can be calculated [21].

There are two ways to calculate the touch:

1. By calculating reduction of travel distance of the ultrasound wave through the high Q material.
2. By calculating damping of ultrasound wave.

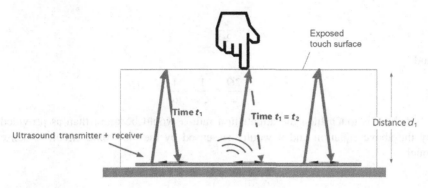

FIGURE 3.44

Ultrasonic touch sensor.

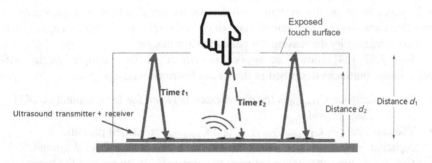

FIGURE 3.45

Compressed/pushed ultrasonic touch sensor.

Method 1 (Fig. 3.45):

$$d_1 - d_2 = \frac{1}{2(t_1 - t_2)}$$

$F(\text{compressing force}) = \text{High } Q \text{ material stiffness } \mu \times (d_1 - d_2) = \mu \times \dfrac{1}{2(t_1 - t_2)}$

Method 2:

The resonant frequency f_0 of high Q substrate can be expressed in radians $\omega = 2\pi f0$

The factors Q, damping ratio ζ, attenuation rate α, and exponential time constant τ are related as

$$Q = \frac{1}{2\zeta} = \frac{\omega}{2\alpha} = \frac{\omega\tau}{2}$$

$$\therefore \zeta = \frac{1}{2Q} = \frac{\alpha}{\omega} = \frac{1}{\tau\omega}$$

$$\therefore \alpha = \frac{\omega}{2Q} = \zeta\omega = \frac{1}{\tau}$$

and

$$\tau = \frac{2Q}{\omega} = \frac{1}{\zeta\omega} = \frac{1}{\alpha}$$

If there is touch then the attenuation rate α would be more than as provided by the above equation and it would be sensed by the electronic circuit to sense touch.

Capacitive touch sensors

Capacitive touch works on the ability to measure a change in capacitance (Fig. 3.46). This change in capacitance based on the touch is relative to the parasitic capacitance of the system (also known as the steady-state capacitance or baseline capacitance). The sensitivity, which is the relative change in capacitance, can be increased by decreasing the parasitic capacitance.

Fig. 3.47 [24] shows an equivalent circuit of an example single self-capacitance button as described in the Texas Instrument design guide.

- The capacitance C_{Ground} is the capacitance between the local ground of DUT and the earth ground.
- The capacitances C_{Trace}, $C_{\text{Electrode}}$, and $C_{\text{Parasitics}}$ are called parasitic capacitance. C_{Trace} is the capacitance between the trace and local ground. $C_{\text{Electrode}}$ is the capacitance between the electrode structures and the local ground. $C_{\text{Parasitics}}$ is the total internal parasitic capacitance of the sensor and circuit components.
- C_{Touch} is the touch capacitance, formed between the user's touch (say a finger) and the electrode. The flat surface of the finger touching the exposed touch surface forms the upper plate of parallel plate capacitance and the electrode forms the lower plate.

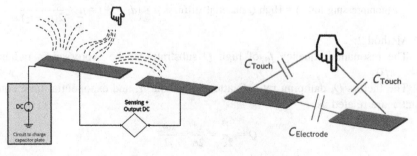

FIGURE 3.46

Capacitive touch sensor.

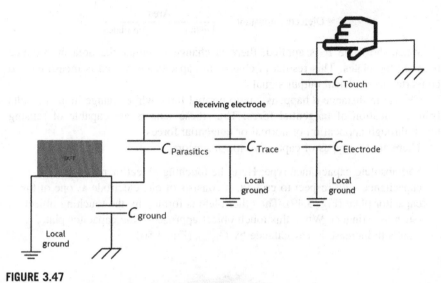

FIGURE 3.47

Equivalent circuitry of capacitive touch sensor.

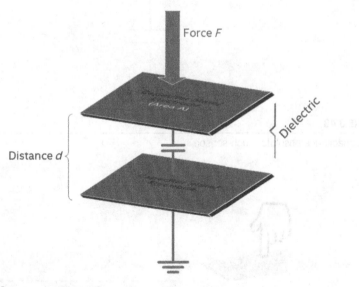

FIGURE 3.48

Simple parallel plate capacitor.

The equation for capacitance in the case of a parallel plate capacitor consisting of two parallel plates with area A and separated by distance d (Fig. 3.48) is given as

$$C = \text{Dielectric constant} \times \frac{\text{Area}}{\text{Distance between plates}}$$

When the force F is applied, there is change in either the area or distance between the plates. This results in change in capacitance, which is measured and converted to electrical output signal.

Change in distance d happens due to normal force while change in area results from application of tangential force. Thus these sensors are capable of sensing touch through application of normal or tangential forces.

There are two types of capacitive touch sensors:

1. Self/absolute capacitance type: Here the touching object increases the capacitance with respect to ground. It consists of one electrode as one of the capacitor plate (Fig. 3.49). The other plate is formed by the touching object (such as a finger). When this touch object approaches the capacitor plate, it results in increase in capacitance by C_{Touch} (Fig. 3.50).

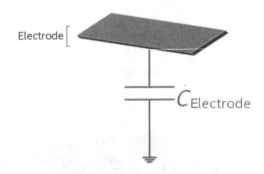

FIGURE 3.49

Self capacitance/absolute touch sensor.

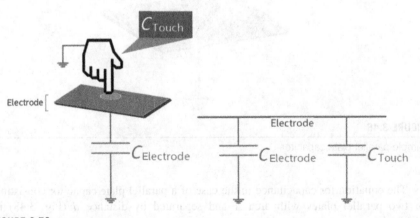

FIGURE 3.50

Absolute capacitance touch sensor with touch object.

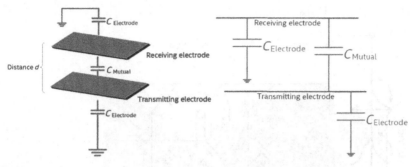

FIGURE 3.51

Mutual capacitance touch sensor.

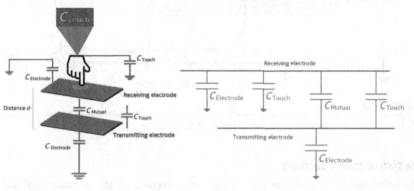

FIGURE 3.52

Mutual capacitance touch sensor with touch object.

2. Mutual capacitance type: Here the touching object changes the mutual coupling of the two electrodes (Figs. 3.51 and 3.52).

In the case shown in Fig. 3.53, the mutual capacitors are arranged in an array [18] and voltage applied to the rows and columns of this array. When a touch object (such as a finger) comes closer to the array, there is a change in capacitance of the array. Through such arrays multiple touch contacts can be detected at the same time. The capacitance change at each separate point in the array is measured to determine the touch location.

C_{mutual} is first measured using the row and column decoders. Voltage V_{step} is applied to row electrode of the sensor to charge the capacitor. When V_{step} is switched to ground, the capacitor charge is transferred to C_F and the change in output voltage is given by:

$$\Delta V_{\text{output}} = -\Delta V_{\text{step}} \times \frac{C_{\text{mutual}}}{C_{\text{feedback}}}$$

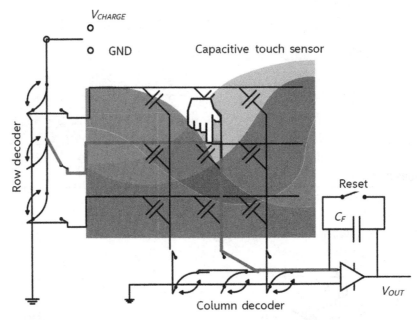

FIGURE 3.53

Mutual capacitance touch sensor in array configuration.

Resistive touch sensors

Resistive touch sensors use the change in resistance of the sensing material to detect and measure touch or contact (Fig. 3.54). The change in resistance can be measured differently depending on the type of resistive sensor:

1. Potentiometer type sensor: change in resistance depends on the position of the touch.
2. Piezoresistive type sensor: change in resistance depends on the contact pressure.

The concept of the potentiometer type of sensors is briefly described using Fig. 3.55.

If the sensor is made of two flexible sheets coated with resistive material placed one on top of the other and separated by air or an insulating material, then when the two sheets are pressed against each other through touch, the second sheet acts as a slider on the potentiometer shown in Fig. 3.56 and this second sheet helps measure the voltage as the distance along the first sheet, thus providing an X-coordinate (Fig. 3.57). Similarly the first sheet helps measure distance in terms of voltage on the second sheet, thus providing a Y-coordinate (Fig. 3.58).

Thus by measuring the above voltages, the exact coordinate of the touch point can be calculated (Figs. 3.57 and 3.58). If a third axis (Z-coordinate) is also measured, then the pressure of touch can also be calculated [24].

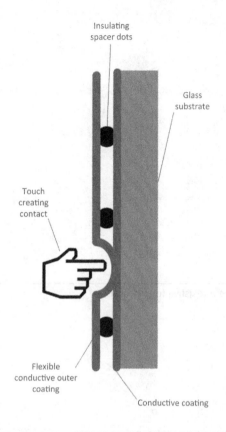

FIGURE 3.54

Resistive touch sensor.

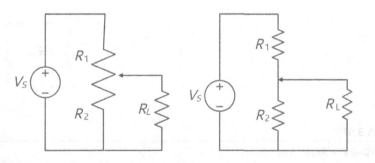

FIGURE 3.55

Potentiometer type sensor.

$$V_L = \frac{R_2}{R_1 + R_2} V_S$$

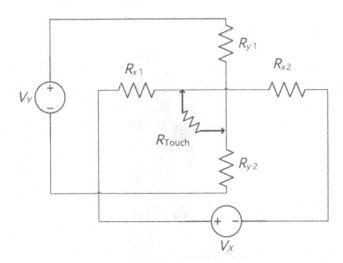

FIGURE 3.56

X- and *Y*-coordinates in a resistive touch sensor.

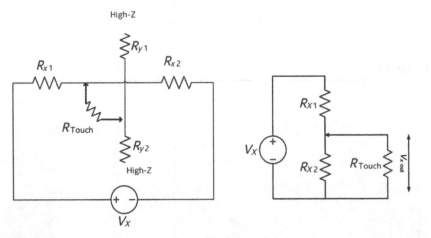

FIGURE 3.57

X-coordinate voltage calculation.

$$V_{xout} = \frac{R_{x2}}{R_{x1} + R_{x2}} V_x$$

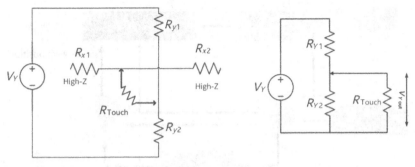

FIGURE 3.58

Y-coordinate voltage calculation.

$$V_{yout} = \frac{R_{y2}}{R_{y1} + R_{y2}} V_y$$

BIOSENSORS

A biosensor consists of:

- A biorecognition component referred to as bioreceptor, a biotransducer component, and electronic system, which includes a signal amplifier, processor, and display. The bioreceptor uses biomolecules from organisms or receptors modeled after biological systems to interact with the analyte of interest.
- A biotransducer, which measures the above-mentioned interaction and outputs a measurable signal proportional to the presence of the target analyte in the sample.
- A bioreader, which outputs the signal from the biotransducer in a user-friendly format.

Bioreceptors can be categorized based on following interactions: antibody/antigen, enzymes, nucleic acids/DNA, cellular structures/cells, or biomimetic materials.

Biosensors can be classified based on following categories of biotransducers: electrochemical, optical, electronic, piezoelectric, gravimetric, and pyroelectric.

Biosensors enable quick, convenient testing at the point of concern or care where the sample was procured.

Based on the different ways that biosensing can occur, the following are the main types of biosensors:

- Affinity sensor: In this kind of sensor the biological element binds to the analyte.

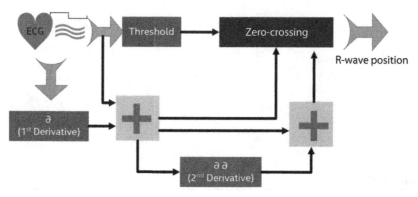

FIGURE 3.59

Heart rate extraction algorithm.

- Metabolic sensor: In this kind of sensor the biological element and the analyte interact and result in a chemical change, which is then used to measure the concentration of a substrate.
- Catalytic sensor: In this kind of sensor the biological element combines with the analyte but does not change it chemically. It instead converts the biological element to an auxiliary substrate.

ECG working principles

An electrocardiogram (ECG) is a recorded data of a user's heart rate produced by electrocardiography. The heart rate can be extracted from the ECG and the continuous evolution of ECG waveforms can be used to diagnose several cardiac disorders.

Example heart rate estimation algorithm [25]

Heartbeat rate measurements can be done by detecting R-wave peaks from the QRS wave, and the interval between two consecutive R-waves can be considered as heartbeat periodicity. One of the many algorithms to detect R-wave peak is to detect zero-crossing of the first derivative of the ECG signal when the original signal (raw) and its second derivative is above a certain threshold value (Fig. 3.59).

The first and second derivative can be estimated using digital signal processing methods. The first derivative measures the rate of change of signal (slope), while the second derivative measures the curvature of the signal. The threshold value depends on the energy of the raw ECG signal and it is adapted continuously.

REFERENCES

[1]   AN3182 Application note, Tilt measurement using a low-g 3-axis accelerometer (STMicroelectronics).

[2]   Goodrich R. Accelerometer vs. gyroscope: what's the difference?

[3]   Wilson E. Virtual gyroscopes [MEng Thesis at Cambridge University]. 2007.

[4]   Wilson E. Explanation of gyroscopic precession [MEng Thesis at Cambridge University]. 2007.

[5]   Gyroscopes, precession, and statics, Lecture PPT, University of Colorado.

[6]   Rotation, torques, precession. UNSW (School of Physics, Sydney, Australia) web page.

[7]   Weisstein E. Gyroscopic precession.

[8]   Fargo Controls Inc. Operating principles for proximity sensors.

[9]   Menke H. Basic operating principle of an inductive proximity sensor.

[10] PC control Learning Zone website. Inductive proximity sensors.

[11] Omron website. Proximity sensors.

[12] Siemens course. Capacitive proximity sensors theory of operation.

[13] PC control Learning Zone website. Capacitive proximity sensors.

[14] Fargo Controls Inc article. Operating principles for photoelectric sensors.

[15] Frigyes G, Myers E, Allison J, Pepperl + Fuchs. Fundamentals of photoelectric sensors.

[16] Omron website. Pressure Sensors.

[17] Sensors online website. Pressure fundamentals of pressure sensor technology.

[18] Dahiya RS, Valle M. Tactile sensing technologies. In: Robotic tactile sensing; 2013. p. 79–136.

[19] Somatosensory system, <http://en.wikipedia.org/wiki/Somatosensory_system>.

[20] Haptic perception, <http://en.wikipedia.org/wiki/Haptic_perception>.

[21] Dahiya RS, Valle M. Tactile sensing for robotic applications. In: Rocha JG, Lanceros-Mendez S, editors. Sensors, Focus on Tactile, Force and Stress Sensors; 2008. p. 444.

[22] Weigel M, Lu T, Bailly G, Oulasvirta A, Majidi C, Steimle J. iSkin: flexible, stretchable and visually customizable on-body touch sensors for mobile computing. CHI 2015, April 18 – 23 2015, Seoul, Republic of Korea.

[23] Schieleit D. Machine design website. New touch sensor uses trapped acoustic resonance technology to monitor contacts.

[24] Gu H, Sterzik C. Texas instruments: capacitive touch hardware design guide, design guide, SLAA576—May 2013.

[25] Luprano J, Sola J, Dasen S, Koller JM, Chetelat O. 2006 International workshop on wearable and implantable body sensor networks (BSN 2006), 3–5 April 2006, Cambridge, MA.

Sensor hubs

INFORMATION IN THIS CHAPTER:

- Types of Integrated Sensor Hubs
- Sensor Hubs From Atmel, Intel, and STMicroelectronics

INTRODUCTION TO SENSOR HUBS

A sensor hub [1−3] is a connection point for multiple sensors that uses a micro controller unit (MCU), coprocessor, or digital signal processor (DSP) to compile and process data gathered from those sensors.

A sensor hub can be the offload engine for the main processor of the device. When the sensors provide environment and ecosystem data, it is gathered and processed by the sensor hub rather than using software (running on the main processor) to process the sensor data. The use of a sensor hub improves power efficiency and battery life of the system while offering better system performance, because it does not require the main processor to continuously run in the background for sensor data processing.

Sensor hubs are generally used:

- when there are multiple sensors, each of which has high requirement for system resources;
- when fusion of multiple sensor data is required (such as combining accelerometer sensor data with gyroscope data for better accuracy);
- in smartphones and wireless sensor and actuator networks.

Sensor hubs [4] are used to perform tasks that need multiple sensors with high demand for resources and for efficiency. Sensor hubs are commonly used in smartphones and on wireless sensor and actuator networks (WSANs). WSANs are formed by groups of sensors that gather information about their environments and use actuators, such as servos or motors, to interact autonomously and instantly with their environment.

Sensor hubs today have increasing military and commercialized applications such as monitoring and control of industrial settings, telemedicine, and scientific development.

With more sensors and sensing applications being to the devices like smartphones, tablets, and wearables, the power needed to run these sensors and process

Mobile Sensors and Context-Aware Computing. DOI: http://dx.doi.org/10.1016/B978-0-12-801660-2.00004-5

the sensor data (into a form useful to humans) increases. The power requirements increases further with more complex sensor data generated from fusion algorithms such as one from fusion of accelerometers, and gyroscopes data.

Sensor hubs are now part of mobile devices and wearables due to battery limitations of such devices and more complex power-hungry applications and processors. Since longer battery life is one of the key factors of such mobile and wearable devices, sensor hubs offload the application process by running sensor fusion algorithms themselves and "waking" the main processor only as needed, thereby increasing the run-time battery life.

With the applications such as context awareness or gesture recognition that requires "always-on" functionality on the mobile devices/wearables, ultra-low power requirements further support the use of sensor hubs in these devices.

Sensor hubs can be implemented using following approaches (including combinations of them):

1. Dedicated microcontroller unit (MCU)
2. Application processor-based hub with integrated sensors
3. Sensor-based hub with integrated microcontroller (MCU)
4. FPGA-based hub.

The approach or combination of approaches is decided based on the application, its price, power, and performance requirements, and its use cases (phone vs wearable device).

For example, a wearable device may have an application processor or separate MCU to perform fusion algorithms in order to keep the main high-performance/high-power MCU from waking up.

A step counter or health/fitness device with context awareness would need to factor in the battery capacity of that device and the type and requirements of applications that would run on the device to select a sensor hub implementation architecture. In such cases, it is important to consider maximum computing power needed for the specific range of applications along with other requirements like display types, connections, synchronization mechanisms, protocols, and additional functions or integrated sensors like pulse or heart rate monitors.

DEDICATED MICROCONTROLLER UNIT

A dedicated microcontroller unit [5] is used as an external hub that handles the data coming directly from the different sensors. This dedicated MCU handles the processing of the sensor data and does not have to wake up the main device processor. For always-on applications, the dedicated MCU can continue to be on in low-power state while the main device processor is sleeping. This helps in better power efficiency and lower latency in handling sensor data. Examples of this approach are TI's MSP430 MCUs and Atmel's SAM G series. Apple iPhone 5, Samsung Galaxy S5, and Motorola Moto X use this approach.

APPLICATION PROCESSOR-BASED SENSOR HUB

This is an integrated sensor hub (ISH) solution where the sensor hub functionality is performed by the main application processor. This solution results in cost savings from elimination of a separate sensor data processor and associate design/device build complexities. The cons of this approach are the challenges of the main application processor (e.g., programming the main DSP application processor instead of the more commonly used MCU). Examples of this approach are Qualcomm's Hexagon DSP embedded in the Snapdragon platform and Intel's Merrifield/Moorefield (Z34XX) architecture.

SENSOR-BASED HUB WITH MICRO CONTROLLER UNIT

In this approach, an MCU is combined with one or more sensors like accelerometer, gyroscope, proximity sensor, and so on. In this architecture, the sensors that are used for fusion algorithms or for tracking user activity and context awareness (gestures, motion or step counting, and so forth) are used. Examples of this approach are STMicroelectronics' iNEMO-A LIS331EB or InvenSense sensor hubs. This solution can be used in high-end mobile device handsets.

This approach reduces the cost through integration and BOM (bill of material) reduction, while helping to achieve lower power through sensor + MCU power flow optimization. Since this architecture tries to do a multitude of functions with sensors that are already integrated, it may not be optimized for one particular function and does not have flexibility of selecting a different set of sensors (from other than what is already integrated in the solution) to go with MCU.

FPGA-BASED SENSOR HUB

This solution provides the ability to reprogram the device while operating at extremely low power. However, designing for FPGA (field programmable gate array) requires a different set of resources and skills.

ATMEL SAM D20 SENSOR HUB WITH MICRO CONTROLLER UNIT

The Atmel SMART SAM D20 [6] is an example of a sensor hub with a dedicated microcontroller. It has 32-bit ARM Cortex-M0 + processor, Peripheral Touch Controller, and six serial communication modules (SERCOM).

The serial communication modules can be configured to support USART, UART, SPI, and I^{2}C. The Peripheral Touch Controller can support up to 256 buttons, sliders, wheels, and proximity sensing. There are two supported sleep modes that can be selected by software: Idle mode and Standby mode.

- Idle mode: In idle mode the CPU is stopped while all the other functions can be kept running.
- Standby mode: In standby mode all the clocks and the functions are stopped except those that are selected to continue running. The SleepWalking feature allows the peripherals to wake up based on some predefined conditions and hence the CPU is awakened only when needed, such as when a threshold is crossed or a result is ready. The peripherals can receive, react to, and send events in standby mode.

Fig. 4.1 is the block diagram of an Atmel SAM sensor hub with MCU followed by brief description of its basic components.

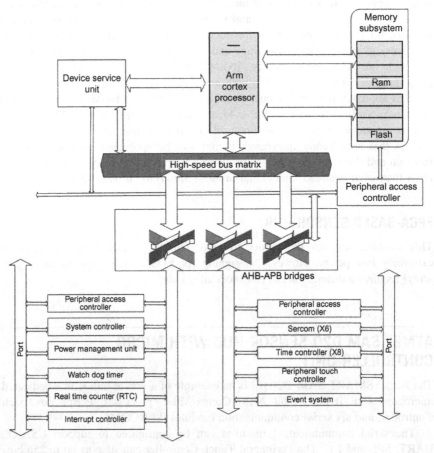

FIGURE 4.1

Block diagram of Atmel SAM series architecture.

CORTEX-M0 + PROCESSOR AND ITS PERIPHERALS

The Atmel SAM D20 device has the ARM Cortex-M0 + processor with two bus interfaces:

- A 32-bit AMBA 3 AHB-Lite system interface that connects to peripherals and all system memory, including flash and RAM.
- A 32-bit I/O port bus that interfaces with the port controlling the I/O pins of the microcontroller.

The following peripherals are connected to the processor:

- System Control Space: This space houses registers that the processor can use for debug.
- System Timer (SysTick): This is a 24-bit system timer.
- Nested Vector Interrupt Controller (NVIC): There are 32 external interrupts connected to this interrupt controller block. Each of the interrupt signals is connected to one peripheral (such as SERCOMs, timers/counters, and the power management unit). This block prioritizes the external interrupts connected to it.
- System Control Block: This block provides information about system implementation and control (such as configuration, control, and system exceptions).
- High-Speed Bus Matrix: This is a symmetric crossbar bus switch that enables concurrent accesses between multiple masters and slaves with a 32-bit data bus width. The two masters on this crossbar switch are the cortex processor and the DSC (device service unit). The internal flash memory, internal SRAM, and AHB-APB bridges are the slaves on this bus matrix (Fig. 4.2).
- AHB-APB Bridge: These bridges are AHB slaves on the high-speed bus matrix that provide the interface between high-speed AHB bus matrices and programmable control registers of APB peripherals. These bridges have

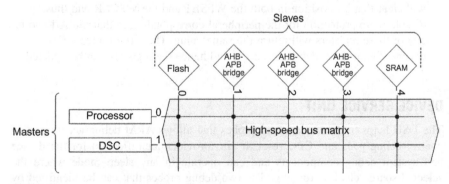

FIGURE 4.2

High-speed bus matrix masters and slaves.

Table 4.1 Write-Protection Registers

Bit	7	6	5	4	3	2	1	0	Comments
WPSET	Reserved	EIC	RTC	WDT	GCLK	SYSCTRL	PM	Reserved	Writing one will set bits for the peripherals
WPCLR	Reserved	EIC	RTC	WDT	GCLK	SYSCTRL	PM	Reserved	Writing one will clear bits for the peripherals

capability to add wait states, report error, and provide transaction protection along with features such as sparse data transfer (byte, half-word, and word), cycle merging (merge address, and data cycles into single cycle).
- Peripheral Access Controller (PAC): Each AHB-APB bridge has one PAC that provides register write protection for each of the peripherals connected to that particular AHB-APB bridge. The bus clock to PAC is controlled by the power management unit controls. The peripherals such as interrupt controller, real-time counter (RTC), watchdog timer (WDT), clock controller (GCLK), system controller (SYSCTRL), and power management (PM) can have the write protection. A write-protected peripheral will return an access error on receiving a write. No data is written to the peripheral in this case.

Write Protect Clear register (WPCLR) and Write Protect Set (WPSET) are the two 32-bit memory mapped I/O registers associated with write protection (Table 4.1):

0: Write-protection is disabled
1: Write-protection is enabled

Writing a one to any bit 6:1 in WPSET register will set that bit position in both the WPSET and the WPCLR and thus enable write protection for the peripheral corresponding to that bit. Writing a one to any bit 6:1 in WPCLR will clear that bit position in both the WPSET and the WPCLR and thus disable write protection for the peripheral corresponding to that bit. A Read to any of these registers will return the same value. The write protection is disabled/ignored for debugger access and hence the registers can be updated.

DEVICE SERVICE UNIT

The DSU helps to detect debugger probes that allows ARM debug access port to control debug pads and CPU reset. It also provides identification for the device and system debug components and can operate in any sleep mode where the selected source clock is running. The two debug probes that can be identified by the DSU are cold plugging and hot plugging. Cold plugging refers to the detection of debugger when the system is in reset and hot plugging refers to the detection of debugger when the system is not in reset. The DSU also supports the extension of CPU core reset after the release of external reset to ensure that CPU does not execute any code while the debugger is getting connected to the system.

POWER MANAGEMENT UNIT

The Power Management (PM) unit has three main functions: reset control, clock generation, and sleep modes of the microcontroller sleep mode management. These functions are described briefly here.

- Reset Control: The PM unit combines the resets from multiple sources such as power on reset (POR), external reset (RESET), WDT reset, software reset, brown out detector resets (BOD12, BOD33), and generates a reset to initialize the microcontroller to its initial state.
- Clock Control: The PM unit provides and controls synchronous clocks to the CPU, AHB, and APB modules. It also supports clock gating and clock failure detection.
- Power Management Control: The PM unit supports different sleep modes that can be selected to save power depending on the requirements of an application. The supported modes are:
  - *ACTIVE mode*: In this mode all the peripherals are operational and the software executes normally because all the clock domains are active.
  - *SLEEPWALKING*: During sleepwalking, the clocks for the peripherals are started to allow that peripheral to perform a task without waking up the CPU in STANDBY sleep mode. Once the SleepWalking task is done, the sensor hub device can either enter back into the STANDBY sleep mode or it can be awakened by an interrupt (from a peripheral involved in SleepWalking).
  - *SLEEP modes*: A WFI instructions activates the sleep mode and the sleep level (IDLE or STANDBY) is selected based on setting IDLE bits in the Sleep Mode register (SLEEP.IDLE) and the SLEEPDEEP bit of the System Control register of the CPU (Table 4.2). The brief description of the two sleep level is given here.

Table 4.2 Sleep Mode Entry and Exit

Mode	Level	Mode Entry	Wake-Up Sources
IDLE	0	SCR.SLEEPDEEP = 0	Asynchronous interrupt, synchronous (APB, AHB) interrupt
	1	SLEEP.IDLE = Level	Asynchronous interrupt, synchronous (APB) interrupt
	2	WFI	Asynchronous interrupt
STANDBY		SCR.SLEEPDEEP = 1 WFI	Asynchronous interrupt

- IDLE mode: In this mode, the CPU is stopped and for further reduction in the power consumption the clock sources as well as clocks to the various modules can also be disabled. This mode allows power optimization with the fastest wake up time. The voltage regulator operates in normal mode under IDLE mode. A nonmasked interrupt with sufficient priority can cause exit from this mode. On exit the CPU and the modules that were impacted are restarted.
- STANDBY mode: In this mode, all clock sources are stopped. Refer to Table 4.3 to understand the effect of the oscillator ONDEMAND and RUNSTDBY bit on the clock behavior in STANDBY mode. This mode helps to achieve very low-power consumption. Since the voltage regulator operates in low-power mode in STANDBY mode and cannot be overloaded, the user must ensure that a significant amount of clocks and peripherals are disabled before entering STANDBY mode.

Fig. 4.3 shows the entry and exit flows for IDLE mode. The SCR refers to the system control register in the ARM cortex CPU. The interrupt required to wake up the system should be of the appropriate priority and not masked in the NVIC module.

Fig. 4.4 shows the entry and exit flows for STANDBY mode along with the IDLE mode. The PRIMASK (priority mask register) configuration register is in the ARM cortex CPU. On exit from STANDBY mode, the device can either execute the interrupt service routine or continue the normal program execution according to the Priority Mask Register configuration.

SYSTEM CONTROLLER

The SYSCTRL provides a user interface to the clock sources, brown out detectors, on-chip voltage regulator, and voltage reference of the device. The interrupts from this module can be used to wake up the device from sleep modes.

WATCHDOG TIMER

The WDT monitors correct program operation and helps to recover the systems from error conditions (such as runaway or deadlock) by issuing a system reset. It can be configured in normal mode or window mode. The following bits/registers are used to enable different mode/capabilities of the WDT:

- Control Register: Enable bit to enable the WDT, Always-on bit to enable always-on capability and Window mode enable bit to enable window mode.
- Config Register: Window mode timeout period bits and timeout period programming bits to program the timeout values.
- Early Warning Control Register: Early Warning Interrupt Time Offset bits to program the WDT to issue an early warning interrupt to indicate an upcoming watchdog timeout condition.

Table 4.3 Clock Behavior During Sleep Modes in Atmel SAM Sensor Hub

Mode	Level	CPU Clock	AHB Clock	APB Clock	Oscillator Bit Setting (RIR Means Run If Requested)			
					ONDEMAND = 0		ONDEMAND = 1	
					RUNSTDBY = 0	RUNSTDBY = 1	RUNSTDBY = 0	RUNSTDBY = 1
IDLE	0	Stop	Run	Run	Run	Run	RIR	RIR
	1	Stop	Stop	Run	Run	Run	RIR	RIR
	2	Stop	Stop	Stop	Run	Run	RIR	RIR
STANDBY		Stop	Stop	Stop	Stop	Run	Stop	RIR

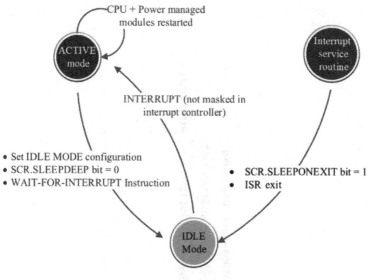

FIGURE 4.3

IDLE mode entry and exit for Atmel SAM sensor hub.

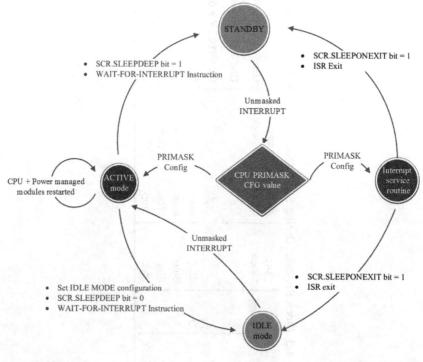

FIGURE 4.4

STANDBY mode entry and exit for Atmel SAM sensor hub.

When enabled, the WDT is constantly running in active mode and all sleep modes. It is asynchronous and runs from a CPU independent clock source. Hence the WDT will continue to run and issue system reset or interrupt even if the main clocks fails.

The WDT functions in Always-on mode when the Always-on bit is set in the control register. In this mode the WDT runs continuously irrespective of the enable bit status in the control register. The time period configuration of WDT cannot be changed (bits become read-only) and the Always-on bit can only be cleared at POR. The early warning interrupt can be enabled or disabled but the early warning timeout value cannot be altered.

The two modes of WDT are described briefly here.

- *Normal mode*: The WDT is enabled and configured to a predefined timeout period. A system reset is issued if the WDT is not cleared within the timeout period. The WDT can be cleared at any time during the timeout period in this mode. If early warning interrupt is enabled then an interrupt is generated before timeout occurs. Fig. 4.5 shows the operation of WDT in normal mode.
- *Window mode*: In this mode, a time slot window can be defined within the total timeout period. There are two timeslots defined in this mode: a closed window timeout period and the normal timeout period. The total duration of the timeout period equals the closed window timeout period plus the open window timeout period. A system reset is issued if WDT is cleared during the closed window timeout period because the WDT can be reset only during the normal timeout period and not during the closed window timeout period. Compared to the normal mode, this feature can help identify situations where

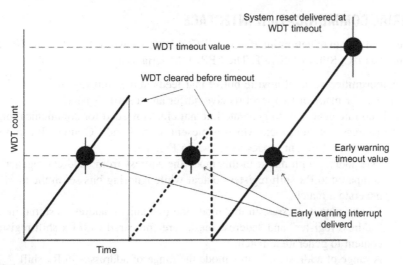

FIGURE 4.5

Normal mode of watchdog timer.

a code error causes the WDT to be cleared frequently. Just as in normal mode, a system reset is issued if the WDT is not cleared within the total timeout period. Fig. 4.6 shows the operation of WDT in normal mode.

REAL-TIME COUNTER

The RTC is a 32-bit counter that runs continuously to keep track of time. It can run in three modes: 32-bit counter mode (Mode 0), 16-bit counter (Mode 1), and clock/calendar mode (Mode 2). This module can generate different events to wake up the device from sleep modes such as an alarm event, a compare event, a periodic event, and an overflow event.

EXTERNAL INTERRUPT CONTROLLER

The External Interrupt Controller (EIC) helps to configure the external pins as interrupt lines. The external pins can be used as asynchronous interrupts to wake up the device from sleep modes where all clocks have been disabled or to generate event pulses that are connected to the event system. A separate nonmaskable interrupt (NMI) is also supported by this module. The NMI line is connected to the NMI request of the CPU, and hence can interrupt any other interrupt mode.

EIC can mask the interrupt lines or generate interrupts based on different levels or edges at the interrupt lines (such as rising, falling or both edges, or on high or low levels). To prevent false interrupt/event generation each external pin has a configurable filter to remove spikes.

SERIAL COMMUNICATION INTERFACE

The serial communication interface (SERCOM), as shown in Fig. 4.7, can be configured as I^2C, SPI, or USART. The SERCOM serial engine consists of:

- A transmitter made of a write buffer that feeds into a shift register.
- A receiver made of two-level receive buffer and a shift register.
- A baud rate generator to generate internal clocks needed for communication.
- An address matching logic which is present for SPI and I^2C mode. It can be used in three different modes as shown in Fig. 4.8:
  - One address with mask: In this mode the address from "address register" is compared to Rx shift register content while ignoring bits set in the mask to generate a match.
  - Two unique addresses: In this mode the two unique addresses stored in "address register" and "address mask" are compared with Rx shift register content to generate a match.
  - A range of addresses: In this mode the range of addresses in Rx shift register that lies in between (and including) the address in "address register" and in "mask register" will generate a match.

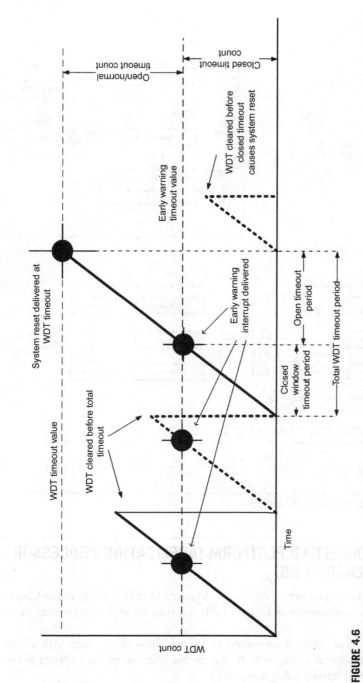

FIGURE 4.6

Window mode of watchdog timer.

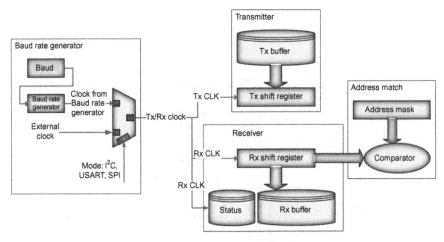

FIGURE 4.7

SERCOM serial engine block diagram.

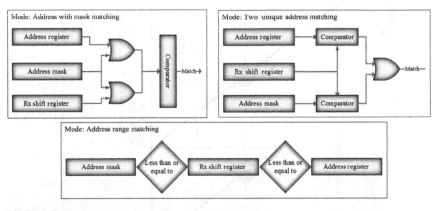

FIGURE 4.8

Address matching modes in SERCOM.

INTEL MOOREFIELD PLATFORM (APPLICATION PROCESSOR-BASED SENSOR HUB)

The Moorefield platform [7,8] with Moorefield SOC (System-On-Chip) is designed for smartphones or tablets. Table 4.4 lists the main components of such platforms.

Here the main SOC is connected to various subsystems along with a sensor subsystem as shown in Fig. 4.9. It also offers interconnection between sensors, audio, and connectivity subsystem.

Table 4.4 Moorefield Platform Components

Subsystem	Component
Processor and memory	Intel Moorefield SOC
Modem subsystem	Intel cellular modem
Power management	Intel's power management integrated circuit
Wireless subsystem	NFC, Wi-Fi/Bluetooth/FM module, GPS/GLONASS receiver
Audio subsystem	Audio codec, microphones, speakers, audio jack
Sensor subsystem	Integrated low-power sensor hub + Accelerometer/ compass, gyroscope, pressure sensor, 2 + skin thermal sensors, ambient light sensor/proximity sensor
Display subsystem	4.7-in., 1080p (1920 × 1080) HD command mode LCD panel, capacitive touch panel
Imaging	MIPI front and back camera

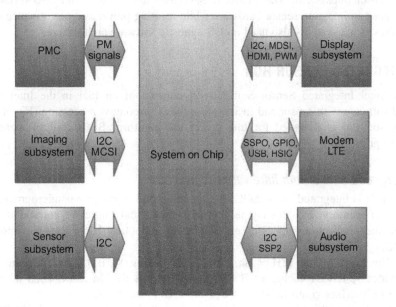

FIGURE 4.9

SOC-subsystem block diagram.

The Moorefield platform's audio subsystem has a comprehensive set of mixing, recording, and playback capabilities for telephony audio, music, and alerts routed between multiple audio sources and sinks including the internal speaker and microphone, a stereo headset, a mono speaker/microphone headset, HDMI or Bluetooth. The wireless/connectivity subsystem has Bluetooth, WLAN, FM Radio, GNSS (Global Navigation Satellite System), NFC (Near Field Communications), and so on.

Context-aware computing is used to differentiate mobility products, so such products and platforms will enable features that use continuous context sensing to deliver unique uses while increasing user experience by making intelligent autonomous decisions based on available sensor data. Below are some of the examples of use cases with integrated sensor hub [9] (as in case of Moorefield platforms):

- Classifying the user's activities, such as meeting, talking, walking, sitting, and running.
- Classifying the user's environment—speech, music, noisy, or quiet.
- Detecting gestures—right/left-hand holding, shake, and rotation.
- Assisting the user based on the user's calendar and location.
- Giving the user recommendations based on the user's cloud information and location.
- Profiling the user's context and knowing the user's requirements.

Context-aware computing depends on consistent and continuous sensing from the sensor subsystem. The Platform Services Hub in SOC like Moorefield is designed to integrate sensor hardware while meeting power and performance constraints. Such systems also need an OS-agnostic software architecture.

INTEGRATED SENSOR HUB

The Intel Integrated Sensor Solution [9] consists of an ISH in the Intel SOC and software with sensor and fusion algorithms for context processing (Fig. 4.10). The solution is designed for low power and platform BOM (bill of material) cost optimization.

Integrated sensor hub hardware architecture

The ISH is integrated in the SOC. It is composed of a low-power microprocessor, internal memory, I/Os for connection of sensors, and fabric for communication with the application processor or main CPU and other IPs embedded into the SOC.

The heart of the ISH is an X86 CPU running at 100 MHz. The memory includes 32 KB L1 cache, 8 KB ROM, and 640 KB SRAM. Low-speed IO ports (sensor interface controllers) are I²C, SPI, UART, and GPIO.

In addition, there is a power management and clocking unit as well as a debug interface. The hardware architecture is depicted in Fig. 4.11.

Integrated sensor hub power management

The ISH is designed as an autonomous subsystem that can operate while the rest of the SOC is in low-power mode.

The active power consumption of the ISH is comparable to the SOC retention and sleep power (estimated for a CPU running at 100 MHz with 32 KB of L1 cache and 640 KB of SRAM for code and data storage). This means that

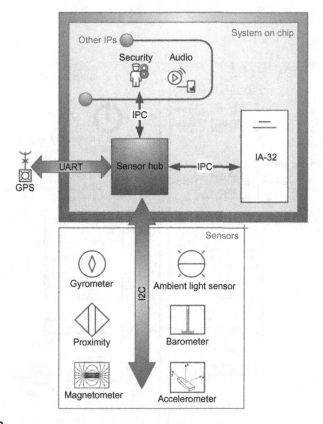

FIGURE 4.10

Moorefield platform sensor hub connections.

continuous sensing through the ISH (sensor data acquisition, sensor algorithms and capable of fusion) can be performed with no or very minimal impact to the battery life of the mobile device.

The ISH autonomously manages its power states, depending on the sensor sampling frequency and the time between processing of sensor data in general. Following are the possible power management states (additional description and transitions arcs are explained in Chapter 5: Power Management):

- D0 is the active state during which the ISH processes workloads.
- D0i1, D0i2, and D0i3 are idle states with wake latencies of 10 µs, <100 µs, and <3 ms, respectively.

In D0ix idle states ISH internal logic is put into low-power mode (CPU in HALT state, memory logic clock gated, in retention or power gated, and so on). The deeper the power state, i.e., the more logic including memories is in low-power mode, the higher the time the wake latency (in particular linked to the time to restore the

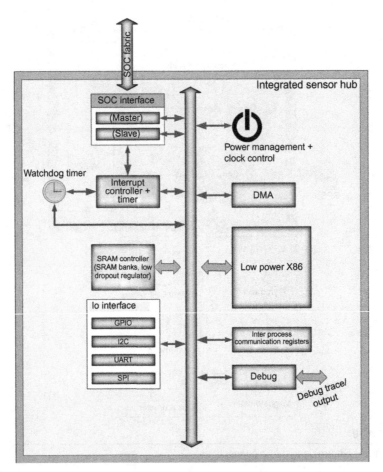

FIGURE 4.11

Integrated sensor hub architecture.

memory in D0i3), as illustrated in Fig. 4.12. All ISH device states (including the active state D0) allow the rest of the SOC to stay in deep sleep mode.

The ISH wakes up the application processor through interrupt when ISH side processing is finished and the OS application has data available to process.

The sensor hub autonomously manages its device based on the processing load and time between workloads. For example, during processing intensive periods of accelerometer sensor data, the sensor hub will go into either D0i1 or D0i2 state as the time between workload processing is low. During sample acquisition periods with low or no processing the sensor hub goes into its lowest power state, D0i3. The D0i3 state requires context save and restore as the memory is power gated and memory content lost during this state.

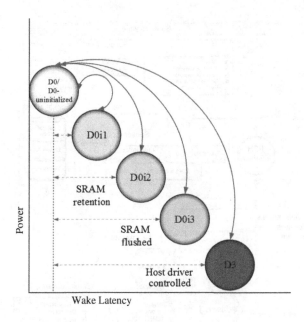

FIGURE 4.12

Power versus wake latency for integrated sensor hub.

Platform and sensor hub firmware architecture

Fig. 4.13 is the basic block diagram of associated firmware of the ISH and its interaction with the SOC firmware/software stack.

Supported sensors

The Integrated Sensor Solution is the hub for many sensors to the system. It enables "always-on" sensing usages and new ranges of applications (e.g., in the domain of health through support of biosensors). The "always-on" usages are possible due to its optimized power management architecture. Many applications including monitoring of heart rate, blood oxygen, glucose in the domain of health, and air quality (CO, CO_2, and so on) in the domain of environmental sensing can be enabled.

Some of the possible sensors are listed (and there can be many more):

- Inertial: three-axis accelerometer, three-axis magnetometer, three-axis gyroscope;
- Environmental: pressure, humidity, temperature, ambient/RGB light, UV, CO, CO_2;
- Proximity: RF/SAR proximity, IR proximity, human presence;
- Biosensors: heart rate, oximeter, ECG, glucose.

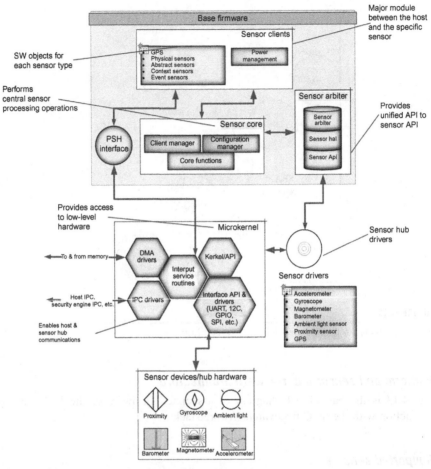

FIGURE 4.13

Firmware block diagram for sensor hub and platform interaction.

Security with integrated sensor hub

New types of sensors such as ECG and glucose for health provide sensitive personal data to applications (with storage on the device or in the cloud). Secure capture, processing, and storage can be achieved on the device by using a Trusted Execution Environment (TEE).

The TEE is a secure area of the main processor of a smartphone (or any connected device including tablets, set-top boxes, and televisions). It guarantees code and data loaded inside to be protected with respect to confidentiality and integrity. The TEE and the Security engine to which the sensor hub is connected form a

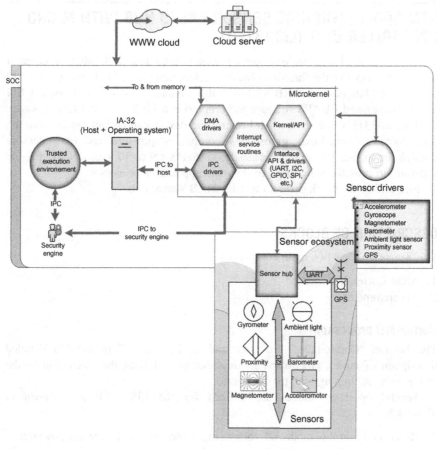

FIGURE 4.14

Sensor data protection mechanism.

Trusted Computing Base (TCB) that enables secure sensing. The TCB carries out software and firmware authentication.

The sensor data on the device is transferred from the ISH through the security engine to the application processor using secure channels (encryption and/or certification of data), as shown in Fig. 4.14.

The data also needs to be secured for transfer and processing in the cloud. The confidential data is protected through user sign-on credentials and session encryption keys generated by the cloud service. User data aggregation (decryption, integrity check, filtering, and logging) is based on the hardware certificate associated with the user.

STMICROELECTRONICS SENSOR-BASED HUB WITH MICRO CONTROLLER UNIT (LIS331EB)

The LIS331EB [10] is an example of sensor-based hub with MCU because it includes sensors like the three-axis linear accelerometer with MCU like Cortex-M0 core with 64 KB flash, 128 KB SRAM, 8 dual timers, 2 I^2C (master/slave), 1 SPI (master/slave), and 1 UART (transmitter/receiver) in a $3 \times 3 \times 1$ mm LGA package.

The LIS331EB is a sensor hub because the device can collect inputs from the accelerometer (embedded), gyroscopes, compasses, pressure, and other sensors through the master I^2C and elaborates/fuses together 9 or 10 axes (iNemo Engine software) to provide quaternions to the main application processor.

Fig. 4.15 is the block diagram of LIS331EB sensor hub.

DESCRIPTION OF BLOCKS

This sensor hub has two main components:

1. ARM Cortex-M0 core
2. Accelerometer

Cortex-M0 processor

The Section "Cortex-m0+ Processor and its Peripherals" provided a detailed description of cortex processors, so this section will limit the discussion to the processor's functioning with the accelerator.

Several operating modes are defined for the LIS331EB and shown in Table 4.5:

1. Reset mode: In this mode, all voltage regulator, and clocks are not powered and the LIS331EB sensor hub is in the ultra-low power mode. The sensor hub enters reset mode by asserting the external reset signal.
2. Two low-power modes:
   a. Low-power wait-for-interrupt (WFI) mode: In this mode the LIS331EB CPU is stopped, all peripherals except one timer are disabled and the high-frequency 80 MHz RC oscillator is powered down. The power consumption is about 800 µA with a 1 kHz clock.
   b. High-power WFI mode: In this mode, the CPU is stopped but all peripherals are enabled. The peripherals can interrupt and wake up the CPU. The high-frequency 80 MHz RC oscillator is powered up. The response time for an interrupt to wake up the CPU is faster in this mode but the power consumption is also higher compared to lower power WFI mode (around 2 mA with an 80 MHz clock).
3. Active mode: In active mode the LIS331EB is fully operational with MCU core running and all interfaces (such as SPI, I^2C, JTAG, and UART), all internal power supplies and the high-speed frequency oscillator active.

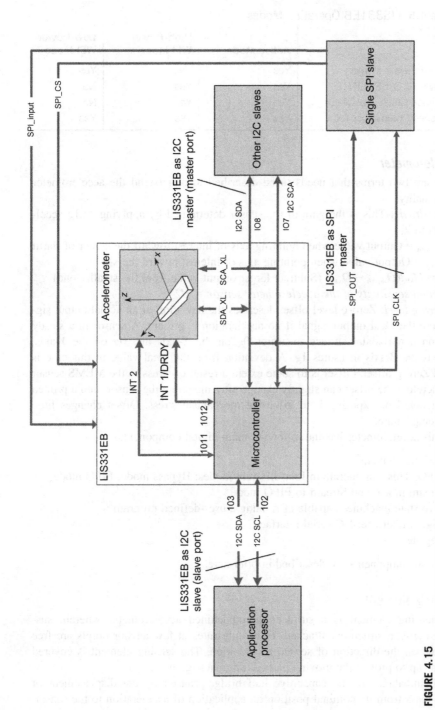

FIGURE 4.15

Sensor-based hub block diagram.

Table 4.5 LIS331EB Operating Modes

IP	Active Mode	High-Power WFI Mode	Low-Power WFI Mode
CPU + Timers + Memory	Yes	Yes	Yes
Interfaces: I^{2}C, SPI, UART	Yes	Yes	No
High-speed internal oscillator	Yes	Yes	No
Low-speed internal oscillator	Yes	Yes	Yes

Accelerometer

There are two terms that needs to be described to understand the accelerometer functionality:

Sensitivity: This is the gain of the sensor determined by applying $\pm 1g$ acceleration to it.

O_{earth} = Output value when pointing axis of interest toward the center of Earth
O_{sky} = Output value when pointing axis of interest toward the sky
$A = Mod(O_{earth} - O_{sky})$ (Subtract larger output value from the smaller one)
Actual sensitivity of the accelerometer sensor = A/2

Zero-g level: Zero-g level offset describes the deviation of an actual output signal from the ideal output signal if no acceleration is present. A sensor in a steady state on a horizontal surface measures $0g$ on the X-axis and $0g$ on the Y-axis, whereas the Z-axis measures $1g$. A deviation from the ideal value in this case is called Zero-g offset. Offset is to some extent a result of stress to the MEMS sensor and therefore the offset can slightly change after mounting the sensor onto a printed circuit board or exposing it to extensive mechanical stress. Offset changes little over temperature.

This accelerometer has the following main digital components:

1. Sensing element
2. FIFO: This can operate in four different modes: Bypass mode, FIFO mode, Stream mode, and Stream-to-FIFO mode
3. Two state machines capable of running a user-defined program
4. Digital interface: I^{2}C serial interface
5. Registers

These components are described in brief here.

Sensing element

The sensing element is a surface micromachined accelerometer wherein suspended silicon structures attached to the substrates at few anchor points are free to move in the direction of sensed acceleration. The sensing element is covered with a cap to protect the moving parts during packaging.

An imbalance in the capacitive half bridge, caused by the displacement of proof mass from its nominal position on application of acceleration to the sensor, is measured by using charge integration in response to a voltage pulse applied to the capacitor. The capacitors have nominal value at steady state in few picofarads, but under acceleration the maximum variation of the capacitive load is in the femtofarad range.

State machine

There are two state machines in the LIS331EB that can run user-defined programs. The programs consist of set of instructions that defines the state transitions. A state n can transition to either the next state $n + 1$ on meeting the NEXT STATE condition or to the reset state on meeting the RESET condition. On reaching an output/ stop/continue state, an interrupt is triggered.

Fig. 4.16 shows the state machine. The state machine can help implement gesture recognition and manage features such as free-fall, wake up, 4D/6D orientation, pulse counter and step recognition, click/double-click, shake/double-shake, face-up/face-down, and turn/double-turn.

FIFO

The LIS331EB has FIFO acceleration data for each of the three output channels, X, Y, and Z. The host processor does not need to poll the sensor data continuously and hence can save power by waking up only when the data is needed. When needed, the processor will burst the data out from FIFO. This FIFO can be used in four different modes: Bypass mode, FIFO mode, Stream mode, and Stream-to-FIFO mode. The mode of FIFO operation is selected by the FIFO_MODE bits. Programmable Watermark level, FIFO_empty, or FIFO_Full events can be enabled

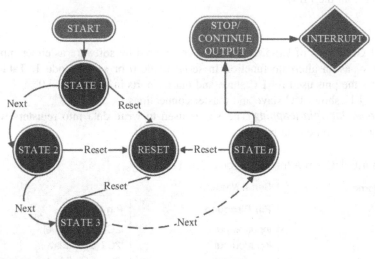

FIGURE 4.16

LIS331EB state machines: sequence of state to execute an algorithm.

to generate dedicated interrupts on the INT1/2 pins internally connected to the microcontroller (DIO11 and DIO12).

Bypass mode In Bypass mode, the FIFO remains empty because it is not operational. Only the first address for each channel is used in this mode, and the rest of the FIFO slots remain empty.

FIFO mode In FIFO mode, the data from X, Y, and Z channels are stored in the FIFO till it gets filled. The FIFO stops storing the data from respective channels once full. A watermark interrupt can be generated (if enabled) when the FIFO gets filled to a specified level set in an internal register.

Stream mode The Stream mode is similar to the FIFO mode, except that when full, the FIFO will discard the older data and continue to accept new data from the channels. A watermark interrupt can be enabled and set just as in the FIFO mode.

Stream-to-FIFO mode In Stream-to-FIFO mode, data from the X, Y, and Z measurements are stored in the FIFO and FIFO continues to accept new data till it is full. Once full, the FIFO will discard the older data and continue to accept new data from the channels (functions as in stream mode). When a trigger event occurs, the FIFO will start operating in the FIFO mode and will not accept new data if full. A watermark interrupt can be generated (if enabled through internal register) when the FIFO gets filled to a specified level set in an internal register.

Retrieving data from FIFO FIFO data is read from the three registers located at their respective address offsets: OUT_X, OUT_Y, and OUT_Z.

In FIFO mode, Stream mode or Stream-to-FIFO mode, a read operation to the FIFO will cause the oldest FIFO data to be placed in the above OUT_X, OUT_Y, and OUT_Z registers. A single read or burst read operations can be used to get the data from the FIFO.

I^2C interfaces

The 11 GPIO pins of LIS331EB can be configured by software as either input or output, or as an alternate function in serial mode 0 or serial mode 1. Table 4.6 indicates the pins used for I^2C slave and master ports in serial mode 0.

Fig. 4.17 shows I^2C slave and master connections.

I^2C terminology/pin mapping The I^2C is used to write data into registers whose content can also be read back.

Table 4.6 I^2C Pin Allocations for LIS331EB

Pin Name	Serial Mode 0	
	Pin Direction	Pin Function
IO2	Input/output	I2C2_SCL (slave)
IO3	Input/output	I2C2_SDA (Slave)
IO7	Input/output	I2C1_SCL (Master)
IO8	Input/output	I2C1_SDA (Master)

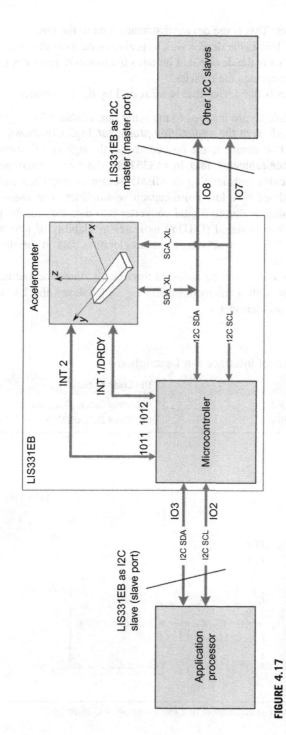

FIGURE 4.17

LIS331EB I^2C connections.

I²C Transmitter: This is the device that sends data to the bus.

I²C Receiver: This is the device which receives data from the bus.

I²C Master: This is the device that initiates the transfer, generates clock signals, and terminates the transfer.

I²C Slave: This is the device that is addressed by the I²C master.

The serial interfaces are mapped to the same pins (Table 4.7).

LIS331EB as I²C slave to the application processor Fig. 4.18 shows the connection of the LIS331EB device to the host controller through an I²C slave port.

I²C to access accelerometer data In LIS331EB, the raw accelerometer data in the form of capacitive unbalancing of MEMS sensor is amplified and converted into an analog voltage by a low-noise capacitive amplifier. The analog voltage is then converted using analog-to-digital converter into data that can be provided to the user. A Data-Ready signal (DRDY) indicates availability of new acceleration data. This signal helps to synchronize the acceleration data in the digital system of the LIS331EB device.

The acceleration data can be accessed through I²C interface and hence can be interfaced directly with a microcontroller. Fig. 4.19 shows the I²C interface of LIS331EB to the accelerometer.

Table 4.7 I²C Serial Interface Pin Description

Pin Name	Pin Description
Master SCL (I²C_SCL)	I²C Serial Clock (SCL_XL)
Master SDA (I²C_SDA)	I²C Serial Data (SDA_XL)

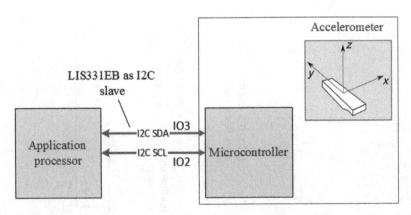

FIGURE 4.18

LIS331EB connection to application processor through I²C slave port.

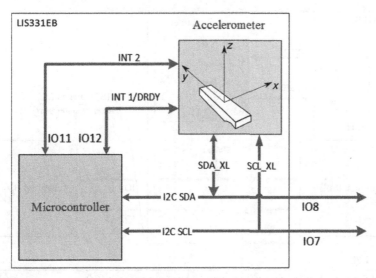

FIGURE 4.19

Accelerometer (embedded) I^2C connections.

The I^2C interface is factory calibrated for sensitivity (So) and Zero-g level. The trim values are stored inside the nonvolatile memory of the device which are then downloaded into the registers when the device is turned on. The values from these calibration registers can then be used during active operation, thus allowing the device to be used with the default factory calibration.

Fig. 4.20 shows the L1S331EB I^2C interface. Through this master I^2C port L1S331EB can collect inputs from the accelerometer (embedded), gyroscopes, compasses, pressure, and other sensors.

SCL_XL is the clock line and SDA_XL is the data line that is used in I^2C operations. The bidirectional SDA_XL is used for sending and receiving the data to and from the interface. When the bus is idle, both the SCL_XL and SDL_XL are pulled high through an external pull-up resistor which connects these lines to an external power supply (VDDA).

The I^2C interface is compliant with fast mode (400 kHz) I^2C standards as well as with normal mode.

I^2C operation The start of I^2C operation is indicated by start signal [ST] transmitted by the master. The start condition is defined by

1. High to low transition on SDA_XL and
2. SCL_XL held high.

After the start condition the bus is considered busy. In the next byte after start condition, the slave address [SAD] is transmitted. For the accelerometer in LIS331EB, the SAD = 0011101b.

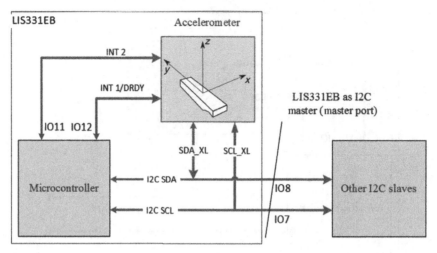

FIGURE 4.20

LIS331EB connection to other I^2C sensors (slaves) in serial mode 0.

[7:1] bits → slave address [SAD].

[7] → Indicates if the master is transmitting to slave or receiving the data from slave.

Read command: SAD [0011101b] + Read [1] = 00111011b = 0 × 3Bh

Write command: SAD [0011101b] + Write [0] = 00111010b = 0 × 3Ah

All devices connected to the bus compares [7:1] bits with their respective address to see if the master is addressing them.

All data transfers must be acknowledged by the receiver. Acknowledge pulse is generated by pulling down SDA_XL during the high period of acknowledge clock pulse. During this acknowledge pulse the transmitter must release SDA_XL. The addressed receiver must generate acknowledge after receiving each byte of data.

The I^2C in the accelerometer is a slave device. It uses the following protocol:

1. Start condition [ST] is delivered by master to accelerometer.
2. Master sends Slave address [SAD] + command [Read or write].
   a. Read/write bit if = 1 (read) then a repeated start [SR] must be issued by master after two subaddress bytes
   b. Read/write bit if = 0 (write) then the Master continues to transmit to slave
3. Accelerometer sends slave acknowledge [SAK].
4. Master then transmits 8-bit subaddress [SUB].
   a. SUB [7:0] = Actual Register address [7:1] + ADD_INC bit in control register CTRL_REG6 of LIS331EB defines address increment [0]

5. Data is transmitted in byte format (DATA). Each data transfer contains 8 bits. The number of bytes transferred per transfer is unlimited. Data is transferred with the most significant bit (MSB) first.
   a. Wait state addition: Receiver can hold clock line SCL low to add wait states (if receiver is busy with some other functions).
   b. Receiver Ready: Receiver will need to release the data lines when it is ready for another byte (data transfer will not continue without this).
   c. Abort: If a slave receiver doesn't acknowledge the slave address (it is busy performing some real-time function) the data line must be left high by the slave. The master can then abort the transfer.
6. A low-to-high transition on the SDA_XL line, while the SCL_XL line is high, is defined as a STOP condition. Each data transfer must be terminated by the generation of a STOP (SP) condition.
7. MAK is Master acknowledge and NMAK is No Master Acknowledge.

   Some examples of the flow are listed in Tables 4.8–4.11.

Table 4.8 Master to Slave 1-Byte Write

Master	ST	SAD + W		SUB		DATA		SP
Slave			SAK		SAK		SAK	

Table 4.9 Master to Slave Multibyte Write

Master	ST	SAD + W		SUB		DATA		DATA		SP
Slave			SAK		SAK		SAK		SAK	

Table 4.10 Master reading 1-Byte From Slave

Master	ST	SAD + W		SUB		SR	SAD + R			NMAK	SP
Slave			SAK		SAK			SAK	DATA		

Table 4.11 Master Reading Multibyte From Slave

Master	ST	SAD + W		SUB		SR	SAD + R			MAK		MAK		NMAK	SP
Slave			SAK		SAK			SAK	DATA		DATA		DATA		

Other components and peripherals

Following are other useful components of LIS331EB.

Memory

LIS331EB has 64 KB of embedded flash memory, two banks of 64 KB embedded SRAM with ECC (data/program), and has memory protection, which prevents read/write access to above memories through JTAG on connecting debug features.

Timers and watchdogs

LIS331EB has eight dual timers (which provide programmable free running counters) for 32-bit or 16-bit operations, one WDG timer: it is a 32-bit counter that generates interrupt/reset on reaching zero, and one SysTick timer: it provides a 24-bit clear on write. It is a decrementing counter and can wrap around on reaching zero.

Communication interfaces: I²C, UART, and SPI

The LIS331EB has two I²C interfaces that can operate in master and slave modes. They can support standard mode and fast mode. The UART interface can operate in UART mode, Infrared data association mode (IrDA), and low power IrDA mode; SPI can operate as master or slave (Fig. 4.21 and Tables 4.12 and 4.13).

Debug

LIS331EB has two embedded debug ports that can be selected by driving IO9 pin during reset.

a. ARM JTAG: It enables debug uses standard JTAG connection (IO9 = 0).
b. ARM SWD (serial wire debug): It enables debug port connection to the CPU (IO9 = 1).

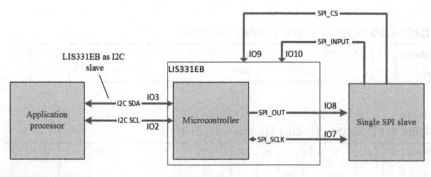

FIGURE 4.21

LIS331EB SPI connection (serial mode 1).

Table 4.12 SPI Pin Allocations for LIS331EB

Pin Name	Serial Mode 1	
	Pin Direction	Pin Function
IO7	Input/output	SPI SCLK
IO8	Output	SPI output
IO9	Input	SPI CS
IO10	Input	SPI input

Table 4.13 UART Pin Allocations for LIS331EB

Pin Name	Serial Mode 1	
	Pin Direction	Pin Function
IO0	Input	UART CTS
IO1	Output	UART RTS
IO2	Output	UART TXD
IO3	Input	UART RXD

REFERENCES

[1] Yurur O, Liu CH, Perera C, Chen M, Liu X, Moreno W. Energy-efficient and context-aware smartphone sensor employment.
[2] Data sheet for STM32F103x4, STM32F103x6. From STMicroelectronics.
[3] Intel® Platform Controller Hub MP30 Datasheet May 2011, Revision 001.
[4] TechTarget sensor hub definition. From IoT Agenda.
[5] Bursky D. MCUs as Sensor Hubs. Digi-key electronics article.
[6] Atmel SAM D20J/SAM D20G/SAM D20E SMART ARM-based microcontroller datasheet.
[7] Tu S. Atom™ -x5/x7 series processor, codenamed Cherry Trail.
[8] Intel Atom Z8000 Processor Series. Datasheet (Volume 1 of 2), March 2016.
[9] Matthes K, Andiappan R, Intel Corporation. eSAME 2015 conference: Sensors on mobile devices—applications, power management and security aspects (Sophia-Antipolis, France), (Espoo, Finland).
[10] LIS331EB datasheet: iNEMO-A advanced MEMS: 3D high-performance accelerometer and signal processor.

Power management

- ACPI Power States
- Power Management in Sensors, Smartphones, and Tablets
- Power Management in the Sensor Hub

INTRODUCTION

Power management (PM) [1] is one of the most crucial aspects of sensor hub architecture and design. In a high-level PM is an architecture and implementation to minimize the average current and in some cases the peak current drawn from the power source. Various factors guide the designer to a target power at which the sensor hub needs to operate. Ultimately it is the expectation of the manufacturer or the user of the length of time the device needs to operate before depleting the power source that is the key factor. This length of time is determined by following two factors:

- Capacity of the energy source powering the device embedding the sensor hub,
- The average current consumed by the device while in operation.

The average current in turn depends on many aspects related to architecture, design, and silicon process. Some of the key aspects are:

- Frequency of operation
- Leakage current
- CPU architecture and efficiency
- Architecture and size of cache and other memory elements
- Architecture and gate counts of elements such as fabrics, I/Os, and so on
- The duty cycle of operation.

PM essentially manages the above elements during the design phase and operation of the device to minimize the average power consumption with minimal impact to the user experience.

Mobile Sensors and Context-Aware Computing. DOI: http://dx.doi.org/10.1016/B978-0-12-801660-2.00005-7

The overall PM architecture of the sensor hub is directed by the system and user experience requirements. These together define the following key factors:

- Average power budget for the sensor hub based on a specific use case or average use over a period of time,
- System power states in which the sensor hub must be capable of operating,
- Maximum latency observed by the high-level software or the use and the system and sensor hub transitions to operating states.

Another aspect of sensor hub PM is how it interacts and coexists with the rest of the system hardware and software. Although a sensor hub can be a standalone device by itself, in most cases it is part of a larger system such a mobile phone, tablet, laptop, or a wearable device. These systems may be running a standard operating system such as Linux, Windows, or Android, which have their own complex system PM architecture to manage: CPU, display, memory subsystem, communication systems (Wi-Fi, Bluetooth, cellular, and so on), various I/Os such as USB, and pretty much every component in the system that is visible to the software, including the sensor hub. Sensor hub PM must coexist with the system software PM schemes.

In the following sections we first look into PM schemes of current mobile systems and then dive into how the sensor hub operates in that environment.

ACPI POWER STATES

ACPI (Advanced Configuration and Power Interface) is an open industry specification developed jointly by Hewlett-Packard, Intel, Microsoft, Phoenix, and Toshiba. ACPI establishes industry-standard interfaces enabling OS-directed configuration, PM, and thermal management of mobile, desktop, and server platforms. When first published in 1996, ACPI evolved an existing collection of PM BIOS code, Advanced Power Management (APM) application programming interfaces (APIs), PNPBIOS APIs, and Multiprocessor Specification (MPS) tables into a well-defined PM and configuration interface specification.

Fig. 5.1 shows the power states as defined by the ACPI Specification.

ACPI GLOBAL POWER STATES

ACPI [2] global power states are described briefly here. Table 5.1 lists these different global power states and their respective properties.

Power State G3: This is the mechanical off state of the system; the state that system enters when powered off using the power button or when the battery is physically removed. The only circuit that may remain powered is the real-time clock (RTC) domain, which is powered by a coin cell battery. The operating system must be restarted to operate from this state and no hardware context is retained.

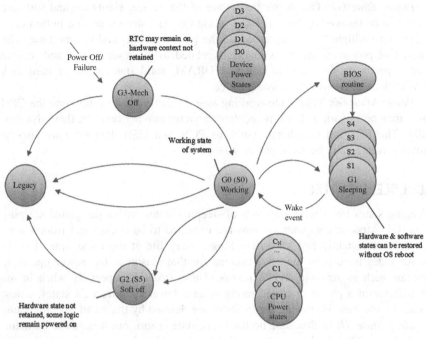

FIGURE 5.1

Global power states and transitions.

Table 5.1 Global Power State Properties [2]

Global System State	Software Runs	Latency	Power Consumption	OS Restart Required	Safe to Disassemble Computer	Exit State Electronically
G0 Working	Yes	0	Large	No	No	Yes
G1 Sleeping	No	>0, varies with sleep state	Smaller	No	No	Yes
G2/S5 Soft Off	No	Long	Very near 0	Yes	No	Yes
G3 Mechanical Off	No	Long	RTC battery	Yes	Yes	No

Power State G2/S5: This state is called Soft Off. In this state some circuitry may remain powered from the battery or main power supply. Like G3, no hardware state is retained and the OS must be restarted to operate from this state. The main difference from G3 is that the system can wake accepting inputs from a LAN, USB device, or a keyboard. Typically, laptop and desktop systems use this state, whereas a mobile device such as a phone or tablet is less likely to use it due to the long resume time.

Power State G1: This is the sleep state of the device. Hardware and software states can be restored without a reboot of the OS. The sleep states are in turn classified into multiple "S" states based on the power savings and resume time. The amount of power consumed is inversely related to the resume time and resume time depends on the medium (such as DRAM, solid state drive, or hard disk drive) selected for saving the system state.

Power State G0: This is the working state of the system. In this state the CPU itself may be in various performance/power states moving between them dynamically. The I/Os and peripherals (such as PCIe and USB devices) may also be moving dynamically between power states.

ACPI SLEEP STATES

Sleeping states (Sx states) are types of sleeping states within the global sleeping state, G1. Modern computer systems are expected to be operational from a low-power state instantly and also yield long battery life at the same time. The Sx power states have been highly optimized for that reason in the newer operating systems such as Android and Windows. These systems, especially when in the form factor of a phone or tablet, rarely enter a lower state than Sx states, unless forced by the user. Following Sleep States are defined by the ACPI Specification.

Sleep State S1: In this state no hardware state is lost, but it needs to be maintained by the OS. Hardware retains all the state, and wake latency is very low, in the order of a few microseconds. Typically this state is where CPU and major hardware blocks (caches, memory fabric, and so on) are clock gated and clock sources such as PLLs (phase-locked loops) are shut off.

Sleep State S2: This is similar to S1 except that the CPU and system cache context is lost. In this state, the cache and CPU may enter a power-gated state.

Sleep State S3: In this state all CPU, cache, and hardware system context is lost and only system memory (DRAM) state is maintained. The operating system is responsible for saving all contexts required to resume in to the DRAM. Typically in general terminology this state is referred to as Standby or Sleep. In Linux kernel documentation S3 is also referred to as Suspend to RAM (STR).

Sleep State S4: The S4 sleeping state is the lowest power, longest wake latency sleeping state supported by ACPI. To reduce power to a minimum, it is assumed that the hardware platform has powered off all devices. Platform context is maintained. Modern computer systems save all hardware/software state to nonvolatile memory such as solid state drive or hard disc drive and power off almost all platform components. This state is referred to as Hibernate in common terminology. The wake latency from this state is several seconds. Most mobile devices (smartphones, tablets, and so on) do not implement this state since wake latency is too high to enable the desired user experience.

Sleep State S5: This state is the same as the S4 state with the exception that in the S5 state the OS does not save any context. The system is in soft-off state and requires a complete reboot on wake.

ACPI DEVICE POWER STATES

Device power states are states of the devices attached to the computer system. This includes the devices attached externally via some interface (such as I^2C, USB, or PCI) to the CPU or SOC and also the devices internal to the main SOC, such as an integrated audio or integrated sensor hub device. The device power state also applies to the interfaces connecting the devices to the main CPU or SOC.

The device states are not necessarily visible to the user. The device power states are managed by the operating system via device driver, using a programming model and other information regarding the wake-up latency and latency tolerance published by the device.

The device power states are distinguished from each other based on following attributes:

- The latency to restart the device to be able to use it,
- How much of the context is saved by the devices and how much needs to be saved/restored by the OS and the driver,
- Power consumed by the device.

Modern systems such as mobile phones and tablets incorporate another form of device PM called autonomous hardware-based device PM. This helped a new class of smartphones to achieve considerably lower power than the traditional laptops. More about these schemes is explained in the later sections. ACPI defines the following device power states:

Device State D3 (Cold): In this state, the device's power has been fully removed and all state and context are lost. The device has to be restarted and reinitialized by the OS and driver. Devices have the longest wake/restore latencies from this state.

Device State D3 (Hot): In this state, the device is expected to be accessible by software to reenumerate (reinitialize) and the device could (optionally) save context. If not, the device is reset by the software as part of restarting. This state is expected to save more power but in most implementations this state is an intermediary state in preparation to a state before the device enters D3 cold.

Device State D2: D2 is a device state expected to save more power than D1 but expected to have lower wake latency than D3. If a device implements D2, it may include power reduction due to shutting of internal PLL, power gating certain internal blocks and so on. This is an optional power state per ACPI and most devices that are strictly compliant to ACPI do not implement this power state. However the devices that implement hardware-autonomous power states are likely to implement a version of this state, but it would be transparent to the OS.

Device State D1: This device power state is expected to save some power but less than D2. However, most devices don't implement this power state, at least as visible to software. Instead this state is indirectly implemented as a hardware-autonomous clock gating in most power-sensitive device implementations.

Device State D0: This is the fully functional state of the device, consuming the highest power.

Table 5.2 Device Power State Properties [2]

Device State	Power Consumption	Device Context Retained	Driver Restoration
D0—fully-on	As needed for operation	All	None
D1	D0 (highest power consumption) > D1 > D2 > D3hot > D3 (least power consumption)	>D2 (more device content retained than in D2)	<D2 (less driver restoration needed than D2)
D2	D0 > D1 > D2 > D3hot > D3	<D1 (less device content retained than in D1)	>D1 (more driver restoration needed than D2)
D3hot	D0 > D1 > D2 > D3hot > D3	Optional (device content retention is optional)	None to full initialization and load depending on amount of device content retention (No driver restoration needed if all device content is retained. Full Initialization and load needed if no device content is retained)
D3—off	0 (no power consumption)	None (device content is not retained)	Full initialization and load

Table 5.2 lists the different device power states and their respective properties.

The ACPI power states described earlier are what can be categorized as traditional power states. Smartphones and tablets have different user experience requirements, such as instant on and longer battery life even with a smaller battery. This is also driven by the different usage pattern of smartphones compared to laptops. A smartphone is expected to come on instantly to be used for a few seconds or a minute and then enter the lowest power state for the next few minutes and so on. Following sections explain how this is achieved in the smartphone and tablets powered by Android and Windows operating systems.

POWER MANAGEMENT IN SENSORS, SMARTPHONES, AND TABLETS

The instant on and longer battery life in smartphones and tablets can be attributed to the following three technologies:

- Android Wakelock-based PM (Android phones/tablets),
- Windows Connected Standby (Windows 8 tablets and Ultrabooks),

- Hardware-autonomous/software-transparent power gating.

Following sections provide further details on each of the above schemes.

ANDROID WAKELOCK ARCHITECTURE [3]

Wakelocks are power-managing software mechanisms that make sure that your Android device doesn't go into deep sleep (which is the state that you should strive for), because a given application needs to use your system resources.

Class PowerManager.WakeLock is mechanism to indicate that the application requires the device to stay on.

The primary API a developer will use is newWakeLock(). This will create a PowerManager.WakeLock object. Methods are used on the wakelock object to control the power state of the device. Table 5.3 shows the wakelock levels and their varying effects on system power. The user can specify only one of these levels since they are mutually exclusive.

Table 5.4 shows additional flags that affects only the behavior. When combined with a PARTIAL_WAKE_LOCK these flags have no effect.

Table 5.5 lists out the constants for wakelock.

Table 5.3 Wakelock Levels

Flag Value	CPU	Screen	Keyboard
PARTIAL_WAKE_LOCK	On	Off	Off
SCREEN_DIM_WAKE_LOCK	On	Dim	Off
SCREEN_BRIGHT_WAKE_LOCK	On	Bright	Off
FULL_WAKE_LOCK	On	Bright	Bright

Table 5.4 Flags for Wakelock

Flag Value	Description
ACQUIRE_CAUSES_WAKEUP	This flag is used to force the screen and/or keyboard to turn on immediately when the wakelock is acquired. For example, it is used for notifications that they user may want to see immediately
	This flag is needed because normal wakelocks don't turn on the illumination but they instead cause the illumination to remain on once it turns on (e.g., from user activity)
ON_AFTER_RELEASE	This flag can be used to reduce the flicker when application is cycling between wakelock conditions. When set, it causes the user activity timer to be reset when the wakelock is released. This causes the illumination to remain on little longer

Table 5.5 Constants for Wakelock

	Constants	
int	ACQUIRE_CAUSES_WAKEUP	Wakelock flag: Turn the screen on when the wakelock is acquired
String	ACTION_DEVICE_IDLE_MODE_CHANGED	Intent that is broadcast when the state of isDeviceIdleMode() changes
String	ACTION_POWER_SAVE_MODE_CHANGED	Intent that is broadcast when the state of isPowerSaveMode() changes
int	FULL_WAKE_LOCK	This constant was deprecated in API level 17. Most applications should use FLAG_KEEP_SCREEN_ON instead of this type of wakelock, because it will be correctly managed by the platform as the user moves between applications and doesn't require a special permission
int	ON_AFTER_RELEASE	Wakelock flag: When this wakelock is released, poke the user activity timer so the screen stays on for a little longer
int	PARTIAL_WAKE_LOCK	Wakelock level: Ensures that the CPU is running; the screen and keyboard backlight will be allowed to go off
int	PROXIMITY_SCREEN_OFF_WAKE_LOCK	Wakelock level: Turns the screen off when the proximity sensor activates
int	RELEASE_FLAG_WAIT_FOR_NO_PROXIMITY	Flag for WakeLock.release(int): Defer releasing a PROXIMITY_SCREEN_OFF_WAKE_LOCK wakelock until the proximity sensor indicates that an object is not in close proximity
int	SCREEN_BRIGHT_WAKE_LOCK	This constant was deprecated in API level 13. Most applications should use FLAG_KEEP_SCREEN_ON instead of this type of wakelock, because it will be correctly managed by the platform as the user moves between applications and doesn't require a special permission
int	SCREEN_DIM_WAKE_LOCK	This constant was deprecated in API level 17. Most applications should use FLAG_KEEP_SCREEN_ON instead of this type of wakelock, because it will be correctly managed by the platform as the user moves between applications and doesn't require a special permission

WINDOWS CONNECTED STANDBY

Starting with Windows 8 and Windows 8.1, connected standby is a new low-power state that features extremely low power consumption while maintaining Internet connectivity. When the user presses the power button of the mobile device then the smartphone enters primary *off* mode. This primary off mode is the connected standby power state. The Windows user interface exposes the connected standby power state to the end user as the system "sleep" state.

In the device supporting connected standby:

- The device can instantly resume from sleep,
- The device is always connected to the Internet,
- The applications are automatically updated while the device is in connected standby mode. This ensures that the critical information (e-mail, messages, and so on) are already synced when the device is turned on.

Benefits and value

There are many benefits of connected standby over the traditional ACPI Sleep (S3) and Hibernate (S4) states. Following are some of the prominent benefits:

1. Instant resume from sleep. A connected standby device resumes extremely quickly. The performance of a resume from connected standby is almost always faster than resuming from the traditional Sleep (S3) state and significantly faster than resuming from the Hibernate (S4) or Shutdown (S5) state.
2. Keeps the Wi-Fi device turned on in a very low-power mode. The Wi-Fi device automatically searches for known access points and will connect to them according to the user's preference. This feature allows the system to maintain connectivity seamlessly between various locations like home, work, bus, and coffee shop.
3. The Wi-Fi device is already connected to the network when the user turns on the system. Hence the user does not have to wait to connect to a Wi-Fi access point and then wait for e-mail to sync. Since Wi-Fi is already connected, the e-mail is already synced.
4. With a constant Wi-Fi connection, a mobile device with connected standby also maintains constant connectivity with the cloud. Communications applications (such as Skype and Lync) notify the user in real time of an incoming request or call while the system is in connected standby. Applications can also deliver push notifications to alert the user to news events, weather alerts, or instant messages.

A connected standby device automatically roams between all available network types and can use the available networking option (mobile broadband (MBB; cellular) connection and wired LAN/Ethernet) that is the cheapest and uses the least power.

Connected standby is the foundation of the modern mobile experience. Users expect all of their electronics devices to instantly turn on, have long battery life, and always be connected to the cloud. All smartphones and the overwhelming majority of tablets support a sleep mode that is always on and always connected.

What does connected standby do?

Connected standby is a screen-off sleep state. So when the device screen is off, the device is considered to be in connected standby mode.

While the system is in connected standby, it can pass through various hardware and software operating modes. The hardware is in a low-power state and the software is paused or stopped most of the time while in the connected standby mode. However the system intermittently powers up to process an incoming e-mail, alert the user to an incoming Skype call, or perform other application-related background activities.

Differences between connected standby and traditional Sleep and Hibernate

Table 5.6 summarizes a few differences between Sleep or Hibernate and connected standby mode.

Platform support

Implementation of connected standby power mode affects all levels of system design. Low power consumption, long battery life, and constant connectivity require devices that have low-power hardware like a power-efficient SOC (or chipset), low-power memory (DRAM), low-power-capable networking (Wi-Fi, MBB) devices, and so forth. A low-power system design forms the foundation of long battery life during sleep in a connected standby device, and has significant benefits even when the system is in active use. For example, the device should be able to safely save or store an e-mail that arrives at any time without any disc damage during writes that can occur while the handheld mobile device is moving in the user's hand.

HARDWARE-AUTONOMOUS POWER GATING [4]

Here the hardware automatically regulates the power through various mechanisms like power gating individual logic if not used, keeping memory/SRAM in power gating mode, turning off LDO (low dropout voltage regulators). Since the system automates the PM, the users do not need to be aware of the details. A set of predefined sensor characteristics are used to initiate Automatic Power Gating/Management. The automation prevents inefficient power control by user-level PM and provides better energy efficiency by taking sensor-specific information into account. It also reduces user intervention and application development time.

The automatic PM system used for sensors/sensor network is meant to automatically reduce the energy consumption for each sensor or sensor hub (controller of all sensors/data processor) while guaranteeing the quality of service, which means that sensors should be able to capture all events that occur and the sensor hub should be able to process all data received from the sensors.

Table 5.6 Differences Between Connected Standby and Traditional Sleep and Hibernate

Feature	ACPI Sleep (S3) and Hibernate (S4) States	Connected Standby Mode
System activity	• Completely pause all activity on the system when the processors are turned off • Activity remains paused until the user turns the system back on by pressing the power button, keyboard, or touchpad	• Automatically pause/resume system activities while device screen is off to maintain connectivity and cloud-content sync • Amount of activity is tightly controlled to achieve low power consumption and long battery life
Connectivity	• Do not maintain connectivity on the network (Wi-Fi, LAN, or cellular) • The networking devices are turned off until the user powers the system back on	• Keeps networking devices powered on in an extremely low-power mode to maintain connectivity • Device's Wi-Fi can automatically roam between user-preferred networks and alert OS to important network traffic
Applications and driver services	• Completely pause all application, service, and driver activity when the processors are powered off	• Allows applications, services, and drivers to keep running in a controlled manner to save power and extend battery life • E-mail sync and tile updates are performed by apps in a controlled manner
Power consumption	• Has more average power consumption to maintain memory in self-refresh and enable the platform to wake on user input	• Use low-power memory and power-optimized embedded controllers to consume much less than power in most configurations
Battery life and entry/exit	• Reduced battery life compared to connected standby mode • Differences in resume performance (exit latency, and so on) and power consumptions between Sleep and Hibernate	• Has longer battery life • No worries about battery life tradeoff between Sleep and Hibernate, or about the differences in resume performance • Shutting lid or pressing the power button makes system enter a low-power mode and maintain connectivity

A single automated PM strategy for all sensors is not efficient, because the characteristics of sensors vary significantly in terms of wake-up latency, power consumption, and operation latency. We can however discuss a few factors as an example for sensor PM.

A few factors for sensor-specific autonomous power management

Most sensor platforms are equipped with diverse types of sensors. These sensors communicate through standard interfaces like I^2C or SPI but their internal hardware architectures are different. Hence there is significant variance in the sensor sensitivity, hysteresis, wake-up latency, and so on between the sensors.

A few factors like wake-up latency, break-even cycle, and inrush current can be considered for sensor-specific PM, because these features are related to shut down or power-up. For sensor-specific PM, the autonomous PM system stores information about these factors in flash memory and makes a decision based on the stored characteristics.

Wake-up latency

The wake-up latency [4] is the time required for a sensor to reach the ready state after a stable power supply is provided. In the ready state a sensor can generate the correct value. A task is required to wait for the wake-up latency after requesting the kernel to turn on the sensor, otherwise the task will receive a wrong value. Wake-up latency varies significantly in each sensor type. Wake-up latency is also known as "startup time."

Break-even cycle

The break-even cycle is defined as the rate at which the power consumption of a node with a PM policy is equal to that of nonpower-managed node. There is no loss or gain in energy. The break-even cycle C_{be} is represented as

$$C_{be} = \frac{P_{normal}}{(E_{transtion} + E_{powerdown})}$$

where P_{normal} is the energy consumption of sensor; $E_{transition}$ is the energy consumption when sensor changes state between off and on; and $E_{powerdown}$ is the energy consumption/drawn when sensor is off.

Sensor usage

For automated sensor PM, sensor usage of the applications is an important factor. Typically sensor applications repeat the cycle of sensing, processing, and transmitting. Hence the sensor usage can be classified as: periodic, nonperiodic, and hybrid.

Periodic sensors have periodic sensor usage with low duty cycle. The sensor driver or OS can timestamp the incoming sensor data and determine the sensor usage. For such periodic sensor, the power needs to be applied only when the sensors are needed. For all other times and in-between these sensors can be power gated while considering the efficiency and break-even cycle. The PM schemes should ensure that the power consumption/overhead of switching the sensor from on to off and vice versa does not exceed the power consumption if a sensor is left on.

Nonperiodic sensors are the sensors that do not have predictable cycles. PM techniques that rely on predicting the time when a sensor would be used again next, will not be able to make correct predictions about these nonperiodic sensors. In such cases a PM block provides power to the nonperiodic sensor and related logic when demanded by the need/sensor. The PM schemes however need to ensure that the latency to turn on the sensor from its off state is acceptable to the system, or else such sensors must be left permanently on.

Hybrid sensors are the ones where the sensing cycle varies during operation. Examples include sensors that are normally just monitoring in periodic cycles and transmit data only when thresholds are crossed (and hence change in their duty cycle). The PM schemes would define thresholds for such sensors. When the sensor operation cycles change and the sensed value of parameter is beyond the defined threshold, then the PM unit/scheme will remove any power restrictions to the sensor (allow the needed power to the sensor).

EXAMPLE OF POWER MANAGEMENT ARCHITECTURE IN SENSOR

Following section describes some of the possible PM architectures suitable for implementation in sensors or sensor hubs: autonomous PM architecture, application-based PM architecture, and other PM schemes such as voltage scaling, task-based PM, runtime voltage hopping, and so on.

AUTONOMOUS POWER MANAGEMENT ARCHITECTURE IN SENSORS

Fig. 5.2 shows an example and possible components of autonomous PM architecture in a sensor.

- Sensor property storage: Stores the sensor properties such as power consumption rate, operating voltages, latencies.
- Battery monitor: Observes the residual power in the battery.
- Application monitor: Classifies sensor usage type: periodic, nonperiodic, or hybrid, and also monitors sensor latencies against the required response time to ensure sensors data remains valid.
- PM algorithms: This is where the decision on PM is made based on sensor properties, its usage, and latencies from application monitor and the residual available battery power.

APPLICATION-BASED POWER MANAGEMENT ARCHITECTURE [5]

This PM architecture is specifically designed to effectively reduce power usage of communication devices by selecting a short duration of time to suspend communication and shut down the communication devices (such as a Wireless Ethernet card of the mobile phone).

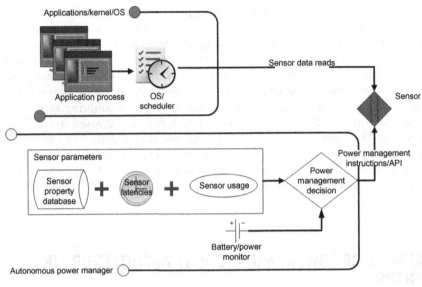

FIGURE 5.2

Example of autonomous power management architecture in sensor.

Power savings are attained by a transport-level protocol, which:

- Manages suspend/resume cycle of the mobile host's communications and the communication device for short periods of time.
- Queues the data transmissions in both the mobile host and any other host trying to communicate with the mobile host during the suspensions.
- Balances the power savings and data delay by identifying when to suspend and restart communications.
- Uses application-specific information to balance power savings and data delay (PM is abstracted at a higher level).

The power conservation is achieved by accumulating power savings from many small idle periods. However, additional energy consumption due to suspend and resume is also taken into account (which negatively impacts the overall power consumption).

Generally mobile communication devices operate in either transmit mode or receive mode. Transmit mode is used during data transmission only, while the receive mode is the default mode for both receiving data and monitoring incoming data. In the receive mode, the mobile communication device is mostly idle. However, some power is used for this reception in the receive mode. If applications are used, then better informed decisions on the use of PM techniques can be made. For software-level power conservation in communication, the time spent in transmission can be reduced using data reduction techniques and intelligent data transfer protocols.

Concept of communication-based power management

In a mobile device, a wireless Ethernet card would be in receive mode when not in use. In communication-based PM, the mobile device would act as master and would tell the base station when data transmission can occur. When the mobile device wakes up, it will send a query to base station to check if it has any data to send. There would be suspend—resume cycles resulting in bursts of data/communication followed by idle/inactivity.

The protocol described later allows a mobile device host to suspend a wireless communication device. Periodically or by request from the application, the protocol wakes up and reinitiates communication with the base station.

The mobile host is the master and the base station is slave, which as a slave is allowed to send data to the mobile device only during specific phases of the protocol. The slave queues the data during nontransmit phases of protocol, while waiting for commands from the master mobile device. Idle timers detect idle time for both the mobile device master and the slave base station.

Input messages to the mobile device or base station are the incoming message/data or timeout and output messages are the outgoing messages/data.

The following are the timers that are needed in the application-based PM architecture.

Timeout period

The timeout timer is set with a fixed period. When the timer expires and no communication has occurred since the last expiration, the protocol concludes that there is an idle period in the communication. Sufficient care should be taken to ensure that the timeout periods are not too short or long. Shorter timeout periods will cause SLEEP earlier than desired causing poor response from applications, while longer timeout periods will cause the communication devices to remain active for unnecessarily longer time resulting in energy/power wastage.

Sleep duration

This timer determines the duration of communication suspension by the master. Longer sleep periods will result in longer lags in any interactive applications, while shorter sleep periods may not extend battery lifetime significantly.

Fig. 5.3 shows the state transitions for slave (base) station in communication-based PM architecture. The slave (base) station comes up in sleeping mode and will transition to other states after receiving a wake-up message from the mobile device (master).

If the base station (slave) has data to send then it will be in the send/receive state. Once it is done sending the data, the slave will enter into the receiving state. If the slave has new data to transmit to the mobile device (master) then the slave can do so after it is done receiving all data from the mobile device and receives a wake-up message from the mobile device.

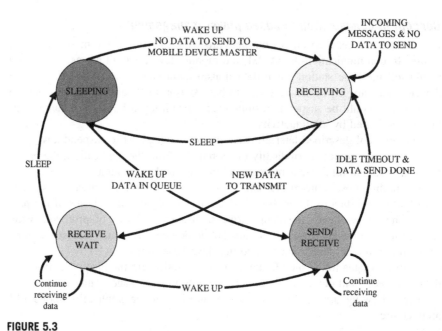

FIGURE 5.3

State transitions for slave device.

Table 5.7 summarizes the conditions for state transitions and corresponding data transfers for the slave device (base station in this example).

The mobile device (master) state machine can be partitioned into three sets. The first set consists of SLEEPING state. The second set consists of SENDING_WAIT, WAITING, and WAIT_FOR_OK. The third set consists of SENDING, SEND/RECV, and RECEIVING.

1. SLEEPING: The master mobile communication device is sleeping in this state and the device can be woken up by the following two conditions (Table 5.8 and Fig. 5.4):
   a. WAKE UP message (through wake-up timer) and sends new data to the slave.
   b. If it has new data before WAKE UP timer expires then the master mobile device can wake itself up or keep accumulating the new data until it wakes up on the wake-up timer expiry.
2. SENDING WAIT, WAITING, and WAIT FOR OK: The master in these states is waiting for a response from the slave. When the master receives a response from the slave in the form of a DATA or a NO DATA message, the master enters the appropriate state in the third set as shown in Table 5.9 and Fig. 5.5.
   a. SENDING WAIT: The master is transmitting data. If an idle timer expires (while the master device is in SENDING WAIT mode) indicating that the master has no more data to send, the master enters the WAITING mode and continues waiting for a response from the slave.

Table 5.7 State Transitions for Slave Device (Base Station)

Current State	Next State	Condition	Data
SLEEPING	SLEEPING	Initialized in this state	None
SLEEPING	RECEIVING	WAKE UP received from master and no data to send	Receives data, no data to send
SLEEPING	SEND-RECEIVE	WAKE UP received from master and has data to send	Receive and send data
RECEIVING	RECEIVING	Till incoming data is being received and no outgoing data/message	Receives data, no outgoing data
RECEIVING	SLEEPING	Receive SLEEP message	None
RECEIVING	RECEIVE-WAIT	When there is new data to be transmitted. NEW DATA CMD sent by slave (need to wait for WAKE UP before sending new data)	Receives data, cannot send data
SEND-RECEIVE	RECEIVING	When no more data to send; sends DONE message	Receives data, no data to send
SEND-RECEIVE	SEND-RECEIVE	Will continue data transfer	Receive and send data
RECEIVE-WAIT	SLEEPING	When receive SLEEP command (there can be data in the buffer but not transmitted)	None
RECEIVE-WAIT	RECEIVE-WAIT	Keep receiving data but waiting to send new data (can only send when it gets WAKE UP message)	Receives data, waiting to send data
RECEIVE-WAIT	SEND-RECEIVE	Receive WAKE UP and has data to send	Receive and send data

Table 5.8 State Transitions for the First Set of Master Mobile Computing Device States

Current State	Next State	Condition	Data
SLEEPING	SLEEPING	Initialized in this state	If the mobile communication device has new data before WAKE UP timer expires then the device can wake itself up or keep accumulating the new data until it wakes up on the wake-up timer expiry
SLEEPING	SENDING WAIT	WAKE UP and has data to send to slave	The master is transmitting data in next state of SENDING WAIT
SLEEPING	WAITING	WAKE UP but no data to send	The master mobile device has no data to transmit

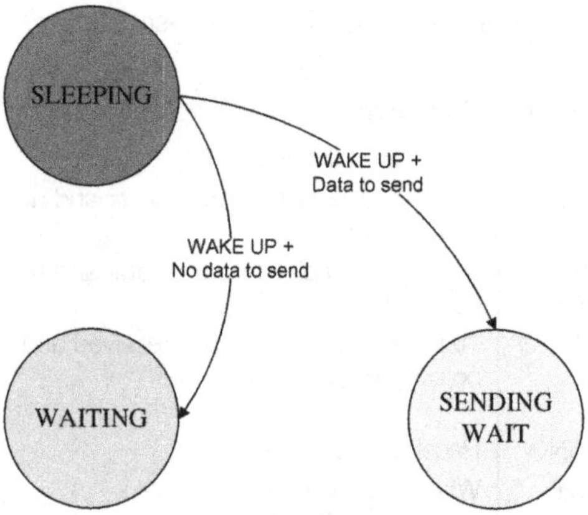

FIGURE 5.4

State transitions for the first set of master mobile computing device states.

Table 5.9 State Transitions for the Second Set of Master Mobile Computing Device States

Current State	Next State	Condition	Data
SENDING WAIT	SENDING	No data to be transmitted (but IDLE timer not expired)	
SENDING WAIT	SEND/ RECV	Data needs to be transmitted (but IDLE timer not expired)	
SENDING WAIT	WAITING	An idle timer expires indicating that the master has no more data to send (Queue empty)	continues waiting for a response from the slave
WAITING	SENDING WAIT	Master mobile device has data to transmit (Queue filled)	
WAITING	RECEIVING	Master mobile device has data to receive from slave	Receives data from slave
WAITING	WAIT FOR OK	Asks slave to SLEEP, waiting for SLEEP OK message	No data
WAIT FOR OK	SLEEPING	Receives SLEEP OK message from the slave device	No data transfers

    b. WAITING mode: The master has no data to transmit.

    c. WAIT FOR OK: The master in this state has told the slave that it should sleep and is waiting for a SLEEP OK message.

3. SENDING, SEND/RECV, and RECEIVING: The master in these states is actively sending and/or receiving data.

    a. SENDING: The master may receive a NEW DATA message from the slave. The master responds with a WAKE UP message and enters the SENDING WAIT mode.

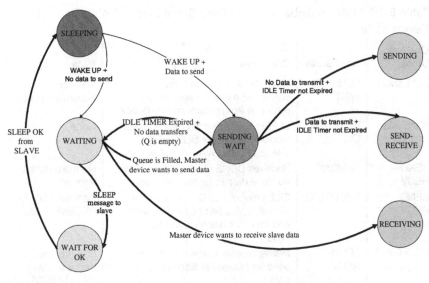

FIGURE 5.5

State transitions for the second set of master mobile computing device states.

b. When neither the master nor the slave have any more data to send, the master sends a SLEEP message and enters the WAIT FOR OK mode.

Table 5.10 summarizes the state transitions and corresponding data transfers for the third set of master mobile device states.

Based on the transport-level protocol described here and shown in Fig. 5.6, a mobile device can appropriately suspend and restart its communication devices (such as a wireless Ethernet card), inform the base station using appropriate commands, can queue data during noncommunication phases, and not lose any data. Based on experimental results from an implementation of this protocol by Robin Kravets and P. Krishnan showed power savings of up to 83% for communication.

POWER MANAGEMENT SCHEMES

Below are the various PM schemes [6] that can be deployed on the mobile devices' sensors and sensor hubs to achieve varying magnitudes of power savings and power control.

Dynamic voltage scaling

This scheme directly controls and varies the supply voltage of the devices to control their power consumption.

Table 5.10 State Transitions for the Third Set of Master Mobile Computing Device States

Current State	Next State	Condition	Data
SENDING	SENDING WAIT	NEW DATA message from Slave, WAKE UP message sent out as response from master mobile device	The master is transmitting data
SENDING	WAIT FOR OK	SLEEP message from master. Master would now wait for SLEEP OK message in the WAIT FOR OK state	None
SEND-RECV	SENDING	Receives DONE message from Slave; no more data to be sent to Slave	No more data to transfer
SEND-RECV	RECEIVING	IDLE timeout and Queue is empty. Master device has nothing to send and can continue receiving from the slave	Receives data in RECEIVING state
RECEIVING	SEND-RECV	Master mobile device now has data to send and Queue is filled with some data	Data transfers in the next state (SEND-RECV)
RECEIVING	WAIT FOR OK	Done and SLEEP message sent from the master mobile device to the slave. Master would now wait for SLEEP OK message in the WAIT FOR OK state	None

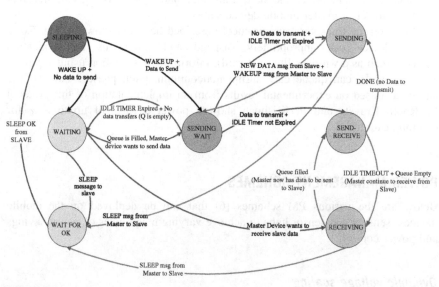

FIGURE 5.6

State transitions of master mobile computing device.

Dynamic power management

This scheme changes the voltage states of devices if it is idle for longer than predetermined time. This scheme requires correct prediction of device idle time in order to administer power reduction/saving schemes on the device.

Task-based power management

This scheme utilizes operating system to manage power of the devices and utilizes the device usage pattern for each task to optimize the power consumption per task. Each task reports to the OS task scheduler with its own device utilization. The scheduler then rearranges the execution order of tasks so that changes in power states can be avoided to reduce overhead as far as possible.

Low power fixed priority scheduling

This scheme is a hybrid between dynamic voltage scaling (DVS) and the dynamic PM scheme. Here the supply voltage of the devices is changed dynamically to operate the device in the power-down mode when the device is idle for longer than predetermined time. This scheme cannot incorporate workload-variation slack times of the task (time between execution time and worst-case execution time) because supply voltage cannot be adjusted dynamically within a particular task.

Runtime voltage hopping [7] (Sakurai)

The DVS scheme reduces the supply voltage dynamically to the lowest possible state where proper operation is still possible but the required performance of the system, device, sensor, or what have you is lower than the maximum possible performance. In the conventional DVS system as shown in Fig. 5.7, the output frequency of a ring oscillator is compared with the desired clock frequency and supply voltage is adjusted by a frequency−voltage feedback loop. However, voltage−frequency modeling of the critical path as ring oscillator is not accurate (critical paths may be different inside the same chip, and/or the chip fabrication process may be different, resulting in different circuit delay characteristics, and so forth), hence this DVS does not provide efficient control of supply voltage. Also, since system clock frequency can have different and arbitrary values, it can result in data exchange issues at the interface. These problems can be resolved by making the following modifications in the conventional DVS system:

- Supply voltage controlled by software feedback instead of hardware feedback,
- Supply voltage determined based on physical voltage−frequency relationship of chip/sensor/device,
- System clock frequency restricted to a discrete level, which could be obtained by dividing the highest system clock frequency vs having arbitrary values.

Fig. 5.8 shows the architecture of the modified DVS scheme known as a runtime voltage hopping scheme. This scheme uses the timeslot concept. In this

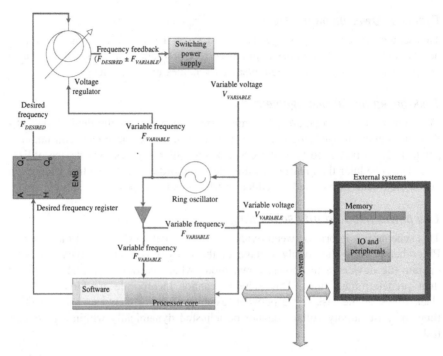

FIGURE 5.7

Conventional DVS system architecture.

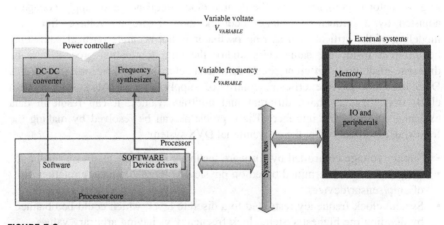

FIGURE 5.8

Runtime voltage hopping DVS system architecture.

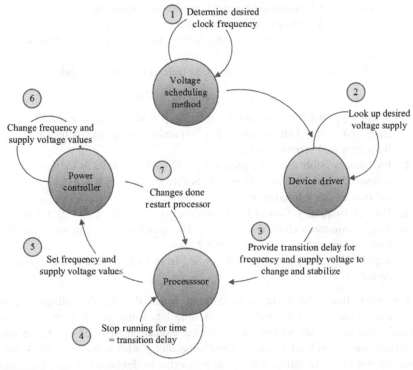

FIGURE 5.9

Runtime voltage hopping mechanism.

scheme, the relationship between clock frequency and supply voltage is measured by experiment and is stored as a lookup table in the device driver. The scheme then controls clock frequency and supply voltage by software feedback (instead of hard-wired feedback). It partitions the task in several timeslots and then dynamically controls supply voltage to the device on timeslot-by-timeslot basis. This helps fully utilize workload-variation slack time.

The device driver shown in the processor block of Fig. 5.8 has two lookup tables, which are prepared using actual characteristics of the device. The first lookup table has the voltage—frequency relationship of the target device, and the second lookup table contains the transition delay needed to change the clock frequency and the supply voltage.

Fig. 5.9 shows the basic mechanism followed in the runtime voltage hopping scheme that can be deployed on a mobile computing device. The voltage scheduling method that can be used to determine the desired clock frequency and corresponding supply is described here:

1. Compile time steps:
   a. A task is divided into N timeslots and
   b. Following parameters are obtained through either analysis or direct measurement

T_{WC}: WCET (worst-case execution time) of whole task;
T_{WCi}: WCET (worst-case execution time) of ith timeslot;
T_{ri}: WCET (worst-case execution time) from $(i+1)$th to N timeslots.

2. Runtime steps
   a. For each timeslot, the target execution time is obtained through:

$$T_{TAR} = T_{WC} - T_{WCi} - T_{ACC} - T_{TD}$$

   where T_{TAR} = target execution time; T_{ACC} = accumulated execution time from first to $(i-1)$th timeslots; T_{TD} = transition delay to change clock frequency and supply voltage.
   b. For each possible clock frequency $F_j = F_{CLK}/J$ ($J = 1, 2, 3 \ldots$), the estimated maximum execution time is calculated as $T_j = T_{Wi} \times j$. F_{CLK} is the master clock frequency.
   c. If clock frequency $F_j \neq$ clock frequency of $(i-1)$th, then $T_j = T_j + T_{TD}$.
   d. F_{VAR} = minimum clock frequency F_j whose estimated maximum execution time T_j does not exceed target time T_{TAR}.
   e. Supply voltage V_{VAR} is then determined from lookup table in the device driver.

Fig. 5.10 shows the basic steps through which the supply voltage can be controlled within each task and for each timeslot, while ensuring that each of the tasks still completes within its worst-case execution time. This scheme thus effectively uses workload-variation slack time along with worst-case slack time where the workload-variation slack time arises due to deviation of task execution time from its worst-case execution time.

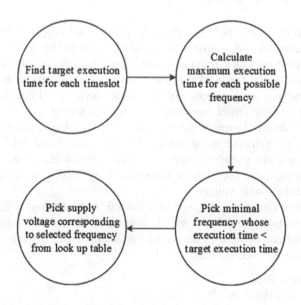

FIGURE 5.10

Runtime voltage hopping steps.

Adaptive power management system

The duration of the power-down state of the device should be long enough to justify the overheads involved in putting the device in that power-down state. The period during which the device remains in power-down mode is called BET (break-even task).

There are two main overheads of putting a device into a power-down mode:

1. Time delays due to the need to frequently wake up the device from its power-down mode and
2. Additional power consumption by the device to wake up.

The time delays resulting from the above two overheads cannot be handled by the runtime voltage hopping scheme.

Adaptive PM scheme uses the features of dynamic PM, DVS, pattern analysis algorithm, and BET time-based task partition scheduling. The following steps are executed in this PM scheme:

1. The task is split based on BET to reduce power consumption of applications in mobile environment.
2. The usage pattern of devices/sensors is analyzed.
3. The results of the analysis are applied to task scheduling to further reduce the power consumption.

Fig. 5.11 shows the basic building that are the blocks of this adaptive PM system.

Analysis Module: This module analyzes the runtime usage pattern of the devices. Algorithms like expectation-maximization (EM) can be used to identify the maximum likelihood from the list of input patterns. When an application executes, the analysis module extracts the pattern stored in the pattern information database. If this pattern matches the usage model of the application that would be run, then the existing pattern is retrieved/used instead of analyzing the pattern again for the application. This saves overhead of pattern analysis.

Instead of collecting all patterns for the device, the existing patterns are updated every time a new pattern is collected. This goes on until the pattern is finalized as the representative pattern.

To revise undetermined representative patterns, the following are used:

- The usage counts of individual peripheral devices.
- The total usage counts of all the peripheral devices in the EM algorithm.

If revised undetermined representative patterns satisfy the reference value of the EM algorithm, they are finalized as representative patterns. No additional patterns are collected once the representative patterns are chosen. This helps reduce the storage requirements.

Scheduling Module: This module has two components:

- Slack time calculator: $T_s = T_d + T_e$ where T_d = deadline time of the time slot and T_e = execution time of the timeslot.

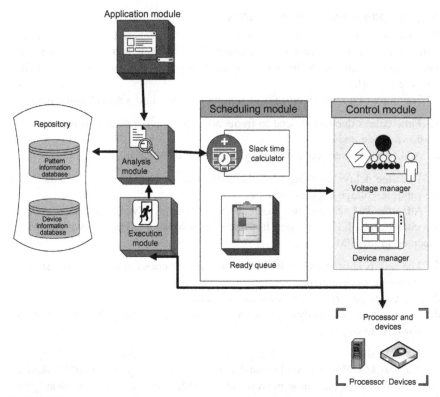

FIGURE 5.11

Adaptive power management system.

- Ready Queue: It manages the timeslots for execution using break-even time-based task partitioning scheduling. It identifies the timeslots during which the specific device is to be utilized, either simultaneously or consecutively. It modifies the processing sequence of timeslots to minimize the change in power state of the device. This module also checks if device would be used for more than one timeslot consecutively. If it is likely, then this module schedules the timeslot such that the device/logic doesn't sleep in between to avoid wake-up overheads.

Fig. 5.12 shows that the scheduling module will chose the next task such that it uses the same devices (devices 7, 8) as in last timeslot (in this example timeslot 2 of the previous task).

They can be also scheduled as shown in Fig. 5.13, where devices 7, 8 can remain idle during Task 1 if they are not participating in Task 1.

In Fig. 5.14 devices 7 and 8 go to idle and then have to be brought back up for next task. This results in higher power consumption due to switching (from on to off in idle time and then on again) or they would have to be stopped from going

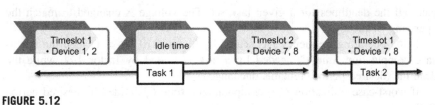

FIGURE 5.12

Effective timeslot execution orders using same devices consecutively.

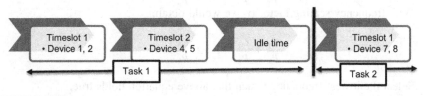

FIGURE 5.13

Effective timeslot execution orders using same devices consecutively.

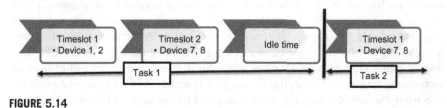

FIGURE 5.14

Effective timeslot execution orders using same devices consecutively.

into idle state and left on between the two tasks. Such scheduling will consume more power.

Each task, T_i, has an associated period, P_i, and a worst-case computation time, C_i. The task is released (put in execution) periodically once every P_i time units (actual units can be seconds or processor cycles, or whatever) and it can begin execution. The task needs to complete its execution by its deadline (by the next release of the task). A real-time scheduler can guarantee that the tasks will always receive enough processor cycles to complete each invocation in time as long as each task T_i does not use more than C_i cycles in each execution.

Control Module: This module has

- Voltage scaling manager: adjusts the supply voltage of device using DVS schemes.
- A device manager: manages/actually controls the device based on the information provided by the other components of the PM system.

In a simplistic version of static voltage scaling [8], the lowest possible operating frequency is selected for the device such that it allows the scheduler to meet all the deadlines for a given task set. The voltage is changed to match the operating frequency.

If the operating frequency f is scaled by factor α $(0 \leq \alpha \leq 1)$ then the worst-case computation time C_i needed by a task is scaled by factor $1/\alpha$, while the deadline (desired period) remains unchanged.

If worst-case utilization $U_i =$ computational time C_i divided by desired period P_i then

$$\frac{C_1}{P_1} + \frac{C_2}{P_2} + \ldots + \frac{C_n}{P_n} \leq 1$$

With frequency scaling factor α, we would obtain:

$$\frac{C_1}{P_1} + \frac{C_2}{P_2} + \ldots + \frac{C_n}{P_n} \leq \alpha$$

Select the lowest frequency f such that above equation holds true.

When a task is released for its next execution, it is not known how much computation it will actually require, so a conservative assumption is made that it will need its specified worst-case processor time. When the task completes, the actual number of processor cycles used is compared to the worst-case specification. Any unused cycles that were allotted to the task would normally (or eventually) be wasted, idling the processor. Instead of idling for extra processor cycles, the *DVS* algorithms avoid wasting cycles (cycle conserving) by reducing the operating frequency. The surplus time is used to run other remaining tasks at a lower CPU frequency rather than accomplish more work. So if a task completes earlier than its worst-case computation time, the excess time is reclaimed by recomputing utilization using the actual computing time consumed by the task. This reduced value is used until the task is released again for its next execution. At each scheduling point (task release or completion) the utilization is recomputed using the actual time for completed tasks and the specified worst case for the others, and the frequency is set appropriately.

If a task T_i completes its current execution after using cc_i cycles (much smaller than its worst-case computation time C_i), then cc_i can now be considered its worst-case computation bound temporarily. With the reduced utilization specified for this task, a smaller scaling factor (and hence a lower operating frequency) can be found for which the task set remains schedulable [8] (meaning remaining tasks are executed at lower frequency of the device). It may be necessary to increase the operating frequency again for the next task set.

Repository: This module has

- Device information database: contains representative usage pattern of the applications that would be run on the device(s).
- Pattern information database: contains the device/sensor properties and attributes like device state (on, off, running, idle, wake up, power consumption, and so on). The power consumption information is gathered by

the analysis module and stored in this repository module. It also contains the BET of the device, which is calculated using the following formula:

$$BET = \frac{2 \times T_w \times (P_w - P_p)}{P_p - P_i}$$

where T_w = wake-up time of sensor/peripheral device; P_w = power consumed during wake-up of sensor/peripheral device; P_p = power consumed by operating sensor/peripheral device; and P_i = power consumed by idle sensor/peripheral device.

POWER MANAGEMENT IN A TYPICAL SENSOR HUB

Earlier different ACPI power states were discussed. When a sensor hub is used in the SOC, the following power states can be supported. Table 5.11 correlates the sensor hub device D-state and system/SOC states from an OS perspective.

Table 5.11 The Sensor Hub Device D-State and System/SOC States

SOC System State	Sensor Hub States	Notes
S0i0	D0–D0i3, D3	The sensor hub is on and running. It is receiving full power from the system and is delivering full functionality to the user. The sensor hub can enter D0i1–D0i3 in S0i0 to do power savings during the normal duty cycle
S0i1	D0*	The sensor hub cannot access system memory in S0i1 but it can maintain context in SRAM or DRAM staying in D0i1–D0i3
	D0i1–D0i3, D3	*The sensor hub could be in D0 while in S0i1, but as soon as it has to bring code or data page from system DRAM it forces system transition to S0 to activate path to DRAM
S0i2	D0*	The sensor hub cannot access system memory in S0i2 but it can maintain context in SRAM or DRAM staying in D0i1–D0i3
	D0i1–D0i3, D3	*The sensor hub could be in D0 while in S0i2, but as soon as it has to bring code or data page from system DRAM it forces system transition to S0 to activate path to DRAM
S0i3	D0*	The sensor hub cannot access system memory in S0i3, it can maintain context in SRAM or DRAM
	D0i1–D0i3, D3	*The sensor hub could be in D0 while in S0i3, but as soon as it has to bring code or data page from system DRAM it forces system transition to S0 to activate path to DRAM
S3–S5	D3	No sensor hub context is maintained; the sensor hub is in D3

Here is the detailed description of states that can be implemented for any sensor hub.

D0—This is the normal operation state. All the sensor hardware components are powered and performing. The active firmware pages are located in the sensor hub SRAM and on-demand paging with system DRAM is active.

D0u—This uninitialized state of the sensor hub is where a single sensor hub SRAM bank can be on to enable start of the firmware loading process. The DRAM can be accessed by the sensor hub, but there is no loadable firmware present. The main difference between D0 and D0u is the fact that system power state change events need to be handled by sensor hub ROM rather than by loadable firmware. The sensor hub power consumption in this state is also lower than D0 due to fact that all SRAM banks except one are powered off.

D0i1—This is a shallow power-savings state wherein the sensor hub hardware can be clock gated with SRAM in drowsy mode maintaining the content. Transition back to D0 state is triggered by interrupts such as timer, GPIO alert from sensor(s), host, or any other engines that can talk to the sensor hub through a defined internal communication protocol.

D0i2—This is a medium power-savings state wherein the sensor hub hardware is clock gated or power gated (depending on particular hardware block power-saving capabilities). Wake reasons are similar to D0i1. SRAM content is preserved, while actual SRAM power state depends on the sensor hub hardware capabilities. Transition back to D0 state is triggered by interrupts such as timer, GPIO alert from sensor(s), host, or any other engines that can talk to the sensor hub through a defined internal communication protocol.

D0i3—This is a deep power-savings state wherein the sensor hub hardware is clock gated or power gated. SRAM content is evacuated to DRAM. Wake reasons are similar to D0i1. The sensor hub hardware power consumption would be lower while resident in D0i3 compared to D0i1 and D0i2, but resume latency is higher due to the need to refill SRAM with content evacuated to system DRAM on D0i3 entry. Power savings of D0i3 state compared to D0i2 depend on D0i3 residence time. The D0i3 exit flow has significant impact on system power consumption as it is required to wake SOC up to S0 to enable the sensor hub path to system memory for SRAM refill.

D3—This is a power-down state wherein all the sensor hub hardware is shut down, and no firmware context is maintained in SRAM.

Normally the sensor hub duty cycle bounces between D0, D0i1, D0i2, and D0i3 such that it does work in D0 during $x\%$ time of duty cycle and goes to D0i1 or D0i2 for $(100 - x)\%$ time of duty cycle. The sensor hub can wake up in any system power state depending on operating system, software, and firmware support. The power state of sensor depends on the availability of the hardware resources during a particular system power state. The sensor hub hardware cannot operate in D0 state with paging from DRAM because the system is in S0i2, and in S0i2 the system DRAM is not available. If there is use case that requires it, then the sensor hub can exit sleep state and cause the system to wake from S0i2 into a state where it can access the system DRAMs.

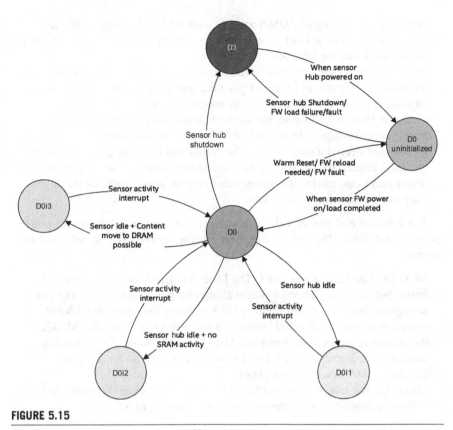

FIGURE 5.15

Possible sensor hub power state transitions.

Fig. 5.15 shows possible power state transitions in a sensor hub. Some of the possible key PM device states are D0, D0-uninitialized (D0u), D0i1, D0i2, D0i3, and D3.

D3 to D0u: The transition from D3 to D0u occurs when the sensor hub hardware is powered on from D3 state. As mentioned earlier, in D0u state only certain banks (typically 1) of SRAM bank can be left on from which firmware can be loaded.

D0u to D0: The transition from D0u to D0 state occurs when the sensor hub firmware load process has completed.

D0 to D0u: The transition from D0 to D0u state occurs when the sensor hub firmware undergoes Warm Reset. Warm Reset can occur if there is an explicit request from software to reload the firmware or if there is a firmware fault due to some protection failures/violations or watchdog timer expiration.

D0 to D0i1 and Exit From D0i1: The transition from D0 to D0i1 state occurs when the sensor hub firmware identifies a potential idleness period and decides to enter the shallow power-saving state. If at the moment of idleness detection there is ongoing DMA activity with SRAM, the only available power-savings state is D0i1. The resume from D0i1 to D0 is triggered by any sensor hub hardware interrupt.

D0 to D0i2 and Exit From D0i2: The transition from D0 to D0i2 occurs when the sensor hub firmware identifies potential inactivity period and there is no ongoing DMA activity with SRAM in progress requiring SRAM to be available. In such a situation, the sensor hub firmware decides whether to target power-savings state in D0i2 or D0i3 based on projected sleep duration. If projected sleep duration exceeds the "minimum sleep for D0i3" threshold and D0i3 resume time is shorter than the latency tolerance set by the current sensor hub usage model, the sensor hub firmware selects D0i3 as the target sleep state, otherwise it enters D0i2.

The entrance and exit of D0i2 flows depend on sensor hub hardware power-savings capabilities. The exit is triggered by any enabled sensor hub hardware interrupt.

D0 to D0i3 and Exit From D0i3: The D0i3 entrance is performed when the sensor hub firmware detects a potential idleness period justifying D0i3 power savings as described earlier. During D0i3 entrance the sensor hub SRAM content is copied to allocated sensor hub space in the system DRAM. After the content is copied, the sensor hub DRAM is shut down. This operation requires system exit from S0iX to S0 and residence in S0 until sensor hardware DMA operation completes.

D0 to D3: The transition from D0 to D3 state occurs when the sensor hub is to be shut down due when the system enters from S3 to S5.

EXAMPLE OF POWER MANAGEMENT IN ATMEL SAM G55G/SAM G55 [9]

In general, sensor hub implementation can be done using the following options:

- A dedicated microcontroller (MCU) with ultra-small footprints and ultra-low power
- An application processor-based hub with integrated sensor
- A sensor-based hub with an integrated MCU
- FPGA-based solutions.

The following section discusses PM on a sensor hub implemented using integrated MCU from Atmel.

Main components of Atmel SAM G55G/SAM G55

The Atmel SMART SAM G55 is a flash microcontroller using a 32-bit ARM Cortex-M4 RISC processor with an Floating Point Unit. It operates at a maximum speed of 120 MHz and has 512 KB of flash and up to 176 KB of SRAM.

It has following peripherals:

- eight flexible communication units (USARTs, SPIs, and I^{2}C bus interfaces),
- two three-channel general-purpose 16-bit timers,
- two I2S controllers,
- one-channel pulse density modulation,
- one eight-channel 12-bit ADC,
- one real-time timer (RTT) and one RTC, both located in the ultra-low-power backup area.

Supported sleep modes and wake mechanism

The Atmel SMART SAM G55 devices have three software-selectable low-power modes: Sleep, Wait, and Backup.

- Sleep mode: In this mode the processor is stopped while all other functions can be kept running.
- Wait mode: In this mode all clocks and functions are stopped but some peripherals can be configured to wake up the system based on events, including partial asynchronous wake-up (SleepWalking).
- Backup mode: In this mode RTT, RTC, and wake-up logic are running.

For power consumption optimization, the flexible clock system offers the capability of having different clock frequencies for some peripherals. Moreover, the processor and bus clock frequency can be modified without affecting the peripheral processing.

The Cortex-M4 processor sleep modes reduce the power consumption:

- Sleep mode stops the processor clock.
- Deep sleep mode stops the system clock and switches off the PLL and flash memory.

The SLEEPDEEP bit of the system control register (SCR) selects which sleep mode is used.

Entering Sleep Mode: The various mechanisms that software can use to put the processor into sleep mode are mentioned below. The system can generate spurious wake-up events, e.g., a debug operation wakes up the processor. Therefore the software must be able to put the processor back into sleep mode after such an event. A program might have an idle loop to put the processor back to sleep mode.

1. *Wait for Interrupt (WFI)*: The wait for interrupt instruction causes immediate entry to sleep mode. When the processor executes a WFI instruction it stops executing instructions and enters sleep mode.
2. *Wait for Event (WFE)*: The wait for event instruction causes entry to sleep mode conditional on the value of a one-bit event register. When the processor executes a WFE instruction, it checks this register:
   - If the register is 0, the processor stops executing instructions and enters sleep mode.

- If the register is 1, the processor clears the register to 0 and continues executing instructions without entering sleep mode.
3. *Sleep-on-Exit*: If the SLEEPONEXIT bit of the SCR is set to 1 when the processor completes the execution of an exception handler, it returns to Thread-mode and immediately enters sleep mode. This mechanism is used in applications that only require the processor to run when an exception occurs.

The various mechanisms that can be used to wake up the processor are mentioned below.

1. *Wake Up From WFI or Sleep-on-Exit:* Normally, the processor wakes up only when it detects an exception with sufficient priority to cause exception entry. Some embedded systems might have to execute system restore tasks after the processor wakes up, and before it executes an interrupt handler. To achieve this, set the PRIMASK bit to 1 and the FAULTMASK bit to 0. If an interrupt arrives that is enabled and has a higher priority than the current exception priority, the processor wakes up but does not execute the interrupt handler until the processor sets PRIMASK to zero.
2. *Wake Up From WFE*: The processor wakes up if:
   - It detects an exception with sufficient priority to cause an exception entry.
   - It detects an external event signal. The processor provides an external event input signal. Peripherals can drive this signal, either to wake the processor from WFE, or to set the internal WFE event register to 1 to indicate that the processor must not enter sleep mode on a later WFE instruction.
   - In a multiprocessor system, another processor in the system executes an SEV instruction.
   - In addition, if the SEVONPEND bit in the SCR is set to 1, any new pending interrupt triggers an event and wakes up the processor, even if the interrupt is disabled or has insufficient priority to cause an exception entry.

Power management controller of Atmel SAM G55G/SAM G55

The power management controller (PMC) controls the clocks to various peripherals and the Cortex-M4 processor. One of the feature supported by PMC is asynchronous Partial Wake-up (also known as SleepWalking).

The asynchronous partial wake-up (SleepWalking) wakes up a peripheral in a fully asynchronous way when activity is detected on the communication line. The asynchronous partial wake-up can also trigger an exit of the system from Wait mode (full system wake-up) under some user configurable conditions.

The asynchronous partial wake-up function automatically manages the peripheral clock. Through the use of this function, the peripherals (FLEXCOM0-7, ADC) are clocked only when needed and hence it improves the overall power consumption of the system. The peripheral selected for asynchronous partial wake-up must be first configured so that its clock is enabled by setting the appropriate register bits.

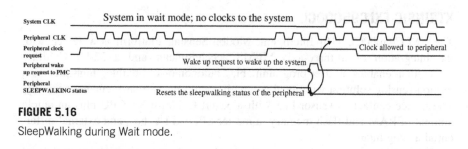

FIGURE 5.16

SleepWalking during Wait mode.

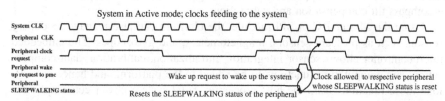

FIGURE 5.17

SleepWalking during Active mode.

When the system is in Wait mode (Fig. 5.16), all clocks of the system (except slow clock (SLCK)) are stopped. When an asynchronous clock request from a peripheral occurs, the PMC partially wakes up the system to feed the clock only to this peripheral. The rest of the system is not fed with the clock, thus optimizing power consumption. Finally, depending on user-configurable conditions, the peripheral either wakes up the whole system if these conditions are met or stops the peripheral clock until the next clock request. If a wake-up request occurs, the Asynchronous Partial Wake-up mode is automatically disabled until the user instructs the PMC to enable asynchronous partial wake-up by setting PIDx in the PMC SleepWalking Enable Register (PMC_SLPWK_ER).

When the system is in Active mode (Fig. 5.17), peripherals enabled for asynchronous partial wake-up have their respective clocks stopped until the peripherals request a clock. When a peripheral requests the clock, the PMC provides the clock without CPU intervention. The triggering of the peripheral clock request depends on conditions which can be configured for each peripheral.

If these conditions are met, the peripheral asserts a request to the PMC. The PMC disables the Asynchronous Partial Wake-up mode of the peripheral and provides the clock to the peripheral until the user instructs the PMC to reenable partial wake-up on the peripheral. This is done by setting PIDx in the PMC_SLPWK_ER.

If the conditions are not met, the peripheral clears the clock request and PMC stops the peripheral clock until the clock request is reasserted by the peripheral.

XTRINSIC FXLC95000CL

The FXLC95000CL [10] Intelligent, Motion-Sensing Platform is a device with the integration of a three-axis MEMS accelerometer and a 32-bit ColdFire MCU that enables a user-programmable, autonomous, flexible, high-precision motion-sensing solution with local computing and sensors management capability. The device can act as sensor hub with a 32-bit ColdFire V1 CPU plus an ample amount of RAM and flash memory, a master SPI and I^2C bus, and external differential analog inputs.

The user's firmware, along with the hardware device, can make system-level decisions required for applications, such as gesture recognition, pedometer, and e-compass tilt compensation and calibration.

Using the Master I^2C or SPI module, the platform can also manage secondary sensors such as pressure sensors, magnetometers, and gyroscopes. The embedded microcontroller allows sensor integration, initialization, calibration, data compensation, and computation functions to be added to the platform, and hence can offload those functions from the host processor. Total system power consumption is significantly reduced because the application processor stays powered down for longer periods of time.

Power management modes of FXLC95000CL

The ColdFire MCU architecture has several modes of operation such as Reset, Run, Stop, and Halt (debug). At the device level there are three main phases, namely, analog phase, digital phase, and idle phase as shown in Table 5.12.

The MCU of the device has only a single STOP operation, but there are additional levels of distinction at the device level as shown in Table 5.13.

Table 5.12 FXLC95000CL Device Power Phases

Phase	Title	Description
Φ_A	Analog phase	All analog (C2V and ADC) processing occurs in this phase. The CPU and associated peripherals are "quiet" during this mode
Φ_D	Digital phase	The CPU and peripherals are active, analog in low-power state
Φ_I	Inactive or idle phase	Most of the device is powered down for minimal power consumption

Table 5.13 FXLC95000CL Device Level STOP Phases

Stop Phase	Title	Description
$STOP_{FC}$	STOP—clock in fast mode	Nominally used for Φ_A
$STOP_{SC}$	STOP—clock in low-speed mode	Nominally used for Φ_I
$STOP_{NC}$	STOP—all clocks disabled	Nominally used for the SLEEP phase

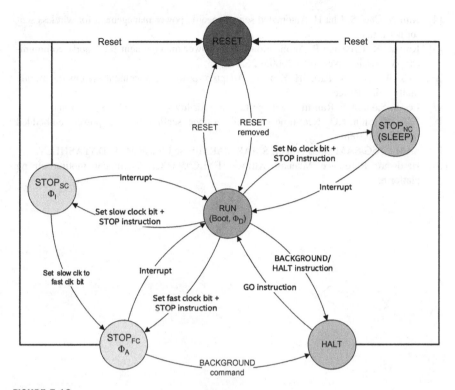

FIGURE 5.18

Possible state transitions in FXLC95000CL sensor hub.

Fig. 5.18 shows various power state transitions and mapping of device phases to the ColdFire MCU operation modes. Boot and Φ_D (functionally identical) are mapped into the MCU Run mode, while the Φ_A, Φ_I, and Sleep phases are mapped into the ColdFire STOP mode on this device.

REFERENCES

[1] Yurur Y, Liu CH, Perera C, Chen M, Liu X, Moreno W. Energy-efficient and context-aware smartphone sensor employment.

[2] Hewlett-Packard Corporation, Intel Corporation, Microsoft Corporation, Phoenix Technologies Ltd., Toshiba Corporation, Revision 4.0a April 5, 2010. Advanced configuration and power interface specification.

[3] Android reference, <https://developer.android.com/reference/android/os/PowerManager.html>.

[4] Kim N, Choi S, Cha H. Automated sensor-specific power management for wireless sensor networks.

[5] Kravets R, Krishnan P. Application-driven power management for mobile communication. Wireless Networks 2000;6:262–77.

[6] Park SO, Lee JK, Park JH, Kim SJ. Adaptive power management system for mobile multimedia device.

[7] Lee S, Sakurai T. Run-time voltage hopping for low-power real-time systems.

[8] Pillai P, Shin KG. Real-time dynamic voltage scaling for low-power, embedded operating systems.

[9] SAM G55G/SAM G55J Atmel. SMART ARM-based Flash MCU DATASHEET.

[10] Hardware Reference Manual. Xtrinsic FXLC95000CL intelligent motion-sensing platform.

Software, firmware, and drivers

6

INFORMATION IN THIS CHAPTER:

• Windows Sensor Software Stack
• Android Sensor Software Stack
• Sensor Hub Firmware Architecture

INTRODUCTION TO SOFTWARE COMPONENTS

Today's mobile devices have sensors, sensing components, or sensor hubs that can use continuous sensing, including context-aware sensing, to add intelligence to the devices and deliver a unique user experience. Such user experience depends on sensor hardware—software integration and a software environment, i.e., OS agnostic.

A typical mobile or context-aware device has built-in sensors like accelerometers, gyroscopes, and magnetometers that take measurements or detect changes in their respective parameters and provide raw data in the form of signals with certain configured precision, accuracy, and duration. This raw data is then interpreted by associated software or firmware components, including applications, into some meaningful contexts: gestures or motions (such as the detection of the tilting the device, the unintentional dropping of the device, or the hand gestures during a game) or inferring the environment around the device (using temperature, pressure, or humidity sensors [1]).

OS platforms for mobile devices such as Android and Windows support three main categories of sensors: motion sensors, environmental sensors, and positioning sensors. These sensors can be accessed using software/firmware components, configuration, or a framework (such as the Android sensor framework, Windows basic driver configuration, or Windows sensor hub configuration). The main blocks of this software can be grouped into [2] the following layers as shown in Fig. 6.1:

• Physical sensing and control layer: This layer interfaces with physical or hardware sensors. It configures, activates, controls, and reads the sensors to provide raw sensor data to higher layers of software or firmware.
• Sensor data processing layer: This layer processes the raw sensor data in the form of voltage or current into a value or data that can be evaluated by the

Mobile Sensors and Context-Aware Computing. DOI: http://dx.doi.org/10.1016/B978-0-12-801660-2.00006-9

evaluation layer. It uses various error estimation mechanisms to remove sensor data uncertainty and noise.
- Sensor data evaluation layer: This layer connects the sensor data to higher application layers. It evaluates the processed sensor data using various algorithms and models into a more meaningful context that applications, devices, and humans can understand and use.

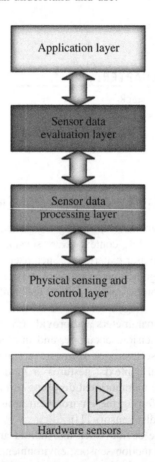

FIGURE 6.1

Sensor data processing basic software/firmware stack.

WINDOWS SENSOR SOFTWARE STACK

The Windows OS native sensor software stack [3] consists of following main components:

- Sensor driver: This component or layer communicates directly with the underlying sensor devices/hardware.

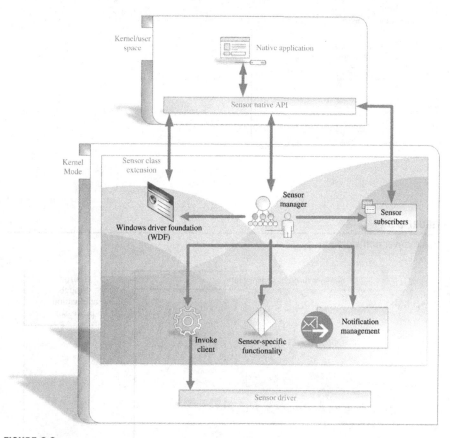

FIGURE 6.2

Windows sensor class extension components.

- Sensor native application programming interface (API): This component provides a sensor-specific API to native applications.
- Sensor class extension: This component manages multiple instances of the same hardware sensor when the same sensor needs to be used. Each open sensor class extension instance is unique to the sensor it manages, even when there can be multiple sensor class extensions open on the system as in basic driver configuration shown in Fig. 6.2. The two main functions of the sensor class extension are notification management and power management.

SENSOR DRIVER CONFIGURATION

There are two possible configurations in the Windows sensor driver model: the basic driver configuration and the hub configuration.

In the basic driver configuration, the individual hardware sensor is controlled by individual driver for that sensor as shown in Fig. 6.3.

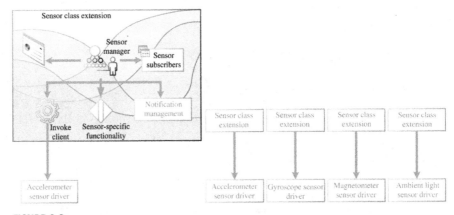

FIGURE 6.3

Basic driver configuration.

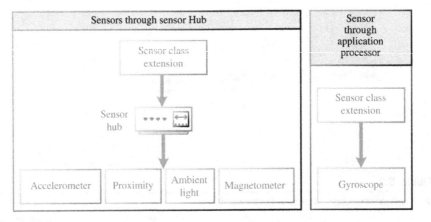

FIGURE 6.4

Hub configurations using sensor hub and application processor.

In the hub configuration, many hardware sensors are controlled by a dedicated sensor hub and therefore accessible only through that hub. Some other individual hardware sensors are accessible directly through the application processor. Fig. 6.4 shows the configuration with a sensor hub as well as with an application processor.

SENSOR CLASS EXTENSION IMPLEMENTATION

The sensor class extension consists [4] of the Windows Driver Foundation (WDF), sensor manager, sensor-specific functionalities, sensor subscribers, notification management, and Invoke client module (Fig. 6.2). Fig. 6.5 shows the interaction between the components of sensor class extension.

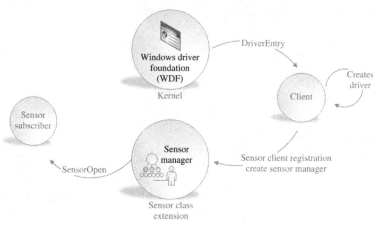

FIGURE 6.5

Interactions between sensor class extension components.

WDF: This module implements the fundamental features of a Windows driver.
Sensor manager: The WDF creates this object on calling the DriverEntry [5] function (it initializes the driver) of the client's driver.
Sensor subscriber: The sensor manager creates this object when SensorOpen [6] (a function used to open a sensor) is called. There could be many subscribers to the sensor driver.
Sensor-specific functionality: This module implements sensor-specific functionalities that cannot be implemented by the generic sensor manager like validating a notification.
Notification management: This component manages all active notifications and aligns operating frequencies to make the sensor more power efficient while serving different applications.
Invoke client [7]: This module connects the client driver and the sensor class extension and defines the communication interface (data structures such as SENSOR_TIMING and SENSOR_CLIENT_REGISTRATION_PACKET, and functions such as ClientDrvInitializeDevice and ClientDrvQueryDeviceInformation).

Sensor class extension notification management

The sensor class extension manages the application needs related to the sensor.

As indicated in Fig. 6.6, following steps describe the notification management scheme [8]:

- The various applications request a particular sensor to operate and provide the sensor data at Requested or notification rates of R_1, R_2, R_3, and R_F. R_F is the fastest requested rate among all the Requested rates from various applications.
- The sensor class extension causes the underlying sensor to operate at the fastest common frequency R_c.

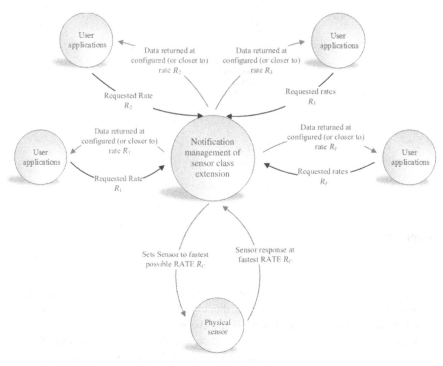

FIGURE 6.6

Notification management in Windows sensor class extension.

- The sensor class extension provides the sensor data to various applications at their respective requested rates possible or at the rate closest to the requested data rate. This is the configured notification rate.
- The sensor class extension also informs the application if their respective configured events occur during the sensor data procurement/processing such as data crossing high or low threshold set by the applications or data crossing a configured range.

Let us consider the following example, where $R_1 = 3$ ms, $R_2 = 6$ ms, $R_3 = 9$ ms, and $R_F = 12$ ms.

Case 1: The sensor sample rate is 3 ms. In this case, since the sensor data is available at an interval of 3 ms, each application would be provided data as per their requested rate (3, 6, 9, and 12 ms, respectively).

Case 2: The sensor sample rate of the sensor is 5 ms. In this case, the sensor data would be available at the intervals of 2 ms (2, 4, 6, 8 ms, and so on). The sensor class extension tries to provide the sensor data to the respective applications at the rate closest to their requested rate. Hence in this case, the sensor class extension will respond to applications at 5 ms for $R_1 = 3$ ms, 5 ms for $R_2 = 6$ ms, 10 ms for $R_3 = 9$ ms, and 10 ms for $R_F = 12$ ms. So some of the applications will either gate data earlier or later than what they requested for. The applications therefore depend on the timestamp of the sensor sample data rather than on the configured notification rate.

Sensor class extension power management

The sensor class extension can be the owner of the power policy for the sensor. It can start or stop the power to the sensor. It uses functions like SensorStart [9], SensorStop [10], or SensorGetData [11] to achieve this.

SENSOR STATES

As shown in the Fig. 6.7, Windows supports four possible sensor states: Initialization, Idle, Active, and Error [12].

Initialization: The sensor enters into this state as the startup and will transition to Idle state only when it is ready to respond to native API calls.

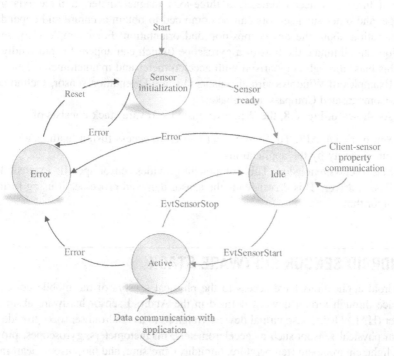

FIGURE 6.7

Windows sensor states.

Idle: The sensor enters this state when it is ready to respond to client application for requests and configuration of sensor capabilities/properties and data field ranges.

Active: The sensor enters into this state when the client application calls EvtSensorStart [13]. This causes sensor to start with its default properties or with the properties set by sensor class extension. In this state the sensor will take active measurements of its sensor parameter(s) and send data to the requesting agent as per the set configuration. The sensor will transition to Idle state when the application calls EvtSensorStop [14] to stop the sensor.

Error: The sensor can enter into this state from all of the sensor states at the occurrence of any error. User intervention/reset may be needed to recover from this state.

SENSOR FUSION

Sensor fusion refers to the process of combining data from multiple sensors into information that is more accurate, complete, and dependable than each of the individual contributing sensors' data.

In the mobile computing systems or smartphones, the sensor data from sensors like a three-axis accelerometer, a three-axis magnetometer, a three-axis gyroscope, and other such sensors can be combined to obtain accurate and dependable information about the device position and orientation. For example [15], sensor fusion can eliminate the bias of a gyroscope (which can appear to spin wildly due to this bias) through comparison with accelerometer and magnetometer data.

Examples of Windows virtual sensors [15] are Orientation sensor, Inclinometer, Tilt-Compensated Compass, and Shake.

As shown in Fig. 6.8, the Windows fusion software stack consists of:

- Sensor native API: This component is used to access fusion features and functionality by the applications.
- Sensor class extension: This component provides sensor-specific extensibility.
- Fusion driver: This driver reads the sensor data and processes it using fusion algorithms.

ANDROID SENSOR SOFTWARE STACK

Android applications have access to the physical sensors of the mobile computing device through virtual devices defined in the Android sensor hardware abstraction layer (HAL) [16]. These virtual devices (referred to as Android sensors) provide data from physical sensors such as accelerometers, magnetometers, gyroscopes, proximity, light, environment (temperature, humidity), pressure, and biosensors (heart rate).

The physical sensors may be connected through a hardware sensor hub over I^2C or SPI protocol. The Android sensors are defined in sensors.h and the

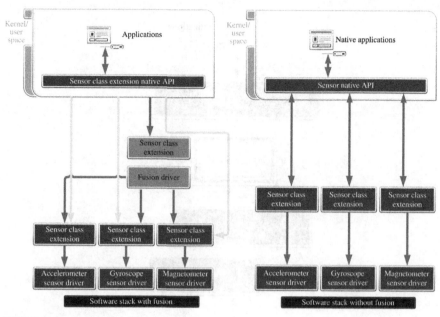

FIGURE 6.8

Software stack with and without fusion support.

Android software stack consists of applications, software development kit (SDK) API, Framework, HAL, and drivers. Drivers then connect to underlying physical sensors or a sensor hub. Android applications use sensor-related APIs to identify sensors and their capabilities and to monitor sensor events. Fig. 6.9 shows the Android sensor software stack components.

SDK: Applications above the SDK layer can access the sensors through the SDK API. This layer has various functions that can be used to list the available sensors and register a sensor with required sensor properties or requirements such as latencies or sampling rate.

Framework: This layer links various applications to HAL. Since HAL is single client, the multiplexing of applications to connect to single-client HAL must happen in the framework.

HAL: This API connects the hardware drivers to the Android framework. It contains one HAL interface provided by Android (sensors.h) and one HAL implementation provided by the Android device manufacturer (sensors.cpp).

Drivers: The drivers communicate with underlying physical sensors and are provided by the hardware manufacturers.

Sensor hub and sensors: These are the physical sensors that take measurements of various parameters and provide sensor data to the software stack above them. A sensor hub can also be part of the device that can

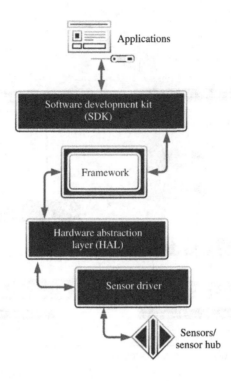

FIGURE 6.9

Android sensor stack.

process the sensor data, while the main processor or system on chip is in power management mode. Sensor fusion functionality can be part of this sensor hub.

ANDROID SENSOR FRAMEWORK

The Sensor Framework [17] is used to find out which sensors are available on the mobile device, access those Android sensors, find out their capabilities, and obtain raw sensor data. It also provides a default fusion implementation for some of the composite sensors such as a Gravity sensor, which is a fusion of accelerometer and gyroscope, or geomagnetic rotation vector, which is a fusion of accelerometer and magnetometer.

The Sensor Framework links various applications to HAL through multiplexing such that all applications can be supported for their requested sensor latency and sampling rates. The HAL then would communicate with respective sensor drivers. The applications cannot directly communicate with the sensors or sensor drivers and hence cannot directly configure the sensors.

The applications can only request to configure the sampling frequency and the maximum reporting latency of the underlying sensors and that too with the help of the Sensor Framework. They are not allowed to configure any other parameters in order to prevent one application from configuring the sensors in a manner that could break the other applications. The Sensor Framework prevents the applications from requesting conflicting modes of the sensor. For example, it would be impossible to support two applications when one of the application requests high-accuracy/high-sampling mode while another application requests low-power mode of the sensor, because the sensor cannot operate in low-power mode while supporting higher accuracy or faster sampling rates.

As shown in Fig. 6.10, each application would request a specific sampling frequency and maximum reporting latency for the underlying sensor. When multiple applications try to access the same underlying sensor with different sampling frequencies and maximum latency, the Framework would help set the underlying sensor to:

- Maximum sampling frequency (from among all the requested sampling frequencies): In this case even the application whose requested sampling frequency is lower than some other application will receive the data from sensor at a faster rate.
- Minimum reporting latency (from among all the requested reporting latencies): In this case some of the applications would receive the data from the sensor at a latency that is less than their requested latency.

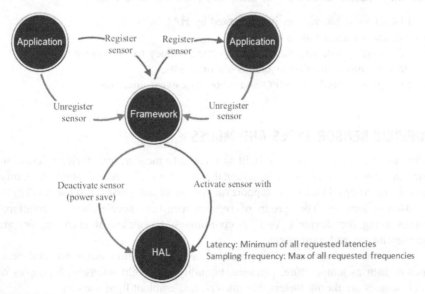

FIGURE 6.10

Android application-framework-HAL interactions.

The Sensor Framework includes the following:

- Classes: Sensor Manager, Sensor, and SensorEvent
- Interfaces: SensorEventListener.

Sensor Manager [18]: This class helps to access device sensors by creating instances of the sensor service. It provides various methods to access sensors, listen to the sensors, register/unregister sensor listeners, report sensor accuracy, calibrate sensors, or set data sampling rates of the sensors.

Sensor: This class is used to create an instance of the underlying sensor. Sensor capability information can be obtained by methods of this class.

SensorEvent [19]: This class represents a sensor event and holds information such as the actual sensor data, sensor type, and properties of the provided data (accuracy, timestamp, and so on).

SensorEventListener [20]: This interface creates two callback methods (onAccuracyChanged and onSensorChanged) that are used to receive notifications from the sensor manager on availability of new sensor data/event/timestamp change or when there is a change in the accuracy of the underlying sensor.

HARDWARE APPLICATION LAYER

The hardware application layer (HAL) [21] interface is defined in sensors.h for the Android sensor stack. This interface connects the Android framework with the hardware-specific software. The main functions of HAL are to:

- List all available sensors implemented by HAL,
- Activate or deactivate a sensor,
- Set sampling rate and maximum reporting latency for the sensor,
- Provide information on available sensor events,
- Flush sensor hardware FIFO and report that event once done.

ANDROID SENSOR TYPES AND MODES

Most mobile devices will have built-in sensors to measure the device orientation, motion, and surrounding environmental parameters like temperature, humidity, and so on. Android platforms support the following categories of sensors [17]:

Motion sensors: This group of sensors measures acceleration or rotational forces along the device's $X-Y-Z$ coordinates. Examples of such sensors are accelerometers and gyroscopes.

Environmental sensors: This group of sensors measures environmental parameters such as temperature, pressure, humidity, and light intensity. Examples of such sensors are thermometers, barometers, and ambient light sensors.

Position sensors: This group of sensors measures the physical position and orientation of the mobile device. Magnetometers fall under this group of sensor.

The sensor types supported by Android are listed in Chapter 11, Sensor application areas. They are named as TYPE_ < xyz > where *xyz* would be "ACCELEROMETER," "AMBIENT_TEMPERATURE," and so on.

The Android sensor stack has base sensors and composite sensors [22].

Base sensors are not the physical sensors but are given the name after the underlying physical sensors. Base sensor means that these sensors deliver the sensor information after applying various corrections to the raw output from the underlying single physical sensor. Some of the examples of base sensor types are SENSOR_TYPE_ACCELEROMETER, SENSOR_TYPE_HEART_RATE, SENSOR_TYPE_LIGHT, SENSOR_TYPE_PROXIMITY, SENSOR_TYPE_PRESSURE, and SENSOR_TYPE_GYROSCOPE.

Composite sensors are the sensors that deliver sensor data after processing and/or fusing data from multiple physical sensors. Some of the examples of composite sensor types are gravity sensor (accelerometer + gyroscope), geomagnetic rotation vector (accelerometer + magnetometer), and rotation vector sensor (accelerometer + magnetometer + gyroscope).

The behavior of Android sensors is impacted by the presence of hardware FIFO in the sensors. When the sensor stores its events or data in FIFO instead of reporting to HAL, it is known as *batching*. This process of batching [23] is implemented only in hardware and helps to save power because the sensor data or event is obtained in the background, grouped, and then processed together instead of waking up the SOC to receive each individual event. Batching happens when the sensor events of a particular sensor are delayed up to the maximum reporting latency before reporting them to HAL, or when the sensor has to wait for the SOC to wake up and hence has to store all the events till then. Bigger FIFO size will enable more batching and hence potentially more power savings.

If a sensor does not have hardware FIFO or if the maximum reporting latency is set to zero, then the sensor can operate in *continuous operation* [23] mode, where its events are not buffered but are reported immediately to HAL. This operation is the opposite of the batching process.

Based on the capability of the Android sensors to allow the SOC to enter or wake up from the suspend mode, these sensors can be defined as wake-up sensors or nonwake-up sensors through a flag in sensor definition.

Nonwake-up sensors [24]: These sensors do not prevent the SOC from entering the suspend mode and also do not wake up the SOC to report availability of the sensor data. The nonwake-up sensor behavior with respect to SOC suspend mode [23] is listed below.

During SOC suspend mode:

- This sensor type continues to generate required events and store them in the sensor hardware FIFO rather than report it to HAL.
- If the hardware FIFO gets filled, then the FIFO would wrap around just like a circular buffer and new events will overwrite the previous events.
- If the sensor does not have hardware FIFO then the events are lost.

Exit of SOC from suspend mode:

- The hardware FIFO data is delivered to the SOC even if maximum reporting latency has not elapsed. This helps in power saving because the SOC will not have to be awakened soon if it decides to go into suspend mode again. When the SOC is not in suspend mode:
- The sensor events can be stored in the FIFO as long as the maximum reporting latency is not elapsed. If FIFO gets filled before the elapse of maximum reporting latency, then the events are reported to the awake SOC to ensure no events are lost or dropped.
- If maximum reporting latency time elapses, then all events from FIFO are reported to SOC. For example, if the maximum reporting latency of an accelerometer is 20 seconds while that of the gyroscope is 5 seconds, the batches for the accelerometer and gyroscope can both happen every 5 seconds. If one event must be reported, then all events from all sensors can be reported. If sensors share the hardware FIFO and the maximum reporting latency elapses for one of the sensor, then all the events from FIFO are reported even when maximum reporting latency is not elapsed for other sensors.
- If maximum reporting latency is set to zero, then the events can delivered to the application, since the SOC is awake. This would result in continuous operation.
- If the sensor does not have hardware FIFO, then the events will get reported to the SOC immediately resulting in continuous operation.

Wake-up sensors [24]: This type of sensor always has to deliver its data/event irrespective of the SOC power state. These sensors will allow the SOC to go into suspend mode but will wake it up when an event needs to be reported to the SOC. The wake-up sensor behavior with respect to the SOC suspend mode [23] is listed below.

During SOC suspend mode:

- This sensor type continues to generate required events and store them in the sensor hardware FIFO rather than report it to HAL.
- These sensors will wake up the SOC from the suspend mode to deliver its events either before the maximum reporting latency expiry or when its hardware FIFO gets full.
- If the hardware FIFO gets full, then the FIFO will not wrap around like in the case of nonwake-up sensors. Hence FIFO should not overflow (and result in the loss of events) while the SOC takes time to exit suspend mode and start the FIFO flush process.
- If maximum reporting latency is set to zero then the events will wake up the SOC and get reported. This would result in continuous operation.
- If the sensor does not have hardware FIFO then the events will wake up the SOC and get reported. This would result in continuous operation.

Exit of the SOC from suspend mode:

- This sensor type behaves just like nonwake-up sensors and data from the hardware FIFO is delivered to the SOC even if maximum reporting latency has not elapsed.
When the SOC is not in suspend mode:
- This sensor type behaves just like nonwake-up sensors.

Android sensors generate events in four possible reporting modes [25], namely continuous reporting, on-change reporting, one-shot reporting, and special reporting.

In continuous reporting mode the events are generated at a constant rate as defined by a sampling period parameter setting passed to the batch function defined in HAL. Accelerometers and gyroscopes are examples of sensors using continuous reporting mode.

In on-change reporting mode, the events are generated when sensed values change including the activation of this sensor type at HAL. These events are reported after the elapse of minimum time between the two events as set by the sampling period parameter of the batch function. Heart rate sensors and step counters are examples of sensors using on-change reporting mode.

In one-shot reporting mode, the sensor will deactivate itself when an event occurs and then send that event information through HAL as soon as the event is generated. The detected event cannot be stored in hardware FIFO. The one-shot sensors need to be reactivated to send any other event. Sensors that can detect any motion that results in a major change of user location can fall under this category (examples of such motions could be walking or user in moving vehicle). Such sensors are all called trigger sensors. For these sensors the maximum reporting latency and sampling period parameters are meaningless.

In special reporting mode, the sensor will generate an event based on a specific event. For example, an accelerometer can use special reporting mode to generate an event when the user takes a step, or it can be used to report the tilt of the mobile device. Hence the underlying physical sensor is used in special reporting mode as a step detector or as a tilt detector.

ANDROID SENSOR FUSION/VIRTUAL SENSORS

Software-based sensors that derive their data from one or more of the hardware-based sensors are called virtual sensors. Virtual sensors can be formed through the sensor fusion process where data from multiple sensors is converted into useful information that cannot be measured or obtained from a single sensor. Virtual sensors can be considered as a bridge between what can be measured and what is desired to be measured by the developers.

Examples of Android virtual sensors [15] are TYPE_GRAVITY, TYPE_LINEAR_ACCELERATION, TYPE_ROTATION_VECTOR, and TYPE_ORIENTATION.

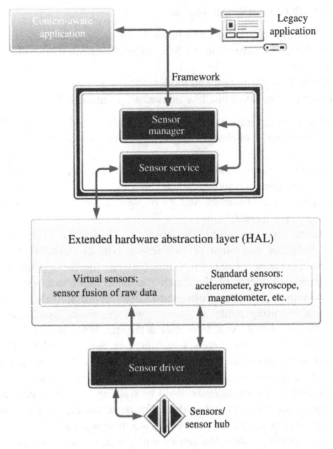

FIGURE 6.11

Android sensor stack extension for sensor fusion/virtual sensors.

A virtual sensor can be created by extending the Android sensor stack. The virtual sensors are integrated into the sensor HAL as shown in Fig. 6.11. The context-aware application will have a library with definitions that can help utilize the virtual sensors.

There are two paths: one is the legacy path for raw sensors and the other is a context-aware path. The sensor manager is the same as in the framework without virtual sensor support. There is no change in the Android framework above the sensor HAL for the support of virtual sensors/fusion.

SENSOR HUB SOFTWARE AND FIRMWARE ARCHITECTURE

Fig. 6.4 illustrates the architecture where sensors are accessed through a sensor hub. In such "sensors through sensor hub" architecture, the kernel will not talk to the sensors using the sensor drivers, but will instead communicate with the sensor hub. The sensor hub will then communicate with underlying sensors, obtain sensor data from them, and pass that data back to the kernel.

These sensor hubs will have their own operating system/firmware and will use various inbuilt libraries/framework to connect to sensors as well as the inbuilt processor or application processors, depending on the type of sensor hub (dedicated microcontroller sensor hub, application-processor—based sensor hub, or sensor-based hub with microcontroller). Hardware architecture of various sensor hubs is discussed in Chapter 4, Sensor hubs.

The core of firmware designed for such sensor hubs is called real-time OS (RTOS). RTOS manages all the sensor hub resources such as timers, interrupts, memory, and power management. The firmware can help configure and access the underlying sensors and their respective data. It can also preprocess the sensor data, flag sensor events, perform sensor data fusion, and implement certain portions of complex sensor algorithms.

The main components of sensor hub firmware are the Viper kernel, sensor drivers, sensor HAL, sensor core, sensor clients, protocol interface, and memory interface.

VIPER KERNEL

The access to underlying hardware sensors is provided by the Viper microkernel. This module does not contain sensor drivers. The kernel can reside on the sensor hub microcontroller ROM. It has DMA drivers to communicate with memory, IPC drivers to communicate with the host, a security engine, interrupt service routines, interface API/drivers for communication protocols like I^2C, GPIO, UART, and SPI (as shown in Fig. 6.12).

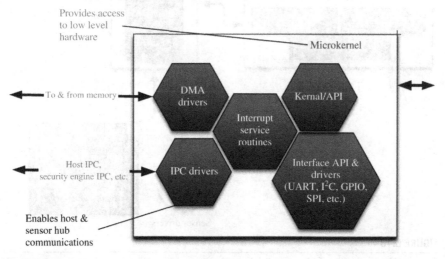

FIGURE 6.12

Viper microkernel.

SENSOR DRIVERS

These modules consist of sensor drivers that can be downloaded from sensor vendor sites/applications. The developers can select different sensors and also develop the drivers.

SENSOR HAL

This layer connects various device drivers to the sensor API. The sensor client uses the sensor HAL to access sensor data and the sensor configuration module uses the sensor HAL to configure the underlying sensor as shown in Fig. 6.13.

SENSOR CORE

This is the processing center that consists of sensor manager, configuration manager, and core functions. It contains a static data model and a running thread model.

Static data model

All physical sensors and all sensing algorithms are abstracted as sensor objects. A sensor object has data entries for attributes, configurations, status, and

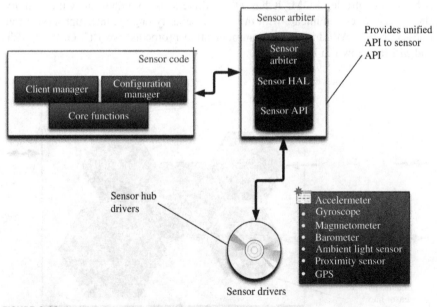

FIGURE 6.13

Sensor HAL connection to sensor client and sensor configuration modules.

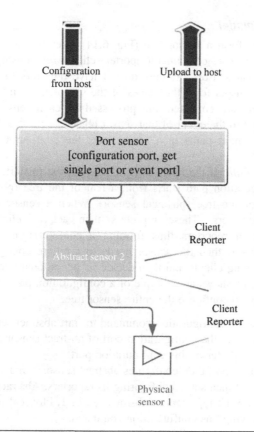

FIGURE 6.14

Sensor tree with clients and reporters.

relationships with other sensor objects. There are three types of sensor objects as shown in Fig. 6.14:

- Physical sensor: This object is for the underlying physical sensor present on the hardware platform. This object directly operates the physical sensor through physical sensor drivers.
- Abstract sensor: This is an abstract object or objects for a data processing algorithm.
- Port sensor: These are abstractions to upload sensor results. These can be configuration port, event port, or get single port type.

Through abstraction all sensor types can be derived from sensor objects. Some of the attributes are: unique sensor ID, sensor status (idle or data ready), data buffer size, and sensor clients (those consuming data from underlying sensor and so on).

Running thread model

The sensor objects form a sensor tree (Fig. 6.14) wherein the sensor objects are linked through producer–consumer (reporter–client) relationships. The roots of the tree are physical sensors (as they do not have reporters to collect any data from) while port sensors form the leaves of the sensor tree. In a sensor tree, the data from reporters are collected and processed by each sensor object and the results are provided to the client of that sensor object.

There are two main paths in a sensor tree: the configuration path and the execution path.

Configuration Path: If the host sends out the request to start, stop, or adjust a sensor, the configuration path starts from a leaf of the tree (port sensor object) toward the root of the tree (physical sensor). When a sensor is configured, it configures its reporters. These reporters then act as clients and further configure their own reporters thus forming a configuration path. If a client configures the sensor, then the sensor needs to arbitrate configuration requests from all of its running clients and then decide its operational parameters (such as frequency). Fig. 6.15 shows an example of a configuration path. The path follows the following steps to configure the entire sensor tree:

1. The host sends the configuration command to start abstract sensor 2.
2. This first configures the configuration port of abstract sensor 2. Abstract sensor 2 is the reporter of this configuration port.
3. The configuration port then configures abstract sensor 2 and starts that sensor.
4. Abstract sensor 2 then starts configuring its reporters. Abstract sensor 1 and physical sensor 3 are reporters of abstract sensor 1. Physical sensor 3 gets started on receiving this configuration command.
5. Abstract sensor 1 then configures its reporters, physical sensor 1 and physical sensor 2.

Execution Path: This path is multithreaded, flows from the bottom of the sensor tree to the top, and is driven by the sensor data. Each physical sensor can be assigned one thread. The thread will start when the underlying physical sensor reports availability of data or when a sensor polling timer is triggered. The arbiter then will use a slide window to determine if the available sensor data needs to be passed on to the clients. On receiving the data, the clients will store the data, buffer it, and then, using their algorithms, will process it. If these clients also have output data, then they will provide it to their running clients down the tree. Finally, the data would reach the port layer from where it would be passed on to the host/IA. This execution path is driven by the sensor data from the root to the leaves of the sensor tree. It is a multithreading model.

Fig. 6.16 shows an example of an execution path. The path follows these steps to configure the entire sensor tree:

1. The physical sensor 2 indicates availability of sensor data using a hardware interrupt. This sensor 2 is the reporter and is connected to its client abstract

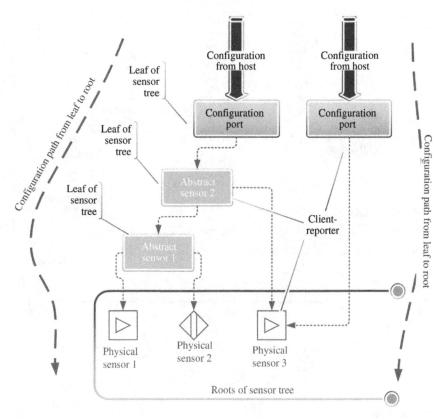

FIGURE 6.15

Configuration path of sensor tree.

sensor 1. If physical sensor 3 reports data availability then arbiter will decide if it wants to pass on the data to its two clients (abstract sensor 2 and port).

2. The client abstract sensor 1 stores the data that it received from physical sensor 2. Abstract sensor 1 will continue to buffer the data from all its reporters (physical sensor 2 and also physical sensor 1 if it reports data too).

3. Abstract sensor 1 will then process the received data from all its reporters once sufficient data is buffered. As a result of the process on the received data, the abstract sensor 1 would either have output data or not have output data. No further actions occur if abstract sensor 1 does not have any output data.

4. If abstract sensor 1 has output data then it will provide that data to all of its active clients. In this case abstract sensor 1 will send out its data to different port sensors (get single port or event port or configuration port) and to the abstract sensor 2.

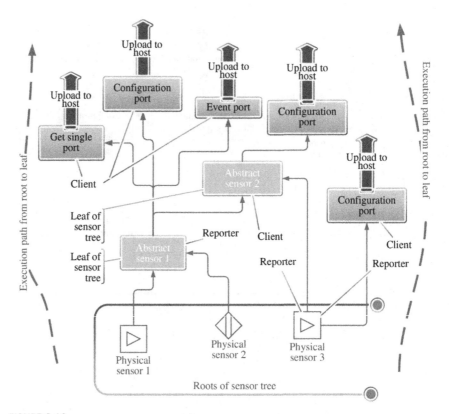

FIGURE 6.16

Execution path of sensor tree.

5. If abstract 2 processes the received data and has output data then it will further pass on the output data to its clients (configuration port in this example).

6. All data/results on reaching the port layer are then uploaded on to the host system.

Thus the execution path moves from the bottom to the top of the sensor tree.

SENSOR CLIENT

This is the main module between the underlying sensor and the platform host/main processor.

PROTOCOL INTERFACE

This interface connects the sensor hub to the host and the sensor core and uses IPC (interprocess interface) to communicate with the host.

Fig. 6.17 shows all the components of the sensor hub firmware architecture.

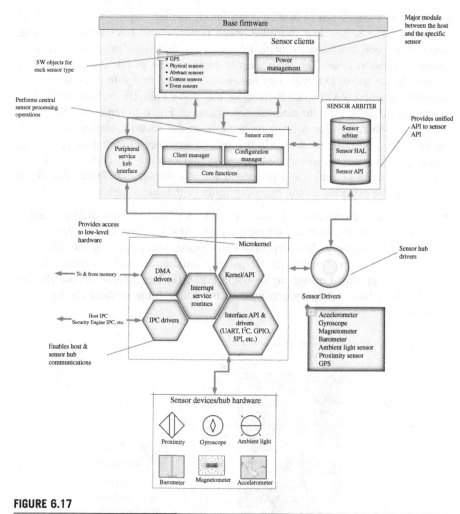

FIGURE 6.17

Firmware architecture block diagram for sensor hub.

FIRMWARE AND APPLICATION LOADING PROCESS

Typical sensor hub firmware is loaded through the following three main stages:

- Load kernel code from security engine nonvolatile memory: This kernel code has an application loader that helps load the applications located on nonvolatile memory and also the ones stored with host software.
- Load application code from security engine nonvolatile memory: These applications have the kernel at their beginning.
- Load applications with help from host software: This step is optional. These types of applications also have the kernel at their beginning.

The above stages can be broken down into following steps:

Step 1: The sensor hub firmware image typically will have kernel code/data, application code/data, and maintenance structures that have information such as image size and location. The main security engine of the mobile computing device containing the sensor hub will copy the entire firmware image from its nonvolatile memory into the DRAM space defined for the sensor hub. The location of the kernel image would be after the maintenance structures. Fig. 6.18 represents this step.

Step 2: There is also a bring-up module in the security engine nonvolatile memory. This bring-up module is in the form of sequence of commands (initialize memory, write data to sensory hub memory, and execute the copied code). The support for these commands is preloaded into the sensor hub ROM. The ROM content can be executed by the microcontroller of the sensor hub.

- The initialize command will initialize the sensor hub memory/SRAM(s) and will set up the destination addresses to copy the code from security engine nonvolatile memory. This step would also ensure that turning on the SRAMs does not exceed the mobile device power consumption limits by turning on the banks in staged manner as shown in Fig. 6.19. The SRAMs should also be brought in known state by erasing the bank before bring-up code can be loaded.

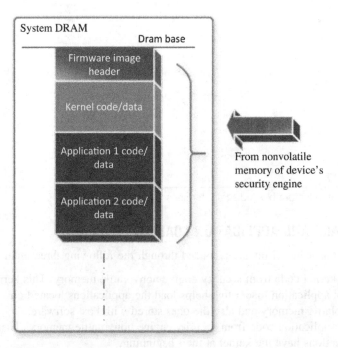

FIGURE 6.18

Firmware image components loaded into system DRAM by security engine.

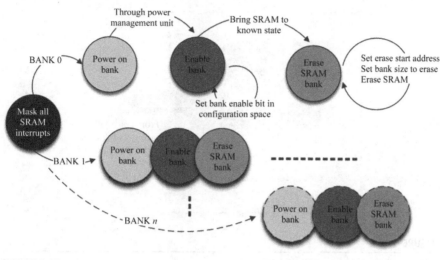

FIGURE 6.19

SRAM initialization flow.

- With the help of write commands the bring-up code is then copied from security engine nonvolatile memory to the sensor hub memory/SRAM(s). The write commands will have the memory location of where data needs to be copied from, the actual data to be transferred, and the size of data being transferred.
- Next the execute command will hand over the control to the loaded bring-up code in the sensor hub memory (SRAM).

Fig. 6.20 represents the step of loading bring-up code into sensor hub SRAM. The bring-up code will contain DMA driver to access the system DRAM. It can also contain drivers to communicate with the mobile computing device's power management unit to ensure that the sensor hub has sufficient access to system DRAM during any DMA transfers between its SRAMs and the system DRAM.

Step 3: The bring-up code will then request the security engine for the location of the sensor hub firmware image present in the host DRAM (result of Step 1). The security engine will then send the sensor hub the requested DRAM location, send the size of the firmware image, and will also identify the sensor hub SRAM(s) that can be used as the destination for the firmware.

Step 4: The bring-up code will seek permission from the device's power management unit to access the DRAM and proceed with DMA operation to copy the kernel from the system DRAM to sensor hub SRAM(s) if the DRAM is accessible.

Step 5: The bring-up code will first copy manifest [26] structures that are located in first few kilobytes of the firmware image. It will then parse these structures to obtain information on the location and size of the kernel image along

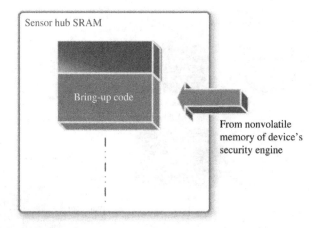

FIGURE 6.20

Loading of sensor hub bring-up code.

with the destination address in SRAM. The kernel code is then copied over to sensor hub SRAM according to the information provided in the manifest.

The firmware image has the kernel placed in the beginning and before the application(s). The kernel is loaded into sensor hub SRAMs first from the host DRAM and then this kernel assumes the control from the bring-up code.

Fig. 6.21 show the steps undertaken to load the kernel from system/host DRAM into a typical sensor hub SRAM.

Fig. 6.22 shows the content of sensor hub SRAM after the kernel code is loaded.

The kernel can then proceed to load applications. The main kernel components that help to load a typical sensor hub application are the kernel space loader and user space loader.

- Kernel space loader: This module helps load and launch applications. The image descriptor located at the beginning of the firmware image in DRAM specifies the location of the application. The kernel space loader checks this header of the sensor hub firmware image to find out these descriptors that contain the offset of applications from the start of DRAM space that is allocated to the sensor hub. Once these applications are loaded the kernel space loader waits for requests to load applications from the host. The requests to load applications come with information on location of that particular application in sensor hub SRAMs/memory.
- User space loader: This module helps load applications from the host. It performs three main functions: it communicates with the sensor hub host driver to receive sensor hub firmware load requests through host embedded controller interface (HECI) firmware, loads the client, authenticates the loaded

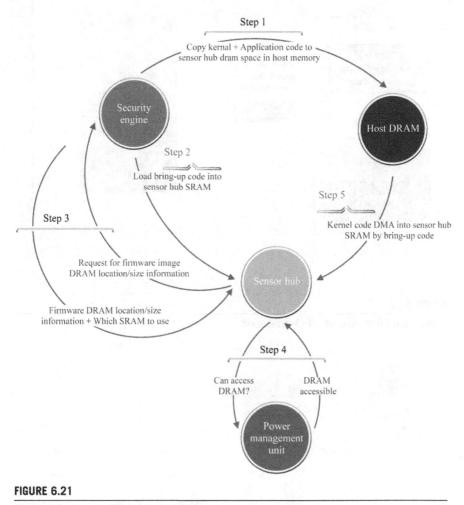

FIGURE 6.21

Sensor hub kernel code loading process.

firmware by communicating with security engines/infrastructure using interprocess communication, and requests the kernel space loader module load and start the authenticated application or applications.

Fig. 6.23 shows possible steps involved in the loading of sensor hub applications:

1. The host sensor hub driver allocates the direct memory accessible range in the host/OS memory and copies sensor hub firmware to that space.
2. The host sensor hub driver then sends a message to the HECI driver to load the sensor hub application.

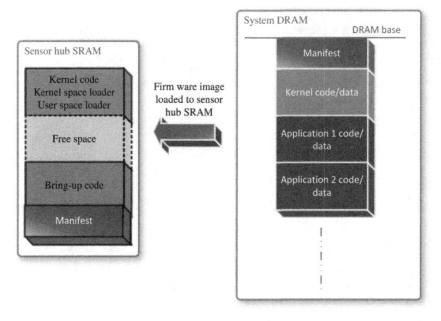

FIGURE 6.22

Sensor hub SRAM loaded with kernel code.

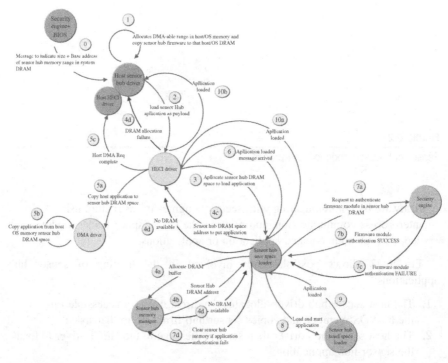

FIGURE 6.23

Application loading process in a typical sensor hub.

3. The HECI driver sends a message to the sensor hub user space loader to allocate sensor hub DRAM space to load the application into it.

4. The sensor hub user space loader requests the sensor hub memory manager to allocate DRAM space. The memory manager responds with a sensor hub DRAM space address if DRAM space is available. This DRAM address is then passed on to the HECI driver by the sensor hub user space loader. If DRAM space is not available, then the user space loader will communicate lack of availability of DRAM to the HECI driver.

5. The HECI driver will copy the application from host OS memory to sensor hub DRAM space using the DMA driver. The host HECI driver is informed of the host DMA request completion.

6. The HECI driver then sends a message to the sensor hub user space loader about the arrival of the application.

7. The user space loader will next request the device's security engine to authenticate the firmware module loaded in the sensor hub DRAM space. If authentication fails then the user space loader will clear out the module from sensor hub DRAM.

8. If the security engine responds with successful authentication of the application, then it will instruct the sensor hub kernel space loader to load and start the application.

9. The kernel space loader will inform the user space loader once the application is loaded.

10. The application load message is then passed on to the host sensor hub driver.

CONTEXT-AWARE FRAMEWORK

Context awareness not only represents the raw status or motions of the device but it also includes additional information such as how the device is carried by the user, what the user's position is, where the device is located, or what the environment is around the device.

A context-aware device will automatically configure itself and adjust to the new context when there is change in a particular context. Sensor hub device firmware/software requires a framework that enables the device to adapt, manage the change or conditions, and respond with appropriate action. This framework is referred to as an aware hub framework. The set of conditions and corresponding set of actions together forms a situation for the device. When all conditions in the situation are met, the actions are taken or executed by the device.

There are three types of plugins that form the situation:

1. Trigger: This is a condition plugin that handles any events that will not result in introduction of logically meaningful state, such as gesture change, timer change, or message receiver.

2. State: This is a condition plugin that handles any events that will result in introduction of logically meaningful state, such as time period, state of display, or activity.

3. Action: This is an action plugin that performs a required action when the condition is met such as message sender or phone manager.

An aware hub framework is a flexible centralized situation manager with a conflict check module that checks and avoids conflicting situations when the same underlying condition is met simultaneously. This modules ensure that the last effective situation is retained if situation conflicts occur.

The aware hub framework consists of the following components as shown in Fig. 6.24:

- Aware hub service: This is the core module that maintains all registered plugins and all incoming situations from multiple clients.
- Situation edit activity: This is the default situation edit activity that can be called up by any activity that does not want to edit a situation directly with the aware hub service. It would perform situation edit.
- Activity: These are the activities requesting the use of the aware hub service. The activity can call the aware hub activity directly and manage all context by itself or it (the activity) can call the situation editor activity to use its built-in default situation.
- Plugins: These are in the separate packages and do not explicitly register into the aware hub service.

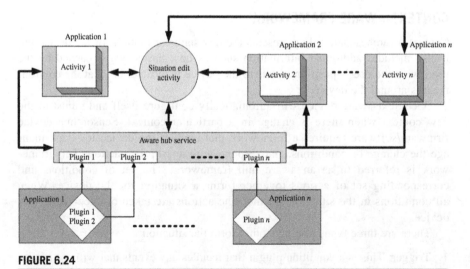

FIGURE 6.24

Plugin-based architecture for aware hub situation framework.

The aware stack supports both the context-aware application and the legacy sensor framework as the basic requirement as shown in Figs. 6.8 and 6.11. "Sensor Fusion" section under Windows and Android describes the details of these framework.

POWER-SAVING FIRMWARE ARCHITECTURE

The details of various power management states and transitions are discussed in Chapter 5, Power management. In this section the focus is on understanding the firmware architecture that enables the minimization of the sensor hub power consumption impact on the overall system power consumption, while maintaining the appropriate and sufficient performance of the sensor hub.

The sensor hub firmware will operate in active phase when it is required to perform various tasks and it will sleep when idle (till it is required to wake up for the next task).

The power state management unit (Fig. 6.17) detects the idle phase, calculates the possible sleep duration, and selects appropriate sleep states for the sensor hub.

Basic firmware power state decision flow is shown in Fig. 6.25. The firmware selects the states based on ongoing DMA activity status and latency tolerance of the sensor hub applications. D0 is the normal active/working state while D0i1, D0i2, and D0i3 are power-saving sleep states.

The power state transition decision making process is triggered in firmware when it detects a projected idleness period. The activity of the sensor hub can be periodic due to applications polling the sensors or be based on events such as interrupts from the sensor ecosystem or hardware.

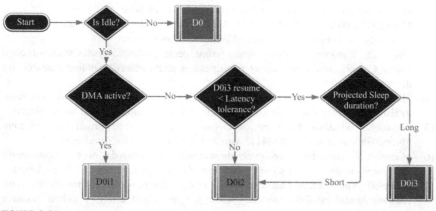

FIGURE 6.25

Firmware power state transition decision flow.

Internal timers can be used to monitor periodic activities of the sensor hub. The RTOS will check scheduled timer events, and firmware can calculate the projected idleness as the time remaining till the nearest expiring timer.

The internal timers cannot be used to monitor event-based activities of the sensor hub and hence a heuristic approach based on the history of events would be needed to calculate the projected idleness duration. The sensor applications can also choose to explicitly inform the firmware about the event-based activities and the time left to the next projected external event. The power management structure of firmware can calculate projected idleness duration by using the next projected hardware event occurrence time.

On detecting projected idleness, the firmware checks if there are any ongoing DMA transfers.

If any DMA transfer is ongoing then the sensor hub SRAM cannot go to D0i2 or D0i3, and hence firmware decides to keep the sensor hub in D0i1.

The firmware will evaluate the projected sleep duration against the latency requirements of application to decide between D0i2 and D0i3.

If D0i3 resume time is more than the current latency tolerance value, then firmware will select D0i2 instead of D0i3. If latency tolerance is more than the D0i3 resume time, then firmware needs to consider the projected sleep duration parameter. If the sensor hub is projected to be in sleep for a short duration then firmware decides to enter D0i2, and it will decide to enter D0i3 for longer projected sleep durations.

REFERENCES

[1] Android. Android developer guide, <https://developer.android.com/guide/topics/sensors/sensors_overview.html>, online resource for developers.
[2] Merrett GV, Weddell AS, Harris NR, Al-Hashimi BM, White NM. A structured hardware/software architecture, for embedded sensor nodes, paper.
[3] Microsoft. Windows hardware development center, <https://sysdev.microsoft.com/Driver_Components/Sensor_driver_configuration_architectures>, online resource for developers.
[4] Microsoft. Windows hardware development center, <https://sysdev.microsoft.com/en-us/Hardware/Sensor_class_extension_implementation>, online resource for developers.
[5] Microsoft. Windows hardware development center, <http://msdn.microsoft.com/library/windows/hardware/ff544113.aspx>, online resource for developers.
[6] Microsoft. Windows hardware development center, <https://sysdev.microsoft.com/en-us/Hardware/oem/docs/Driver_Components/SensorOpen>, online resource for developers.
[7] Microsoft. Windows hardware development center, <https://sysdev.microsoft.com/en-us/Hardware/oem/docs/DDSI_interface__sensor_CX_and_client_driver>, online resource for developers.
[8] Microsoft. Windows hardware development center, <https://sysdev.microsoft.com/en-us/Hardware/Sensor_class_extension_architecture>, online resource for developers.

[9] Microsoft. Windows hardware development center, <https://sysdev.microsoft.com/en-us/Hardware/oem/docs/Driver_Components/SensorStart>, online resource for developers.

[10] Microsoft. Windows hardware development center, <https://sysdev.microsoft.com/en-us/Hardware/oem/docs/Driver_Components/SensorStop>, online resource for developers.

[11] Microsoft. Windows hardware development center, <https://sysdev.microsoft.com/en-us/Hardware/oem/docs/Driver_Components/SensorGetData>, online resource for developers.

[12] Microsoft. Windows hardware development center, <https://sysdev.microsoft.com/en-US/Hardware/Converged_sensors_driver_model>, online resource for developers.

[13] Microsoft. Windows hardware development center, <https://sysdev.microsoft.com/en-us/Hardware/oem/docs/Driver_Components/EvtSensorStart>, online resource for developers.

[14] Microsoft. Windows hardware development center, <https://sysdev.microsoft.com/en-us/Hardware/oem/docs/Driver_Components/EvtSensorStop>, online resource for developers.

[15] Steele J, Sensor Platforms (July 10, 2012). Understanding virtual sensors: from sensor fusion to context-aware applications, newsletter/online.

[16] Android. Android sensor guide, <https://source.android.com/devices/sensors/index.html>, online resource for developers.

[17] Android. Android developer guide, <https://developer.android.com/guide/topics/sensors/sensors_overview.html>, online resource for developers.

[18] Android. Android developer guide, <https://developer.android.com/reference/android/hardware/SensorManager.html>, online resource for developers.

[19] Android. Android developer guide, <https://developer.android.com/reference/android/hardware/package-summary.html>, online resource for developers.

[20] Android. Android developer guide, <https://developer.android.com/reference/android/hardware/SensorEventListener.html>, online resource for developers.

[21] Android. Android sensor guide, <https://source.android.com/devices/sensors/hal-interface.html>, online resource for developers.

[22] Android. Android sensor guide, <https://source.android.com/devices/sensors/sensor-types.html>, online resource for developers.

[23] Android. Android sensor guide, <https://source.android.com/devices/sensors/batching.html>, online resource for developers.

[24] Android. Android sensor guide, <https://source.android.com/devices/sensors/suspend-mode.html>, online resource for developers.

[25] Android. Android sensor guide, <https://source.android.com/devices/sensors/report-modes.html>, online resource for developers.

[26] Android. Android developer guide, <https://developer.android.com/guide/topics/manifest/manifest-intro.html>, online resource for developers.

Sensor validation and hardware—software codesign

7

INFORMATION IN THIS CHAPTER:

- Validation Strategies and Phases
- Sensor Hub Presilicon Validation
- Sensor Hub Prototyping Platforms
- Sensor Test Card Solutions
- Hardware—Software Codesign
- Validation Matrix
- Feature-Based Validation

VALIDATION STRATEGIES AND CHALLENGES

Today's mobile devices have complex components that must be compatible with each other and with the various operating systems. Hence it is important that these devices are validated thoroughly to ensure leading performance, reliability, and compatibility.

Validation begins with the design concept and continues through the entire product life cycle (PLC). All device and sensor components must be exhaustively tested independently as well as with third-party ecosystem and hardware components. As bugs are found, the feedback is provided back to the design to drive improvement in the overall design and manufacturing of these mobile devices.

There are many challenges to validation, such as increasing number of gates, reduced validation budget, complex ecosystems, increased product configurations, and possible test sequences. The issues also need to be found early in the design phase, because any issues, such as compatibility or reliability issues, are costly to resolve in terms of debug time, actual cost, and user experience if found later into the PLC of mobile computing devices.

Mobile Sensors and Context-Aware Computing. DOI: http://dx.doi.org/10.1016/B978-0-12-801660-2.00007-0

GENERIC VALIDATION PHASES

Validation of any component follows its PLC. Based on the general PLC, the key phases of validation are [1]:

1. Design for quality with technical readiness
2. Presilicon simulation
3. Prototyping
4. System validation
5. Analog validation
6. Compatibility validation
7. Software/firmware validation
8. Production qualification
9. Silicon debug.

DESIGN FOR QUALITY AND TECHNICAL READINESS

It is important that the validation phase is completed at the planning and design phase rather than left to be completed at the later phase of the PLC. Such an integrated validation approach is more effective in reducing the number of design iterations and thus ensures product delivery on a predictable and committed schedule. There are three stages during the development phase where validation plays a key role in defining the design process:

- Technical Readiness: In this phase, new technologies are evaluated for their implementation feasibility, keeping in mind the high quality of all involved components in the ecosystem. Factors such as power, performance, die area consumption, cost of design, validation, and so on are evaluated under the feasibility studies. Such technical readiness evaluation including validation enables higher design quality along with an accelerated development cycle and a robust product roadmap.
- Front End Development: This is the phase where the components are designed and implemented. The quality and reliability hooks are implemented along with the logical and physical design so that validation and quality monitoring can be done throughout the PLC. Such a comprehensive development methodology impacts the design flow such as RTL (register-transfer level) generation, synthesis, structural design/layout, and manufacturing process libraries/embedded components. At this stage formal property verification and assertions are used to discover bugs.
- Design and Execution: In this phase efficient design and validation process are put in place through close collaboration of design and validation teams. The design and technology that is ahead of the curve brings new user experience to the market but with it comes the challenge of complex design that pushes the limits (such as that of performance and power). The validation continues on the final design, while every design change is evaluated for its impact on quality and reliability of the product.

PRESILICON SIMULATION

Industry and proprietary tools are used to simulate the design long before the final product is ported to silicon. The design is simulated in software and a variety of test vectors are run on the simulated design to provide a comprehensive coverage of various features as per their priority. The simulation can be done at the unit level, chip level, or system level.

- At the unit level, validation tools, software, and methodologies are used to validate internal functionality of the design. Sequences and test vectors are exercised on the internal design under specific constraints, and outputs are compared with the expected result. Any bugs found at the unit level can be fixed rather quickly with minimal cost to schedule.
- At the chip level, multiple units and interfaces are constrained and validated for their interdependent functionalities and features. Typically, any bugs found at the chip level are a little harder and costlier to fix than those found at the unit level.
- A full operating system and/or production firmware is used to validate the design at the system level. Industry benchmark tests and certification tests can also be part of the validation strategy at the system level. Bugs found at the system level are generally complex and cost more in term of time and impact compared to those found at the unit or chip level.

PROTOTYPING

There are multiple prototyping platforms available for use during this phase. Some of the examples of such platforms are big box emulators, FPGA (field-programmable gate array) systems, virtual platforms using the system C model, or even hybrid platforms that use virtual/software models along with FPGA or emulators. Prototyping helps estimate the behavior and performance of components/devices before silicon production. Prototyping platforms can include actual hardware components, third-party devices, real operating systems, and software drivers, and are therefore the ideal platform to catch system integration bugs in the design that could escape the earlier presilicon simulation phase. The prototyping platforms are expensive but can ensure high-quality design through validation of logic functionality; they can run through BIOS/OS boot and power management flows; they can verify drivers and interoperability with third-party real devices; and they can help with development and cleanup of tests, tools, and processes that are planned for postsilicon use.

During postsilicon validation, these prototyping platforms can be used to reproduce silicon failure and enable deeper debug through better observability compared to silicon. They can also validate proposed fixes for bugs and uncover additional bugs that can be introduced by the previous bug fixes before taking the design through final/another stepping. The use of prototyping platforms can save millions by reducing stepping(s) required to enable on-time, high-quality delivery of a product to the market.

For these reasons, the prototyping phase is one of the most crucial phases of validation that contributes toward the overall quality and time to market of the components/devices.

SYSTEM VALIDATION

This phase starts at the arrival of silicon wherein the actual silicon component is put under comprehensive testing on a real platform. A huge number of iterations and mix of focused, random, and concurrent tests are executed on the silicon, stressing the part in various environmental conditions. Various corners of silicon parts are validated and characterized. Some of the examples of what system validation stresses are:

- Architectural and microarchitecture of the component under test. For example, stressing cache architecture, data space, floating point execution, and so on.
- IO, memory, and intercomponent communication interfaces.
- Power management flows and performance parameters under various conditions, such as concurrent traffic and independently managed power blocks within and outside the component.

ANALOG VALIDATION

In this phase, analog integrity and circuit marginality of device are tested under extreme corners of frequency, voltage, and temperature to ensure that the device functions within the production specifications. Analog integrity tests to ensure that the device and platform are electrically robust. Any issues found are then rectified or fed back into the process or production.

COMPATIBILITY VALIDATION

During this phase the device/hardware is validated for its compatibility with the various other third-party and ecosystem devices/software/firmware and drivers. The devices/components are put through exhaustive compatibility, stress, and concurrency testing with various operating systems (such as Windows, Linux, and Android), platforms, external vendor/test cards, third-party peripheral devices, and numerous applications (such as games, location-based services, sensor-based programs, and industry benchmarks). The device is also put through protocol testing and data coherency checks. Various parameters of devices are tested beyond their normal limits to validate the device/design in the worst-case scenarios.

SOFTWARE/FIRMWARE VALIDATION

Software/firmware components are part of many of the previously discussed validation phases and start mainly along with the prototyping validation phase.

However a focused and rigorous software/firmware validation phase starts once the hardware is validated just enough to enable rigorous software stack validation. During this phase, software/firmware flows, software/firmware interactions with hardware, software/firmware reliability and compatibility, and so on are stressed in the worst-case scenarios. The software/firmware stack is also made to go through various certification tests during this phase. Software, firmware, and drivers are released only after completion of this validation phase.

PRODUCT QUALIFICATION

The previous validation phases are to ensure a high-quality product in terms of architecture, functionality, and features. However, manufacturing materials and processes related to the actual silicon product are just as important in ensuring that the final product is reliable under various environmental conditions and that the product meets or exceeds all operating parameters over the product life. These manufacturing materials and processes are validated during the product qualification phase wherein the components or devices are compared and qualified with the end user expectations in terms of performance, functionality, quality, and reliability. The results regarding design quality, materials quality, manufacturing quality, and operating reliability are documented and reviewed for any issues. If there are issues, then the design is fixed or corrected through design-validation iterations or through advanced debugging tools. The results are also used to evaluate new technologies and process improvements. When the design meets production quality standards, it is released for high-volume manufacturing and sales in the market.

SILICON DEBUG

During this validation phase, the physical and electrical characteristics of the device are observed or changed at the transistor level. A hardware defect can be fixed by changing certain characteristics of the transistor. For example, a laser voltage probe can help to observe physical and electrical characteristics of a single transistor out of many more in the device. By observing these characteristics, any logical or electrical problem can be traced to the physical cause on the silicon. The laser chemical etcher can help isolate the suspected area on the silicon for further validation or repair. The focused ion beam can help to add, delete, or modify transistors and wires to adjust timings. It can also alter digital functionality by adding or bypassing logic cells to fix an issue or a bug. The altered silicon can then go through the validation cycle to confirm if the issue or bug is actually fixed.

Thus different tools can be used to identify, isolate, and fix the bugs/issues in silicon thereby saving or reducing the number of silicon iterations required to achieve acceptable functionality and desirable high-quality devices and components.

SENSOR HUB PRESILICON VALIDATION

A typical sensor hub verification environment would consist of various agents that can access the sensor hub through its interfaces like I^2C, SPI, UART, and so on. These interfaces are used to drive signals including resets into the sensor hub and to observe corresponding outputs, either in form of output signals or memory data updates. A typical test layer for a sensor hub would have the following components:

- *Configuration Layer*: This layer helps to set the test bench topology and various configuration parameters of the sensor hub verification environment. It provides the way to control test bench, simulation, verification components, and test bench topology. It can help set up the subcomponent modes and enable/disable drivers, agents, number of agents (number of instances), monitors, checkers, coverage, and assertions.
- *Test Library*: This contains various tests that can be executed on the sensor hub. The library is collection of sequences like reset, power, configuration read/write, or data receive/transmit sequences.
- *Interface Environment*: This environment contains the bus functional models (BFMs) that act as either slave or master on the respective sensor hub interface along with scoreboards, monitors, BFM drivers, and test sequencers. For example, I^2C and SPI are slaves, JTAG is a master. The interaction steps of these environment components are shown in Fig. 7.1.

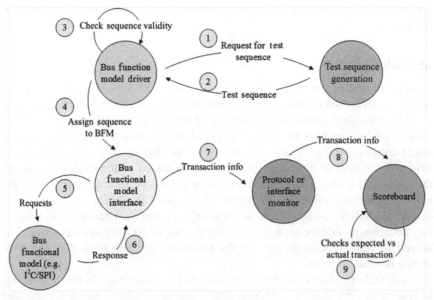

FIGURE 7.1

Interface component interactions.

MONITOR

A monitor is the component of the environment that observes, stores, and, if needed, prints the information related to transactions, data, or commands at an interface to which it is connected. There could also be coverage monitors that observe the protocol signals, interpret the data, and verify the coverage points to ensure tests are covering the intended feature(s). For example, an I^2C monitor connected to an I^2C interface of the sensor hub will have all information regarding I^2C transactions at that input interface.

CHECKER

A checker is the component of the environment that takes information from the monitor(s) it is connected to and checks for any protocol violations. It displays or prints errors in case a violation is noticed. For example, an I^2C checker connected to an I^2C monitor will flag an error on observing an I^2C protocol violation.

SCOREBOARD

A scoreboard is the component of the environment used for checking data that it receives from different interfaces/monitors in the system. It keeps track of transactions or data that are incoming and outgoing at the observation point and compares it with those at the other observation point to which it would be connected. For example, one port of the scoreboard hooked up at the input interface (say I^2C) monitor and the other port to one of the observation points inside the sensor hub would compare the input interface (say I^2C) data with the data observed at the connected observation point inside the sensor hub.

SEQUENCER

The sequencer will generate a sequence item that will contain the parameters required for the BFM to decide on the configuration of a transaction and the commands that need to be used. Hence the sequence is not the exact transaction that reaches the DUT (device under test) but it does decide what the actual transaction will look like.

DRIVER

The driver first requests sequence items from the sequencer and then assigns that as a new configuration to the BFM interface. This sequence is then analyzed and decoded by the wrapper around the BFM. The wrapper then causes the actual BFM to generate a transaction (such as an I^2C or SPI transaction). The driver ensures that the configuration command is first sent to the BFM to program the BFM. The BFM transaction information is also captured by monitors and scoreboards for analysis (Fig. 7.1).

SENSOR HUB PROTOTYPING

Today there are unprecedented challenges from the competitors and hence an urgent need to reduce the postsilicon time to market. To accelerate the postsilicon validation it is essential that all postsilicon tests are ready before the arrival of the silicon device. The time to market after the arrival of the silicon device is crucial and hence this time should not be spent on preparing, debugging, and fixing tests. The high-quality tests should already be available before the first silicon arrival.

The prototyping phase of validation helps to reduce the time to market for a sensor hub by enabling tests and the validation environment long before the silicon arrival. It also provides a platform where both the hardware and software can be designed and validated with the real sensors and sensor ecosystem. The prototyping platforms, also referred to as *early prototyping* (EP) platforms, link software, firmware, and system validation execution to PLC and software/firmware presilicon software (PSS) milestones. Prototyping platforms can also be used for customer enabling/design win demos. Enabling sensor firmware with real sensors and a hardware sensor hub helps to ensure firmware readiness far ahead of silicon arrival.

However, there are challenges in implementing such platforms, and the mitigations to these challenges drive the decisions on the type of prototyping platforms, workflow models, and sensor ecosystem that needs to be used for increased production silicon quality. A carefully defined cross team work model and aligned schedule of all the involved design and validation components is also extremely important, because it helps in prompt debug and disposals of issues, avoids validation duplication, and enables complex validation with hardware—software codesign.

In the following sections a few examples of prototyping platforms are discussed that can be used for prototyping the sensor hub design and to execute various validation phases that were discussed earlier in this chapter along with ongoing hardware and firmware design.

The examples of prototyping platforms are

1. Quick emulator
2. FPGA platform with sensors.

QEMU (QUICK EMULATOR)

QEMU [2] is free and open source software that acts as a hosted hypervisor that runs a virtual machine, and a guest operating system can run on it as a process. It can translate any target code on any host through binary translation (emulating an instruction set by translating binary code) and simulate additional hardware devices.

Fig. 7.2 shows the two main QEMU modules for the sensor hub, namely, the sensor hub simulated hardware and the sensor hub firmware. The sensor hub

Host PC

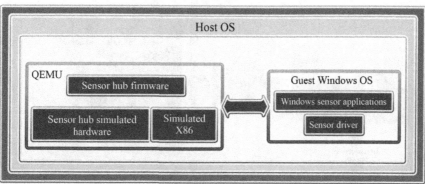

FIGURE 7.2

QEMU set up for sensor hub.

simulated hardware module includes the software model that emulates either the entire sensor hub hardware or just the portions of a sensor hub that are essential for enabling the sensor hub firmware development and debug on this pure software platform. The second module, called sensor hub firmware, is the actual firmware code. The exact same firmware image can also be run on an FPGA prototyping platform. QEMU thus allows an early firmware development and debug in a software environment and then transition to FPGA for running the flows on the real RTL code.

As shown in Fig. 7.2, QEMU also enables running Windows software code developed for the sensor hub, using a virtual machine to connect it to the firmware. This enables to run Windows sensor applications on QEMU.

FPGA PLATFORM

An FPGA system can include the following main components, as shown in Fig. 7.3:

- A host system, which has sensor software and applications along with test content and device drivers to drive the FPGA system connected to its PCIe slot.
- A PCIe bridge that connects the DUT in FPGA to the host PC.
- The sensor hub RTL code as DUT along with its MCU (micro-controller unit) if it is MCU-based sensor hub.
- Additional RTL code for units like security engine or audio subsystem to which the sensor hub interacts and needs to be part of the validation.
- Any RAM and ROM memories in DUT. These needs to be ported to FPGA RAMs.
- Any other interface or routers for communication to the sensor hub.
- Physical sensors that connect to the FPGA board through HAPSTRACK or FMC connectors.

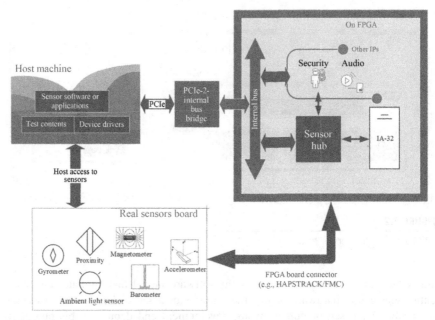

FIGURE 7.3

Sensor hub FPGA prototyping block diagram.

A FPGA system can be based on presilicon simulation models where the clocks, resets, and power control in FPGA are similar to those on the presilicon test benches but are generated using FPGA board PLLs or from the PCIe clock.

Since the sensor hub interacts with the security engine for boot and power management flow, it is important to have a prototyping system that can also emulate the security engine so that the firmware can execute handshake protocols and boot or power management flows.

If the actual security engine cannot be prototyped into the FPGA system due to FPGA resource or timing limitations, then a software emulator can be developed to mimic sensor hub-security engine handshake protocols. Such an FPGA architecture is shown in Fig. 7.4. The software emulator that mimics all the security engine flows and behavior is loaded on the host PC. The security engine emulator will update the sensor hub-security engine handshake registers according to handshake flows (like boot up flow or power management flow) and thus enables a communication channel between the security engine and the sensor hub.

The sensor hub and the register read/write unit can also initiate read/write transfers to the sensor hub-security engine handshake registers. Such a software emulator–based handshake mechanism enables validation of complete firmware/software–hardware interaction flows fairly early in the hardware–software development cycle and finds important interaction bugs.

Fig. 7.5 shows a typical FPGA model build starting from the design RTL database to the final validation report out.

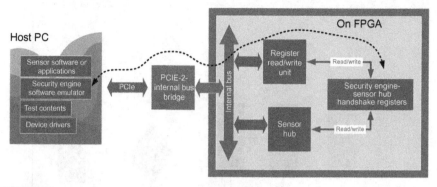

FIGURE 7.4

Sensor hub-security engine software communication model in FPGA.

The process of image generation involves generating a presilicon model, synthesis, partitioning, and bit image generation. During FPGA presilicon model, the RTL is integrated with other FPGA infrastructure components, the embedded memory blocks in design are replaced with FPGA equivalent memories (BRAM), constraints are defined, and clock sources are defined and generated. During synthesis, FPGA vendor synthesis tools (such as SynplifyPro and SynplifyPremier) are used to generate the net list, which is followed by physical synthesis, or PAR (partitioning), (using tools like ISE or Vivado). Finally, the bit file is generated.

Prototype users need to understand the difference between an FPGA model and real silicon. The limitations of the FPGA image needs to be understood and documented for users (such as system validation or software validation teams).

The FPGA image can be qualified with presilicon simulation tests ported to FPGA. This ensures that the users and validation phase are not impacted due to a dead-on-arrival or lower quality FPGA image. For example, 30–40% of presilicon simulation tests can be used as gate tests for quality. Apart from basic FPGA gate tests, the customers and validation teams can also run their acceptance tests to ensure that feature readiness in the released FPGA bit image. Such acceptance testing is important before running automation and executing a large number of tests on the FPGA bit image.

If any test cases fail during the validation phase, then various FPGA debug paths are explored and followed. Some of such paths are shown in Fig. 7.5. Xilinx Chipscope or Synopsys Identify can be used to compile and build an FPGA image with a predetermined debug signal list. These debug signals can then be observed during the test failure. Various protocol analyzers such as I^2C, UART, PCIe, and SPI can also be used for the debug of the failing test case4s.

Once the root cause of the failure is determined, a fix is identified and a new FPGA image is released for verification. The failure is also evaluated for any lessons that can be used to improve the design and validation methodology and infrastructure.

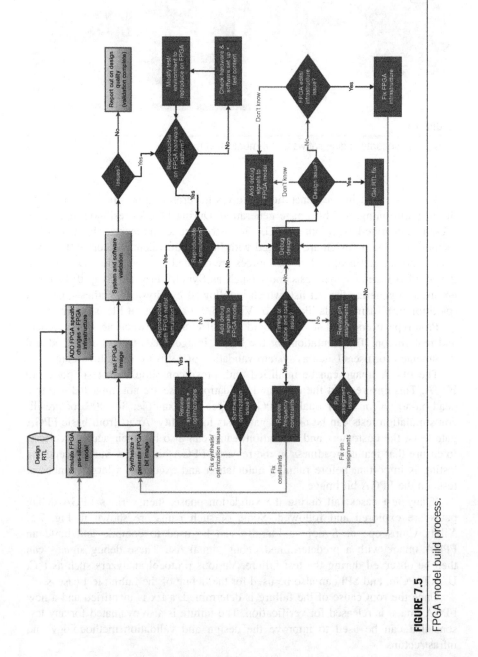

FIGURE 7.5

FPGA model build process.

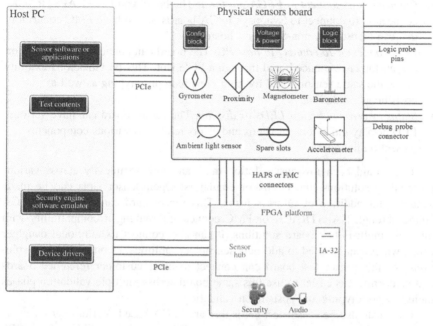

FIGURE 7.6

Physical sensor board connected to FPGA platform and host PC.

SENSOR TEST CARD SOLUTIONS

This section discusses possible design of three different ecosystem/sensor cards that can be used to validate a sensor hub with real physical sensors as well as software simulated sensors.

TEST BOARD WITH PHYSICAL SENSORS

Fig. 7.6 shows a block diagram of a sensor board connected to a host PC and FPGA platform. Such boards will have following main components:

- *Sensor array*: This refers to multiple physical sensors like accelerometer, gyroscope, magnetometer, GPS (Global Positioning System), proximity sensor, ambient light sensor, and so on that are present on the board.
- *Logic analyzer connectors/debug ports*: These ports can be connected to logic analyzers for any debug that may be required during the validation (such as sensor transaction/data observation).
- *Voltage and power supply block*: This block is responsible for supplying power to sensors and components on the board.

- *Connectors to connect to FPGA platform*: The board can have HAPSTRACK connectors to connect to Synopsys FPGA boards or can have FMC connectors that can be used for non-Synopsys boards.
- *PCIe connector to connect to host PC*: The board can connect to a host PC or any customer reference board through a PCIe slot. This provides for flexibility to use the same sensor board for both presilicon prototyping as well as postsilicon validation.
- *Status or error indicator LEDs or display*: The sensor board can have various LED/display indicators for status and errors related to various components present on the board.

This would be a low-cost solution that can work seamlessly across various prototyping solutions like FPGA or emulators. Open sensor slots can be made available for addition of future sensors. This sensor card can connect to FPGA boards through HAPSTRACK or FMC connectors, making it compatibility with multi-IP, multi-FPGA board solutions. It can also connect to additional daughter cards, which can be used to add new sensors, capabilities, or other off-shelf solutions. As this sensor test board can connect to other customer reference boards and platforms, it is easier to use this same board across multiple validation phases including prototyping and postsilicon validation.

There can also be sensor test cards that are FPGA based. Various sensor interface protocols models can be implemented in FPGA such as UART, I^2C, or SPI. These protocol models are used to mimic physical sensor behavior and hence can be used to validate the sensor hub in EP as well as postsilicon validation.

SOFTWARE SENSOR SIMULATOR

The goal of the sensor simulator is to supply an automated environment for sensor validation. It supports several infrastructure layers and thus can work with FPGA and QEMU. The sensor simulator gives the user the ability to control the sensor input (data provider) by selecting from a preprepared list of sensor inputs. This has several advantages such as easily running cycles with the ability to reproduce scenarios\issues and having a low cost in comparison with other options such as automated robots. The following are some of its key features:

- It can inject synthesized data (such as noise).
- It can run along with the real physical sensors.
- It is implemented in software for virtual platforms like QEMU.
- Users can select sensor type and sensor data type for injection into the sensor hub.
- It implements real sensor behavior and can be used to simulate negative (error) behaviors.

Fig. 7.7 shows some of the main components of software sensor simulator.

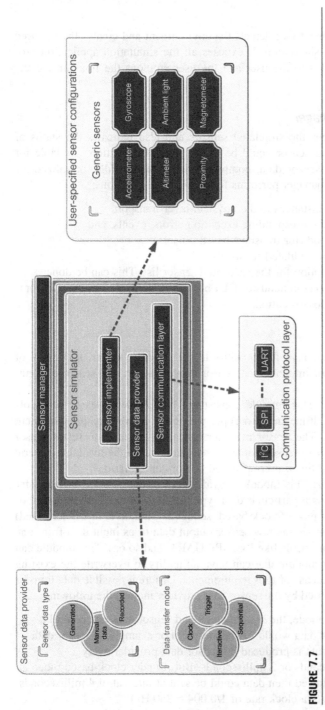

FIGURE 7.7

Software sensor simulator.

Simulation manager

This is the main component that detects the environment and creates the required infrastructure of sensor simulation. It exposes all the simulation application programming interface (API) to the user and the user employs the functions of the simulation manager.

Sensor simulator manager

This component manages the simulated sensors and also indicates the status of each sensor. A particular sensor could be in the state of execution, available for execution, transmitting sensor data, completed data transfer, idle, initialized, or error state. The sensor manager performs following main functions:

- Connects the sensor instances to the physical layer transport.
- Delegates sensor and corresponding execution errors, events, and communication method (for transport-based sensors).
- Sets and validates the emulated sensor list.
- Starts and stops execution for the submitted sensor list. This can be done through start and stop commands or GUI buttons if available once the sensors in the list are ready for execution.

Sensor simulator

This block provides the sensor functionality to the sensor manager. It consists of three components: sensor implementer, sensor data provider, and sensor communication layer.

Sensor implementer: This module consists of basic/generic sensor protocols such as accelerometer, altimeter, gyroscope, proximity sensor, compass, ambient light sensor, and so on. The sensor manager can allow the user to select sensor type and sensor model. The sensor implementer can enhance the available generic sensor protocol with additional user-specified sensor configurations.

Sensor data provider: This module provides control over sensor data transfer rate, number of iterations a particular data type needs to be used in execution or simulation, data transfer mode (clock based, sequential, iterative, or trigger based) and data interpretation mode (as raw sensor output data or as input data from one of the sensor interface protocols like I^2C, SPI, UART, and so on). This module can also act as data injector module that can have an ability to overwrite the existing sensor data with new data as per user requirements. Different possible data transfer modes that can be supported by the sensor data provider include the following:

- *Clock based*: In this mode, the system clock and sensor data rate controls when the next sensor data would be transferred. For example, if sensor data rate is 400 Hz then data is produced by sensor data provider every 1/500 Hz = 0.002 seconds or 2 milliseconds. But if under clock-based mode a lower data rate is allowed then data could be sent at interval of 4 milliseconds (which is equivalent to a clock rate of 1/0.004 = 250 Hz).

- *Sequential*: In this mode, the data is sent by the data provider based on the request it receives through a communication interface like I^{2}C or SPI.
- *Iterative*: In this mode, the data is provided by the data provider based on the user request command through the host machine/GUI.
- *Trigger based*: Under this option the sensor data transition starts based on user selection and zeros are transmitted until the user selects to start transmitting real sensor data.

Sensor communication layer: This component provides a mechanism to communicate over I^{2}C, SPI, UART, and so on. The mechanism to communicate is selected based on the environment (whether it is FPGA with real physical sensors or QEMU).

Fig. 7.8 shows the interaction between various software sensor simulator components including required user interactions.

When start initialization is indicated by the user, the simulation manager initializes and discovers all available sensors. From this available sensor list, the user can select the required sensors for sensor data simulation. The sensor simulator manager then validates the selected sensors along with their respective recorded data (the data that sensor is required to send), and along with their user-selected properties. This sensor validation is a required step to ensure correct sensor simulation behavior. On passing the validation checks, the selected sensors are

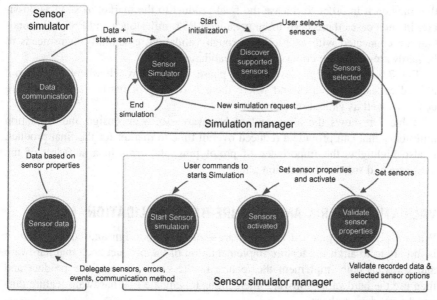

FIGURE 7.8

Software sensor simulator component interactions.

programmed with their respective properties and are activated. The sensors would appear in "ready for simulation" status.

The simulation manager next awaits the user command to start the sensor simulation. On receiving the start command, the sensor simulator manager assigns sensors, errors, events, and communication methods for the sensor simulation.

The sensor simulator then generates data from required sensors as per selected data transfer modes and provides it to the communication layer, which then sends the data to the requesting agent through sensor communication protocols (such as I^{2}C, SPI, and UART) and finally to the user through the simulation manager, which exposes all the simulation API to the user.

VALIDATION STRATEGIES AND CONCEPTS

This section will discuss a few validation strategies and concepts that can help reduce the time to market for a design product.

HARDWARE—SOFTWARE CODESIGN

To align the resource and schedule at the product level, there needs to be a well-defined design and software milestones leading to the final product release. Consider an example where a design needs to be developed along with software that runs on it in order to release the final product to the market as soon as possible. In such cases there need to be presilicon RTL milestones and PSS milestones that are connected with each other through validation; essentially there needs to be hardware—software codesign and covalidation.

Fig. 7.9 shows design development phases of an approach where there is no/limited codesign activities and where there is overlap of hardware and software design as well as validation phases.

Table 7.1 shows the alignment of hardware—software design and validation milestones that can provide a reduced overall time to market for the final product. It also highlights the importance of prototyping platforms in a shift-left of the hardware and software validation phase.

VALIDATION MATRIX AND FEATURE-BASED VALIDATION

When a product is planned for hardware—software codesign and covalidation, it is important to align the feature implementation of the product such that hardware and software both implement the feature in the same phase of the product and then use the hardware—software interactions to validate that hardware feature during the validation phase.

Another important design consideration would be the order of priority to implement and validate the product features. This is called feature prioritization.

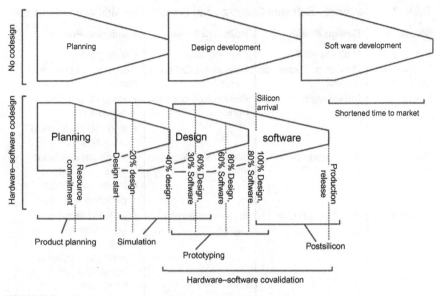

FIGURE 7.9

Hardware—software codesign and covalidation.

The concept of using hardware—software interactions to validate each feature in the prioritized list is known as feature-based validation.

Once the features are prioritized, the next step is to analyze the best suitable platform to validate each of the prioritized feature. For example, it would be easier and more economical to target simple register write and read back validation in presilicon simulation, but a complex flow based on numerous register writes, state transitions, and multiple handshakes with design units including power management checks are best validated on platforms (such as prototyping platforms) that can use software along with hardware. The features that require physical layer interactions or analog design are best validated on real silicon. For example, validation of a low drop-out voltage regulator cannot be done in simulation or prototyping platforms. It has to be done on silicon.

The process of creating a prioritized feature list and identifying the best possible platform to validate that feature is known as a validation matrix. A validation matrix can also mark the depth of validation that can be done for a particular feature across each of the validation platform.

As shown in Table 7.2, the power management feature is of high priority and can be validated with low coverage in presilicon and medium coverage in prototyping, because simulation can validate only the basic flows using behavioral BFMs, while in prototyping platforms the software power management flows can be executed along with power management hardware and even with real sensors in the case of sensor hub validation.

Table 7.1 Hardware–Software Codesign and Covalidation Milestone Alignment

Milestone	Design Phase	Software Phase	Validation Phase
Planning 0	Planning start	Planning start	Planning start
Planning 40 (40% plan)	Resource + Schedule commit	Resource + Schedule commit	Resource + Schedule commit
Design 0	Design start	Architecture definition done	• Bring up presilicon simulation • Bring up prototyping environment
Design 20	20% Design done	Software codesign start	• Presilicon simulation start. • Prototyping/FPGA platforms build start
Design 40	40% Design done	Software ready for covalidation	• 40% Presilicon simulation • Start hardware–software covalidation on prototypes
Design 60	60% Design done	30% Software codesign	• 60% Presilicon simulation • 30% Hardware–software covalidation on prototypes
Design 80	80% Design done	60% Software codesign	• 80% Presilicon simulation • 60% Hardware–software covalidation on prototypes
Design 100	100% Design done	80% Software codesign	• 100% Presilicon simulation • 80% Hardware–software covalidation on prototypes
Silicon arrived	Design bug fixes or workarounds	100% Software done	• 100% Hardware–software covalidation on prototypes • Postsilicon validation start
Production release	NA	NA	• 100% Postsilicon validation done • 100% Software validation done

Table 7.2 Validation Matrix Example

Feature	Priority (1 = High, 2 = Medium, 3 = Low)	Planned Coverage Depth (1 = High, 2 = Medium, 3 = Low)			Coverage Risk (1 = High, 2 = Medium, 3 = Low)	Dependencies (Software, Prototypes, BIOS, Tools, etc.)
		Presilicon	Prototyping	Silicon		
Power management	1	2	2	1	2	
Low drop-out voltage regulator	2	3	2	1	1	Add any dependencies required to validate the feature
Register writes	3	1	1	1	3	

Similarly a low drop-out voltage regulator is a medium priority feature. Since this is the analog portion of the design, it has low coverage in presilicon and on prototyping platforms. Such features can only be validated fully in real silicon. The coverage risk for such features is high since complete coverage is possible only after silicon arrival and any issues found on silicon have a longer bug fix turnaround time and could also result in additional stepping of silicon.

The simple register access feature can be easily validated across all validation platforms and hence has the lowest overall coverage risk. It is possible that validators can completely deprioritize the validation of such features at the prototyping or silicon validation phase and instead decide to get full coverage during the presilicon validation phase. Such decisions are taken considering the return of investment of validating a certain feature on the overall product quality.

REFERENCES

[1] Intel platform and component validation white paper: A Commitment to Quality, Reliability and Compatibility.
[2] Cong K, Xie F, Lei L. Automatic concolic test generation with virtual, prototypes for post-silicon validation.

Sensor calibration and manufacturing

8

INFORMATION IN THIS CHAPTER:

- Motivation for Calibrating Sensors
- Calibration Models
- Manufacturing and Calibration Use Cases

MOTIVATION FOR CALIBRATING SENSORS

A fundamental need of any sensor use case is trust in the data provided by the sensors. Without trust the data provided will be meaningless and discarded. Data errors can appear for a number of reasons—some are added in manufacturing, while other errors are the result of environmental changes. A common example would be a navigational system that a user might simply turn off if they believe that the directions it provided are incorrect.

This type of error can generally be determined through a calibration process. After it is identified, the correction (the opposite of the error) is applied to the received sensor data. Building and designing a calibration process involve both understanding a supply chain and the system design itself. The sensor vendor, system manufacturer, and even the end user may be involved, depending on how the error originates. The range of the products use may also be bounded by how well this error can be corrected through calibration.

SUPPLY-CHAIN STAKEHOLDERS

Sensor vendors, system designers, and system manufacturers form the three main blocks of sensor supply chain. Sensors are manufactured by the sensor vendors, sensor based systems are designed by the system designers and then the final platform or system that has the required sensors is manufactured by the system manufacturers.

SENSOR VENDORS

Sensor vendors strive to be profitable through reaching the right levels of product performance and cost. The path of moving a promising technology from the prototype to high-volume manufacturing stage often requires high levels of capital investment in equipment and factories as well as many years to fine-tune the process of fabricating the sensing devices.

These performance and cost levels are often set by the needs of the device in which the sensor will be placed. This will define the sensor specifications, which often include maximum and minimum levels for each parameter listed. These specifications are often tied to the requirements of the system manufacturer. If the system manufacturer is willing to calibrate and remove the sensor error, then the vendor may be able to widen their specification.

Sensor vendors will therefore fine-tune their manufacturing process such that as many devices as possible will fall within the specification range. Fig. 8.1 shows sensor manufacturing process where the manufactured wafer goes through wafer level testing, followed by packaging and package/sensor level testing. The failed devices that fall outside of the specification during testing will be discarded but will add to the total cost of manufacturing the sensor. This added cost can quickly decrease the profit made with each sensor. For example, if the market price of a sensor is $3 and the cost to make the sensor is $2, the vendor will take 33% of the selling price as profit. However a 20% yield loss would increase costs to $2.50, halving the profits from 33% to 17%.

One method of reducing product variances is to calibrate analog circuits at the wafer test stage (Fig. 8.1). Common adjustments may include adjusting the sensitivity (scale) of each sensor through adjusting the reference voltage of the analog-to-digital converters (ADCs). In this example, the output voltage of the ADC may be tested using a reference voltage. Based on the output, the reference voltages would be programmed through a type of one-time programmable read-only memory.

Adaptive circuits may also be designed into the sensor in order to remove bias (Fig. 8.2). These circuits do not require calibration but use reference circuits to sensor bias error that may change with temperature or other environmental variables. Two common methods of sensing the device error include sampling the sensing device twice, at reset and after a signal has been gathered, and sensing

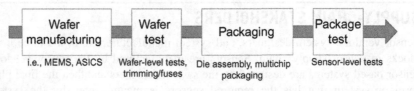

FIGURE 8.1

Sensor manufacturing process.

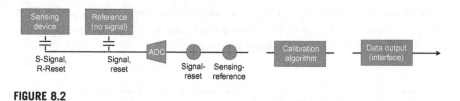

FIGURE 8.2

Example of adaptive circuit to remove sensor bias.

that a reference sensor circuit will not gather signals. In both cases the reference or reset signals are subtracted from the signal effectively adjusting the output for changes in bias [1].

Finally, the sensor vendor may add digital calibration blocks that may be programmed by the equipment manufacturer. These algorithms may include simple look-up tables or polynomial equations to adjust for sensor nonlinearity.

SYSTEM DESIGNERS

Calibration can be a method of enabling a designer to reach ideal product specifications with more flexible design rules and cheaper sensor components. An accelerometer calibration can correct for tilt added when placed in the system mechanical design, or light sensor calibration can adjust for light lost through cover glass that is covering the sensor.

To understand the effect of calibration error and system variations, the designer may choose to evaluate the end use case with a worst-case system. This system could be constructed with sensors that represent the maximum and minimum of the sensor vendor's specification and include other worst-case system variations (e.g., for light sensors, the highest level of attenuation expected through a cover glass).

Finally, the system designer ideally will have design rules that limit the system error added to sensors in the manufacturing process. For example, the designer may be instructed to place a magnetometer sensor a certain distance away from objects that can be magnetized (such as screw holes) or that could add unexpected errors when enabled (such as digitizers).

SYSTEM MANUFACTURER

The system manufacturer will be motivated to minimize the time and labor cost added by sensor calibration in the manufacturing line. To assess the calibration need, the manufacturer may first gather performance data from a batch of prototypes to assess system-to-system variances to determine the need for calibration. This evaluation may also lead to tightening of component specifications such as decreased variances in the cover glass-covering light sensors.

A secondary need is to accommodate sourcing the same type of sensor from multiple vendors. In this case, the manufacturer may develop a common calibration process and tool to cover multiple products.

THE CALIBRATION PROCESS

The goal of the calibration process is to determine the calibration correction so that it is accurate enough to help maintain the data quality of the system under test. Further, the results also must be valid across the range of the product's use.

Designing the calibration process should be based on a comprehensive understanding of the system error sources—both the sources of the error and how each changes across the product's range of use. A useful byproduct of this in-depth study is that it also gives a pragmatic understanding of the product's limitations and can influence changes in the product requirements or design. For example, if it is shown that a sensor bias drift becomes unpredictable at high temperature range, the product planner may either contemplate lowering the product's requirements (i.e., support a lower maximum temperature) or add a more expensive correction circuit or algorithm.

CREATING A SYSTEM MODEL

The first step in defining the calibration process is to understand the product requirements and behavior. This includes understanding how accurate the corrected sensor data should be and the range of the products use.

A second step is to then understand how the product's performance may change—both within its use case (i.e., temperature and input voltage) and within the product-to-product variations. Achieving this often requires studying each component within the system and finding the worst-case error that might result.

After an error model is created for each component, a system-level error model can be created. There are many benefits to this approach, such as providing system designers with insights on where they can reduce errors through selecting the right component (i.e., sensor) and adjusting their manufacturing process.

The error model should also identify how the error will change and reach its maximum across the product's use case. For example, a sensor component's bias error may change significantly across a temperature range, which is often the case for a gyroscope. Or the random noise of a sensor may be the strongest when the sensor is operated at its maximum temperature and minimum input voltage.

ANALYZING ERROR SOURCES

Most error sources within a system can be broken down into two types: systematic or random. Systematic errors in sensors refer to such errors as bias offsets, drift, or scale errors that can be discovered through a calibration process and corrected. On the other hand, random errors (or noise) refer to unpredictable error sources that cannot be calibrated.

It is often found when analyzing error sources that there are both significant systematic and random contributors. In some cases, it can be found that removing the systematic source (via calibration) will leave behind a level of random noise that is tolerable. However, in other cases, the random noise is still significant or dominant such that other means of improving the data (such as digital filters) are required.

The outcome of this analysis can often determine which errors are systematic. And further, which of these system errors can be identified through a calibration process.

DESIGNING THE CALIBRATION PROCESS

Even after a calibration process it is likely that there will still be residual systematic error within the products usage. When designing the process, it is first essential to determine how much residual systematic error (or calibration error) will be allowed within the product. Then the designer should determine how to best minimize this error.

A first step in minimizing this error is defining the correction mechanism and process conditions. This would take into account the system modeling efforts described earlier to identify how the error changes across the use case. For example, if the scale (sensitivity) of a sensor has a nonlinear response across temperature, the system designer may create a nonlinear equation and define the calibration parameters from testing the product across the temperature range. However, if the nonlinear effects are acceptable, a lower cost method could be used where a single measurement is captured at the mid-temperature range to minimize the worst-case error across the product's use.

The error of the calibration process itself must be known and managed. This is essential to ensure that the error of the process is much smaller than the acceptable calibration error. The error of the process itself must be tighter than that of the acceptable calibration error.

DYNAMIC CALIBRATION

In many cases, the calibration process will not encompass all systematic errors that could affect a system. In some cases, there are unpredictable environmental factors such as changes in temperature or fluctuations in external magnetic fields. In other cases, a manufacturer may have selected a cheaper, less comprehensive calibration, trading off product performance for lower manufacturing costs. Finally, the system itself may change over time due to sensor aging and system changes.

A popular method to reducing this varying systematic error is through an adaptive mechanism often called dynamic calibration. This mechanism infers the sensor error through making general assumptions using recent sensor data or input from other sources. A common example would be the gyroscope with an offset that changes with temperature. Therefore a dynamic calibration could be employed in two ways. First, the sensor could reference an on-chip temperature sensor and look up the corresponding temperature offset. Second, if no look-up table exists, an assumption could be made that the gyroscope is not moving when other on-system motion sensors report no movement, and therefore the only signal from the gyroscope will be the offset error.

MANAGING THE CALIBRATION PROCESS AND EQUIPMENT

A key tenet of the calibration process is to ensure the quality of the error correction. For example, if the calibration goal is to minimize the data error to $\pm 10\%$, then the process and equipment used must be less (e.g., $\pm 5\%$). And this level of quality must be maintained over the lifetime of the process's use.

To ensure this level of quality, a separate planning session may be needed. This planning or management would ensure that the calibration process was repeatable. It would ensure that operators received relevant training and would restrict the usage of the calibration equipment.

The equipment selected for calibration will have different qualities relative to the product's usage. It will not need to be rugged or durable and therefore may need to be carefully stored and used. It will also need to be more accurate than the sensors on the product. Maintaining this level of accuracy may require setting conditions on how it is stored and used as well as setting a schedule based on understanding how long the equipment can be used before it must be recalibrated.

The accuracy of the calibration equipment can be maintained in an instrumentation laboratory that contains even more accurate equipment. This instrumentation equipment may be serviced by a standards laboratory containing a more accurate secondary reference. This standards laboratory will have its equipment serviced at a national standards organization that maintains the most accurate equipment. By ensuring that calibration equipment is linked to a national standard through a chain of process and certification, the equipment ensures calibration traceability.

SINGLE AND MULTIAXIS LINEAR CALIBRATION

For the purpose of describing a linear calibration method we will start first describing single and then multiaxis calibration.

When reviewing the light sensor and assuming a linear response, the sensor errors can be broken in two groups:

Scale or Multiplication error (A)—This would describe a multiplication error in the sensor response. For example, if the incident light to the sensor increased by 100% and the measured data increased by 105%, the scale error would be 5%.

Offset or Bias error (B)—This is the error shown by the sensor even without any external stimulation.

A common representation of the linear error can be seen as:

$$V = A^*R + B$$

The requirement measurement process is very simple in that it requires two sensor measurements to isolate contributions from scale and offset.

SENSOR LIMITS AND NONLINEARITY

In a single-axis sensor it is also important to review the maximum and minimum sensor response levels as well as sensor nonlinearity. Fig. 8.3 shows sensor response to a stimulus signal.

Maximum Range: The maximum range is often determined by the internal sensor ADC. For example, a 10-bit ADC would limit the data output from the sensor to 1024 (210). However the sensor response may change as it nears its maximum level therefore lowering the maximum calibration level.

Minimum Range: A similar minimum limit should be evaluated based on the sensor performance. Considerations should include nonlinearity as well as sensor noise. For example, if the standard deviation of the light sensor output (translated to lux) is measured to be 10 lux, the minimum calibration and use-case limit may be set to 10 lux. *Note*: in practice a digital filter may be added in the system to reduce the noise of the sensor.

Nonlinearity: Most sensor systems will have nonlinearity that is represented as "scale error" that varies across the sensor range. If the nonlinearity is great

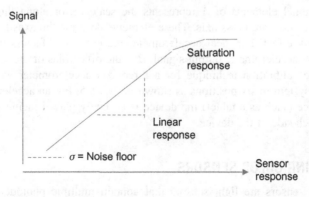

FIGURE 8.3

Sensor response versus signal.

enough ($>1\%$) then the calibration equation can be modified (with an added polynomial equation) to account for the nonlinearity.

$$V(X) = [A^*R + R + i(R)]_{Min\ R}^{Max\ R}$$

The implications of nonlinearity in sensor calibration is that now multiple data points (more than two) are needed to accurately describe the nonlinear effect.

CALIBRATING SENSORS WITH MULTIPLE ORTHOGONAL INPUTS

Sensors representing more complex signals often have multiple corelated sensing devices. One example is the three-axis accelerometer that includes a MEMS sensing device that can detect acceleration across the X-, Y-, and Z-axes.

Based on the previous light sensor example, it could be assumed that each axis could be calibrated separately independent of each other. However the need to determine device orientation and tilt require all three inputs to be calibrated together.

Orientation: Describes how the sensor is placed within the device in terms of direction. In a perfect sensor, an accelerometer may output 9.8, 0, 0 m^2/s when a system is placed flat on a table. However, if the sensor is upside-down within the system, the results would be -9.8, 0, 0 m^2/s requiring an orientation multiplier of (-1, 0, 0). Often this parameter is multiplied into the equation.

Tilt: A 3×3 matrix is required to cover tilt across three axes. Tilt may be expected by design but can occur from variations in the manufacturing process (such as misalignment of silicon die with respect to the package or misalignment of chip with respect to the printed circuit board).

Fig. 8.4 shows the misaligned axes of accelerometer along the Y by α_{XZ} (or α_{YZ}) and Z-axis (by α_{XZ}).

Therefore the equation from a three-axis sensor can be described below where scale and tilt are represented in the 3×3 matrix and bias error in the 1×3 matrix.

$$\begin{bmatrix} V_1 \\ V_2 \\ V_3 \end{bmatrix} = \begin{bmatrix} A_{11} & A_{12} & A_{13} \\ A_{21} & A_{22} & A_{23} \\ A_{31} & A_{32} & A_{33} \end{bmatrix} \times \begin{bmatrix} R_1 \\ R_2 \\ R_3 \end{bmatrix} + \begin{bmatrix} B_1 \\ B_2 \\ B_3 \end{bmatrix}$$

The diagonal elements of A represents the scale factor along the three axes and other elements are cross axis. These elements describe the axes misalignment and cross-talk effect. For ideal accelerometer the cross-axis factors would all be zero. V is the accelerometer output signal. B is the offset/bias of the sensor axis.

A simple calibration technique for a three-axis accelerometer would require placing the system in six positions as shown in Fig. 8.5. For an accelerometer in a mobile device (such as a tablet) the device is typically placed facing up and then down for each side of the device.

CALIBRATING COLOR SENSORS

Color RGB sensors are light sensors that contain multiple photodetectors sampling the red, green, and blue visible spectrums. The sensor provides information

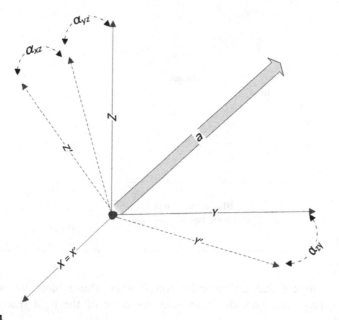

FIGURE 8.4

Geometrical model adopted to describe the misalignment of the sensor axes.

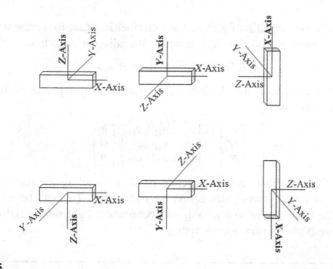

FIGURE 8.5

Three-axis accelerometer calibration positions.

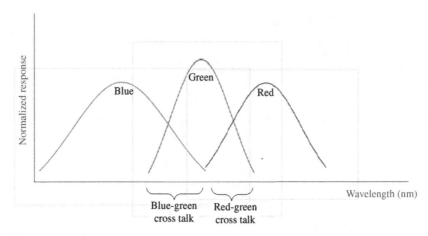

FIGURE 8.6

Color sensor response plot.

on both the light signal and its color composition. This is done by color-filter arrays covering each photodiode to limit the color of the light reaching each photodiode.

The challenge of these types of sensors is cross talk where the red, green, and blue light will leak into each photodiode as shown in Fig. 8.6. For this reason, a calibration must be created for each color filter to understand the light leakage into each.

The calibration equation for each color channel is meant to represent the scale (gain) of the sampled color while subtracting the adjacent cross talk.

$$G' = G^*A_{GG} - R^*A_{GR} - B^*A_{GB}$$

The color correction for all three colors can then be represented in a 3×3 matrix shown below.

$$\begin{bmatrix} R' \\ G' \\ B' \end{bmatrix} = \begin{bmatrix} a_{11} & a_{12} & a_{13} \\ a_{21} & a_{21} & a_{21} \\ a_{31} & a_{23} & a_{33} \end{bmatrix} \begin{bmatrix} R \\ G \\ B \end{bmatrix}$$

Calibration for these sensors typically requires sampling the response of the red, green, and blue photodiodes across the light range. This can be achieved by exposing the RGB sensor to a tunable monochromatic light source and recording the sensor response at each wavelength.

REFERENCE

[1] Nakamura J., editor, Image sensors and signal processing for digital still cameras (optical science and engineering), 2005.

Sensor security and location privacy

9

INFORMATION IN THIS CHAPTER:

- Sensor Attacks
- Security of Sensor Data
- Preserving Location Privacy
- *k*-Anonymity
- Obfuscation
- Cloaking

INTRODUCTION TO MOBILE COMPUTING SECURITY AND PRIVACY

A mobile computing device can be used in a variety of environments and for a variety of use cases. For example, it can be used as a cell phone or computing device, or to access online shopping, databases, and so on. The heterogeneity of hardware, software, communication protocols, variations in resources, and their limitations makes security a major concern for mobile device users and applications. For example, a user can employ a mobile device for online transactions (such as banking, share trading, and shopping) or for communication with peers (using various applications, email, social networking sites) or to access location-based services (LBSs; such as weather reports and maps). In all these use cases, sensitive user data, including user location, is shared. Such use cases require data security and authentication from other users, service providers, or any other infrastructure that the user connects to. The security issues of mobile computing and sensors are related to data confidentiality, data integrity, data authentication, and access control.

Security solutions should have the ability to dynamically change the protocols based on variations in system resource utilizations, hardware resource availability, quality of service (QoS) requirements, and desired data security levels.

The security concerns of mobile computing devices are also related to user data privacy. The user data should be protected and secured during transmission

Mobile Sensors and Context-Aware Computing. DOI: http://dx.doi.org/10.1016/B978-0-12-801660-2.00009-4

and storage. The security solutions for privacy should ensure that the user is notified when sensitive user information is exposed or revealed to any external systems or service beyond the immediate control of the user. It should also keep record of all the instances of exposure, interactions, and exchange of privacy information/data. The privacy security solution should be able to detect any breach or attempt to expose the user privacy data made by an attacking system.

Mobile privacy is complicated because it is difficult to identify the privacy levels of information/data. This makes it difficult to decide on which information/data can be shared or not shared. Moreover, it is also difficult to ensure that the privacy security systems do not mistakenly expose, distribute, or abuse user information.

Fig. 9.1 shows the components of a mobile ecosystem, which can experience security and privacy threats via various communication paths and LBSs such as GPS, Wi-Fi, and RFID (radio frequency identification), which gather and transmit secure user location and hence are susceptible to security and privacy threats.

SENSOR SECURITY

Today's mobile devices and consumer products offer an amazing user experience with the use of many built-in and external sensors on the devices that measure various context parameters such as device/user orientation, acceleration, motions, orientation, and environmental conditions such as pressure, humidity, and so on. Many applications utilize such sensor data in games, LBSs, and social networking.

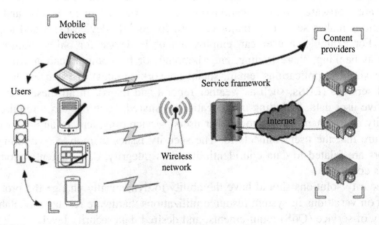

FIGURE 9.1

Mobile ecosystem-privacy and security [1].

For example, Nike's self-lacing sneakers [2] have pressure sensors in the sole. When the user puts a foot inside this shoe, the cables of the internal cable system made from fishing line tightens based on an algorithmic pressure equation.

Sensors like cameras, GPS, and audio sensors provide precise location, voice, pictures, and other sensitive information of the user. Additionally sensors such as motion sensors or orientation sensors also provide detailed device/user information, such as the moving direction of the user. Hence, applications and devices that use such sensitive sensor data may actually be collecting sensitive user data and may be even disclosing it to the other agents in the ecosystem to increase the user experience level. Sensitive sensor data may look irrelevant to the user, and the stealth operations of these sensors can deceive the users into considering the devices and their sensors as safe, but such data can be exploited for identity theft, tracking locating, compromising passwords, and so on.

For example, the user's identify can be inferred by using accumulated long-term sensor data, or a personal location can be exposed by an application, or keyboard inputs can be tracked, or the mobile computing device can be identified by measuring sensor anomalies.

For sensor data to be considered as secure, its confidentiality, source integrity, and availability should be maintained. Whenever any of these three characteristics [3] is not met for the sensor data, then its security is considered to be violated or compromised.

Confidentiality means that the sensor data is provided only to the intended agent and for the intended purpose. No intermediate agents should have access to this sensor data, nor should they be able to read, modify, or understand the data. Source integrity means the sensor data is actually coming from the source it claims it is generated from; otherwise the authenticity and security of the data is compromised. Availability means that the sensor data is accessible when needed by the authorized user/agent in a timely manner. Any denial of data is a security violation because it prevents the authorized agent from accessing the data.

To effectively plan out mitigation solutions for any sensor/sensor data-related security and privacy issues, it is important to understand the different types of threats/attack.

TYPES OF SENSOR ATTACKS

The main security threats [3] can be categorized into location tracking, eavesdropping, keystroke monitoring, device fingerprinting, and user identification. The attacks generally happen on more than one sensor because with more sensors, more types of information, and more data can be obtained.

- Location Tracking: Under this type of threat, the attacks use sensor data to locate the device without using GPS or any other location sensors.

Accelerometer data, e.g., can be used to infer the location of smartphones by using statistical models to obtain estimated trajectory, then use map matching algorithms to obtain predicted location points (within a 200-m radius).

- Eavesdropping: Sensors can leak information not directly measured by them, e.g., motion sensors can leak sound information. Sound samples can be obtained from the gyroscope sensor even when there is no direct access to the device microphone.

- Keystroke Monitoring [4]: Many user inputs can be inferred from sensor data. For example, built-in accelerometers and gyroscopes can expose user inputs, and motion sensor data can be used to infer user keyboard inputs. To infer input keystrokes from raw sensor data, an application obtains raw sensor data from sensors (such as accelerometer, gravity sensor, or gyroscope) of smartphones. The raw data is then preprocessed where signal segments corresponding to user keyboard strokes are identified and extracted from the continuous stream of sensor data. Next the keystroke sensor data is isolated further by matching it with time stamp of start and stop of keyboard clicks. The resulting isolated dataset (which is a collection of features/attributes) is then fed into a classifier, which maps it to appropriate key using machine learning algorithms. Additionally photo sensors can also be used to increase the accuracy of keystroke inference using data related to changes in the light during input of each keystroke.

- Device Fingerprinting: Sensors can provide information that can uniquely identify the device using those sensors. Different mobile computing devices may have the same sensor types or makes but these sensors will have minor manufacturing imperfections and differences that will be unique for each sensor and the device using that sensor. These manufacturing variations and imperfections can be used to fingerprint the device.

- User Identifying: Using sensor data, the attack can identify the user. For example, when a user of devices (such as wearables, intelligent clothing, and other smart devices) walks/runs/climbs with the device, the acceleration signals generated can be used to identify the user in an intuitive and unobstructed manner [5].

SECURITY OF SENSOR DATA

To protect privacy and ensure security of sensor data, the security mechanism should provide following functions [6]:

1. The security mechanism should ensure that sensor data is stored safely so that it is available to the authorized users when needed in timely manner.
2. The security mechanism should increase the cost of attacking and decrease the gain on the compromised sensor, meaning the attack will not be able to obtain significant data from the compromised sensor.

3. In the case of a system of interconnected sensors, the security mechanism should increase the data availability by minimizing the effect of failed or compromised individual sensors.
4. The security mechanism should be implementable with acceptable impact to performance and resource utilization of the sensor/sensor network.

For the security of sensor data, the sensors or sensor nodes in the sensor network can implement some of the methodology mentioned here.

Basic encryption scheme

The sensor data security mechanism must encrypt the data [7] to ensure confidentiality such that only an authorized user can access the data and decrypt that sensor data. The following describes a basic encryption scheme:

1. Generate random session key K_r. Compute keyed hash value h (data, K_r) of the data.
2. Encrypt data, h (data, K_r) with K_r and obtain {data, h (data, K_r)} K_r.
3. Encrypt K_r using the key K_{UV} shared between authorized users and the current sensor node.
4. Store DATA which is equal to {data, h (data, K_r)} K_r, {K_r} K_{UV} and destroy K_r.

This DATA will be provided to an authorized user when required who then will decrypt the original data with key K_{UV} and ensure that h (data, K_r).

This scheme only provides basic security but cannot protect enough against data losses due to sensor compromises or Byzantine failures (arbitrary deviation from processes/data and so on).

Secret sharing scheme

With the basic scheme, the data cannot be protected if the sensor gets compromised or shows behavior that is deviated from its normal. In such cases, the data security can be increased by replicating the sensor data and distributing to neighboring sensors/sensor storage agents. By doing so data can be recovered by authorized users from other sensors/storage agents if one of the sensor gets compromised. A simple replication, however, will result in storage overhead of the number of replications × data and hence will not meet the criteria of being within acceptable limits of resource utilization. To mitigate this problem a secret sharing scheme known as the (k, n) threshold scheme may be used. This threshold scheme is based on the idea that it takes k points to define a polynomial of degree $k - 1$. In this secret sharing scheme, the secret S is divided into n pieces of data $(S_1, S_2 \ldots S_n)$ such that if the user has knowledge of any k or more pieces of data then S can be computed from those pieces of data to recover full secret S. If the user has knowledge of only $k - 1$ or fewer pieces of data (S_i) then the secret S cannot be determined. If $k = n$ then all pieces of data are required to reconstruct the secret S. Thus the data security can be enhanced by ensuring that unauthorized users/hardware cannot get more than $k - 1$ pieces of data.

Partial decryption

The sensor data includes user IDs along with private information such as user location and their path of walking/running. In a partial decryption scheme [8], shown in Fig. 9.2, depending on how the user wants to control the sensor data, some parts of the sensor data can be masked, the user ID can be replaced with an anonymous ID, or the encryption key can be converted to a different encryption key (converted from distribution service key to utilization service key) while the data is still encrypted. The user configures the utilization services provision policy to perform this task. The sensor data remains protected because the data masking and key conversion is done without decrypting the data.

The encrypted data then passes through distribution services where the data gets decrypted using distribution service key and then further gets decrypted using a utilization service key in the utilization service block.

Sliding group watermark scheme

In this scheme, a fragile digital watermark is embedded in the sensor data stream in such a manner that any change/modification in the original sensor data will corrupt the embedded watermark. Such watermarking is known as fragile watermarking because the watermark itself changes on sensor data corruption.

In sliding group watermark scheme [9], steps performed are:

- For each data value S_i, using a secret key k and HASH function, a keyed hash value h of the data is generated (S_i, k). The secret key k is known to the sensor data sender and the receiver. Individual_Hash$_i$ ← HASH $(S_i \| k)$ where $i = 1$, $2, 3 \ldots$ and S_i is sensor data element. Fig. 9.3 shows this step.
- Next, the group hash value is calculated, where the group size is determined based on the data type. For each group the group hash value (Hash group$_i$) is a hash of the concatenation of all individual hash values (Individual_Hash$_i$) of the data values S_i of that group.
  - If there are three groups such that group$_i$ has l individual sensor data, group$_{i+1}$ has m individual sensor data, and group$_{i+2}$ has n individual sensor data. For each of the individual sensor data the individual hash values are calculated as in previous step.
  - Hash_group$_i$ ← HASH $(k \| $ [Individual_Hash$_1$ $\|$ Individual_Hash$_2$ $\| \ldots$ Individual_Hash$_l$]).
  - Hash_group$_{i+1}$ ← HASH $(k \| $ [Individual_Hash$_1$ $\|$ Individual_Hash$_2$ $\| \ldots$ Individual_Hash$_m$]).
  - Hash_group$_{i+2}$ ← HASH $(k \| $ [Individual_Hash$_1$ $\|$ Individual_Hash$_2$ $\| \ldots$ Individual_Hash$_n$]).
- The watermark is calculated as HASH of concatenation of hash values of different groups.

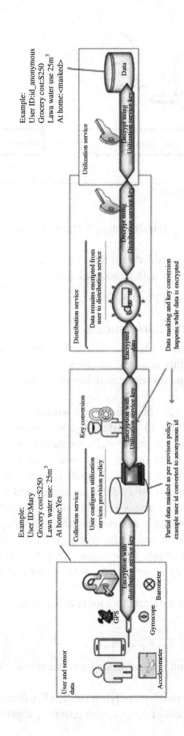

FIGURE 9.2

Partial decryption technology.

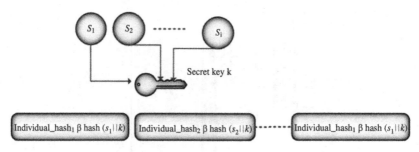

FIGURE 9.3

Sliding group watermark scheme Step 1.

- Watermark $W \leftarrow$ HASH $(k \parallel [\text{Hash\_group}_i \parallel \text{Hash\_group}_{i+1} \parallel \text{Hash\_group}_{i+2} \parallel \ldots])$.
- The watermark W is then embedded into the sensor data by replacing the least significant bit of data elements with watermark bits.

The above process is shown in Fig. 9.4.

Simplified sliding group watermark scheme

Consider sensor data stream $D = \{S_1, S_2, S_3 \ldots S_i\}$. In the simplified sliding group watermark scheme [9] this sensor data stream is organized into groups of different sizes and these groups are delimited based on data readings called the synchronization points.

For each data element S_i of the data stream D, the hash value Individual_Hash$_i \leftarrow$ HASH $(S_i \parallel k)$ is calculated and based on this individual data element hash value, the scheme checks to determine whether the data element is a synchronization point or not. The data element S_i is considered a synchronization point if [Individual_Hash$_i$] mod [secret parameter] $= 0$. The synchronization point is thus based on a secret parameter and a secret key k, and hence it becomes difficult for any attack to determine the synchronization point without the knowledge of the secret parameter and the secret key.

If S_i is a synchronization point and if the group meets the minimal group size requirement (has data elements equal to or greater than the minimum group size requirement) then embedding of watermark is done, otherwise the data is stored in buffer (and not sent).

If there are two such sensor data groups group$_i$ and group$_{i+1}$

$$\text{group}_i \leftarrow (S_1 \parallel S_2 \parallel S_3 \parallel \ldots S_n)$$
$$\text{group}_{i+1} \leftarrow (S_{n+1} \parallel S_{n+2} \parallel S_{n+3} \parallel \ldots S_m)$$

Then the watermark for group$_i$ is calculated as: Watermark $W \leftarrow$ HASH $(k \parallel [\text{group}_i \parallel \text{group}_{i+1}])$.

So the watermark is calculated by applying the HASH function to concatenation of all individual data elements in group$_i$ and group$_{i+1}$ together with the secret

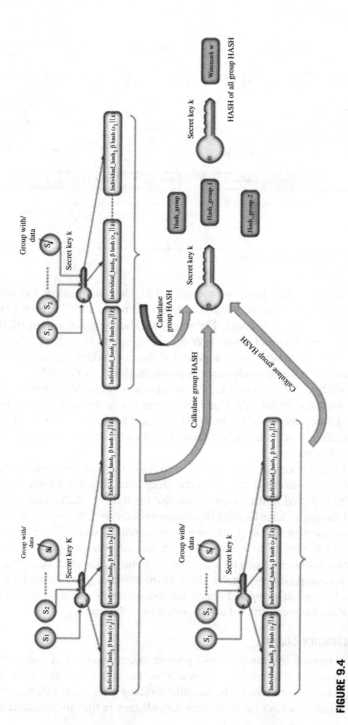

FIGURE 9.4

Slide group watermark scheme process.

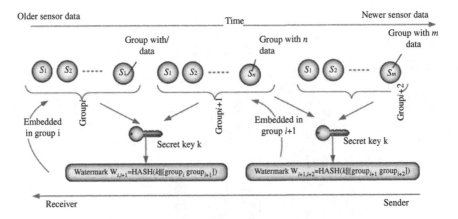

FIGURE 9.5

Simplified sliding group watermark process.

key k, unlike in the sliding group watermark, where the watermark is calculated using the hash multiple times (for individual data elements, then for each group, and then for combination of groups). The simplified sliding group watermark thus saves computing resources and power over the sliding group watermark scheme.

The watermark for $group_i$ once calculated is then embedded by replacing the least significant bits of the data elements in $group_i$ as shown in Fig. 9.5.

After embedding the watermark, the $group_i$ is sent to the receiver. The receiver will need the secret key k and the secret parameter and the minimum group size to detect integrity of the received groups. The receiver will check (just as in the embedding process described earlier) each of the received data elements for synchronization points.

If received data element R_i (corresponding to S_i) is not a synchronization point and the group size is less than the minimum group size, then the received sensor data element R_i is placed in the buffer. Otherwise the received data elements form the $group_i$ and $group_{i+1}$. After forming the groups on receiver side, the watermark W is reconstructed using similar steps as during the watermark embedding process. If the reconstructed watermark on the receiver side matches the extracted watermark (from the received data elements) then the data of $group_i$ is accepted, otherwise the detection mechanism performs a similar check on the previous group before rechecking the results for current group and rejects the data elements if it continues to find mismatch between the reconstructed and the extracted watermarks.

Forward watermark chain

The forward watermark scheme [9] uses a pseudorandom number generator to generate random numbers that are used to determine the data group size instead of using synchronization points as in the simplified sliding watermark scheme. There is no need to calculate a hash value for each data element in the group to determine

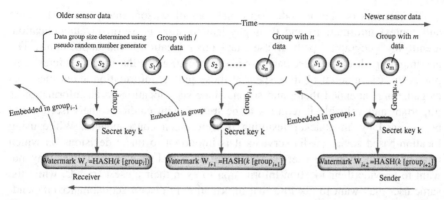

FIGURE 9.6

Forward watermark chain process.

the group size, so the forward watermark scheme has reduced overhead as compared to the simplified sliding watermark scheme. The secret key k, which is known to the sender and the receiver, is used as a seed in the pseudorandom number generator and hence it becomes difficult for attackers to identify the group size.

If a group has n data elements such as $group_i \leftarrow (S_1 \parallel S_2 \parallel S_3 \parallel \ldots S_n])$ then a watermark is generated as a HASH of concatenation of all individual data elements S_i of that one group only instead of two groups together as in the simplified sliding watermark scheme.

Watermark $W \leftarrow$ HASH $(k \parallel [group_i])$

This watermark (for $group_i$) is then embedded by replacing the least significant bits of all data elements in the $group_{i-1}$ as shown in Fig. 9.6.

On receiving the groups of data, the receiver uses the same pseudorandom number generator and secret k to reproduce the group size and organizes the received data into groups similar to the ones on the sender side. The receiver then reconstructs the watermark for $group_i$ and compares it against the received watermark for that group. The received data is considered authentic if the two watermarks match, otherwise the receiver considers the received data as altered/compromised and rejects the data elements of $group_i$.

LOCATION PRIVACY

Location privacy means an ability to prevent unauthorized agents/users from learning the device's current or past location.

LBSs are services that use sensors to identify the device location and other user or device context information (such as the day, time, or environment). LBSs are a requirement today for mobile computing devices, because they offer device users information and services that are relevant to the user/device location.

The sensors or sensor nodes (in a network of sensors that provides location and context information) and their physical location is useful in authentication, identifying geographic path of user, and other location-based applications. The geographic path of the user can provide information on the user's preference of places to visit, amount of time spent at those places, information about meetings or gatherings attended there, and so on. Since such location-based information is important and valuable it requires to be treated with caution, otherwise it could be obtained by an attacker resulting in unforeseen consequences. While using location-based social media services it is important to make decisions on which type of information the user desires to disclose and to whom. A user may not want to provide their location information to even their closest friends, while the same user may want to disclose that information to distant acquaintances depending on the need and purpose.

There are several key factors that needs to be considered for location privacy decisions [10] such as life of information (how long the location context/data will be persistent and discoverable by adversaries), consumer of information (type of data consumer and user's trust level with that consumer), benefits to user (the perceived benefit that user receives after sharing location context with the service provider), user-content relation (content ownership affects privacy perception), culture and environment (differences in privacy perception due to difference in culture and usage environment), personal context (location data used within another context influences privacy perception).

ATTACK-THREAT TYPES

When any LBSs are used, the localization system, which determines the sensor/sensor node or device location, will collect location data and user tracking data. If the sensor/location data privacy is not adequately protected then it becomes a security risk since this data reveals private user/device information (such as location data, routes, and so on) to the service providers, users, and attackers.

Privacy threats related to location sensing systems and LBSs can be categorized into communication privacy threats and location privacy threats.

The types of location privacy threats [11] that arise from disclosed location information are:

- Tracking Threat: In this type of threat the attacker can receive continuous updates of user location in real time, which can be used to identify the user's location routes, predict future locations, and/or frequently traveled routes with sufficient accuracy using a user's mobility patterns.
- Identification Threat: In this type of threat the attacker can receive sporadic updates of user location, which can be used to identify the user's frequently visited locations (such as home or work place) and these places can be used to disclose a user's identity.

- Profiling Threat: In this type of threat the attacker may not have the required information to identify the user but can use the locations to profile the user. For example, an attacker can identify which hospitals or religious places a user visits, or which places the user goes for shopping, and how often.

Through the above location privacy threats an attacker gathers information of user locations through which the attacker can obtain clues about the user's private information such as user lifestyle, time and purpose of movements through different locations, and so on, even if the user does not disclose their identity [12].

Some of the examples of how an attacker can gather information about the user identity are:

- When a user sends a message from a location that exclusively belongs to the user, an attacker, who obtains location coordinates of the origin of message, can correlate the coordinates with existing location database (say to find work or residential address or phone number of the user) and identify the user since it is the user's exclusive location.
- When a user discloses their identity and location information for a legitimate purpose, an attacker can obtain this information. If the user sends an anonymous message next (because the user does not want to disclose their identity), the attacker can link an anonymous message to the user using previously obtained location information and thereby expose the user's identity.
- If an attacker has identified the user at a particular location and if the attacker continues to obtain a series of location updates that can be linked to the user, then the attacker will have information that the user had visited all the locations in the received series of updates. When the user transmits location information too often, then the attacker can link these locations to the same user and identify the user and have knowledge about the user's complete movements.

An attacker's knowledge about the information can be classified into two main categories [13]:

- Temporal information knowledge, where an attacker has information about single snapshot of the user position or has access to multiple user positions accumulated over a time period or has access to the complete movement trajectory of the user.
- Context information knowledge, where an attacker has additional context information above and beyond spatiotemporal information. For example, an attacker can read the user's phonebook to get information about a user's address, type of friends, places of interests, and so on.

Fig. 9.7 shows how an attacker's knowledge can transit between the temporal (time-based) and context space depending on the type of information available to the attacker.

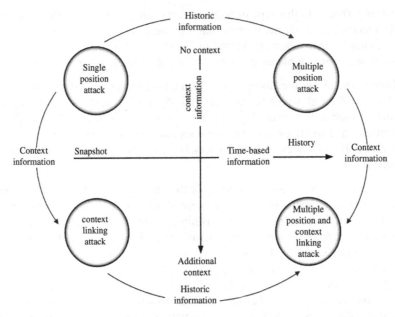

FIGURE 9.7

Attacker knowledge classification.

As shown in Fig. 9.8, location privacy attacks can be classified as single position attack, context linking attack, multiple position and context linking attacks, multiple position attack, and compromised TTP (Trusted Third Party).

- *Single position attack*: In this attack type, the attacker infers private information about the user through analysis of a user location update or a single query that the user/user device generated. There can be two attack types under this category: *location homogeneity attack* and *location distribution attack*.

In *location homogeneity attack*, the user position information gets revealed when the attacker finds that position of k-users (as in k-Anonymity) is almost identical as shown in Fig. 9.9.

The effective area of a user location can be further reduced using maps. As shown in Fig. 9.10, the attacker can identify that users L_1-L_4 are near Interstate 90 on the way to the airport.

If the users are distributed over a larger area then the position information remains protected from this attack type as shown in Fig. 9.11.

A *location distribution attack* can occur if users are found to be distributed nonhomogenously in an obfuscation area (such as in obfuscation area that tries to cover a user with sensitive information located in a lightly populated area and

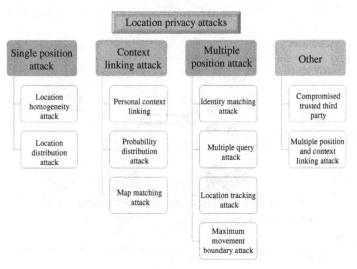

FIGURE 9.8

Location privacy attacks classification.

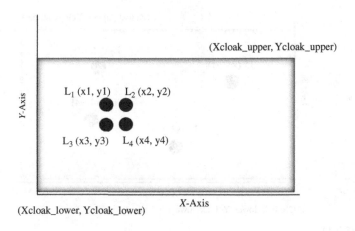

FIGURE 9.9

Location homogeneity (almost identical locations).

away from other nonsensitive users in a densely populated area). As in Fig. 9.12, user L_5 is a sensitive user in lightly populated area, while $L_1 - L_4$ are nonsensitive users in a densely populated area. In this case the attacker can infer that the obfuscated area is extended to cover both the lightly populated and densely populated area to cover sensitive user L_5 because if L_4 was the sensitive user, then the cluster area would be different.

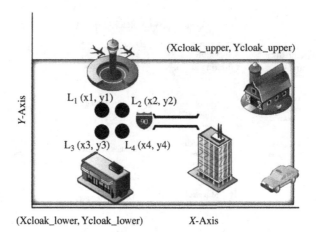

FIGURE 9.10

Location homogeneity with map information.

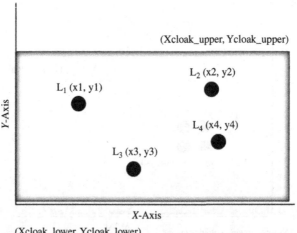

FIGURE 9.11

Location homogeneity example (with distributed location).

- *Context linking attack*: In this attack type, the attacker has context information in addition to spatiotemporal information. Under this category there are two attack types: personal context linking attack and probability distribution attack. The *personal context linking attack* is based on personal context information such as user interests or preferences that an attacker can obtain. For example, an attacker can reduce the obfuscation area to locations of

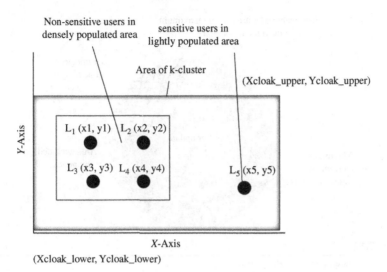

FIGURE 9.12

Location distribution attack.

clinics (within the obfuscation area) to obtain the position information of the user who visits the clinic at a specific time. A *probability distribution attack* uses environmental context information to calculate the probability distribution of the user over an obfuscation area and if the distribution is nonuniform then the attacker has a high probability of identifying the user location areas. The map matching mechanism can be used to restrict the obfuscation area to only certain areas by removing irrelevant areas. In a personal context linking attack, the attacker can use map matching to reduce the obfuscation area to the location of clinic(s).

- *Multiple position attack*: In this attack type the attacker infers user information through correlation of multiple position updates and queries. Identity matching, multiple-query attack, and maximum movement boundary attack are some of the multiple position attack types.

In an *identity matching attack* several user aliases (as mentioned in "Mechanisms to preserve location privacy" section) can be linked to the same identity by linking user attributes, thus breaking the privacy provided by the user aliases. Under a multiple-query attack, there could be a shrink region attack or region interaction attack.

In a *shrink region attack*, the consecutive queries or updates are monitored for change in user members of *k*-anonymity set (refer to "*k*-Anonymity" section) and if the change in user members is such that a common user can be identified among user groups for consecutive queries or updates (other users being different between updates at different instances), then the privacy of that common user can be exposed (refer to historical-*k*-anonymity in "Extensions of *k*-anonymity" section).

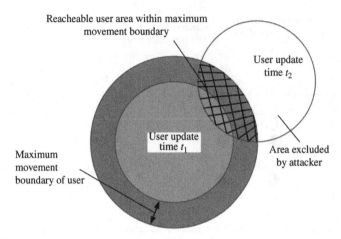

FIGURE 9.13

Maximum movement boundary attack.

In a *region interaction attack*, various user position updates or user queries are used to calculate their intersection from which the attacker can infer privacy sensitive areas of the user or even user location.

In a *maximum movement boundary*, as the name indicates, the attacker calculates where the user could have moved between two successive user positions or queries. Based on this calculation, the attacker can narrow down the region/area that the user can move into and ignore the remaining area of position updates/query. As shown in Fig. 9.13, the user can move only in the shaded area (as bounded by the maximum movement boundary) between the two successive user location updates at time instance T_1 and T_2. The attacker then can ignore rest of the area under time T_2 and narrow down the area of user location.

- *Combined multiple position and context linking*: This attack type is combination or sequence of several different attack types such as map matching with region interaction attack to determine the user position/ movement.
- *Compromised trusted third party*: In this case the attacker obtains user information or data stored at some trusted third party (such as location services) by compromising that trusted third party.

The localization systems depend on communication and information exchange between sensors/sensor nodes and other ecosystem components. Some of the communication privacy attack types that can occur on localization systems are [14]:

- Altering Sensor Data: When a sensor or sensor node is attacked or compromised, the location sensing algorithms can get disrupted or the compromised nodes can alter the location data, causing it to report an erroneous location or causing it to report to unauthorized users.

- Impersonation Attack: Various landmarks are present in many distributed localization systems. In an impersonation attack, the malicious sensor nodes can pretend to be these landmarks and propagate incorrect location information causing those sensors/sensor nodes to localize to wrong locations.
- Modification Attack: If there are multiple sensors involved to provide location and context information (as in a sensor network), then the data exchanged between the sensors can be modified or falsified, which can further result in a spoofing attack where the sensor gets compromised and it impersonates an authorized device or user to steal data or bypass privacy access controls.
- Sinkhole Attack: In this type of attack the sensor/sensor node will attract all traffic to itself by advertising a fake routing update.

PRESERVING LOCATION PRIVACY

To protect a user's location context, the privacy preserving mechanism [15] needs to alter the information that can be accessed, observed, or obtained by an attacker and reduce the amount of information leakage while allowing the user to experience the benefits of LBSs.

Users, applications, and the privacy tools play an important role in preserving the location privacy.

Users and applications are influenced by privacy policies in terms of the amount of information that they can share with mobile ecosystem agents (such as other users, external applications, servers, and so on).

Challenges of preserving location privacy [12]

Here are some of the challenges to preserving location privacy:

1. Privacy threats increase with the increase in data precision and hence a trade-off is needed between QoS from LBSs and location privacy protection.
2. Location updates are frequent and hence privacy threats in location cloaking for continuous location updates should be evaluated and mitigated. The service response time and cloaking time becomes an important consideration because the LBSs are required to meet them for minimal QoS.
3. Privacy requirements are personalized to the users and can vary for that user depending on the location and time of the user. Hence, a varying degree of privacy requirements needs to be handled.
4. If a location is cloaked, the LBSs do not have access to accurate location information. Thus it becomes challenging for LBSs to provide efficient, accurate, and anonymous services based on knowledge of cloaked special regions (instead of accurate location information).

Architecture of privacy tools

There are three main architectures of these privacy protection tools:

1. Distributed: These policy tools can be implemented on user mobile devices such that the policy tools control type, amount, and time of location context that can be shared, visible or observed by external agents/users.
2. Centralized: In centralized policy tools, a trusted server preserves privacy by modifying a user's context information before it can be shared, visible or observed by external agents/users.
3. Hybrid: Such policy tools are a mix of both distributed and centralized architecture.

Mechanisms to preserve location privacy

Fig. 9.14 shows some of the main components of mechanisms that can be used to preserve location privacy.

Users: Users are the members of mobile network with a real identity and aliases. The real identity of the user could be a subset of user's attributes such as name, identity number, and so on, which can uniquely identify a user from all other users. The real identity is unique for each user and will not change over time. If I is set of real identities of all the users then the real identity of a particular user can be represented by a one-to-one correspondence between a set of users and set of identities as $U \rightarrow I$. Each of the users will also have aliases that temporarily identify the user for the purpose of identifying and authenticating that user in a communication without disclosing the user's true identity. These aliases can expire or be rescinded from the system/communication and the real user cannot be identified from the aliases. Examples of aliases would be IP address, application signatures, MAC addresses, and so on.

Event: An event is a function of user identity or alias, the time stamp of the event, and location stamp of the user (location where the user event occurred).

Event = function (id, time stamp, location stamp)

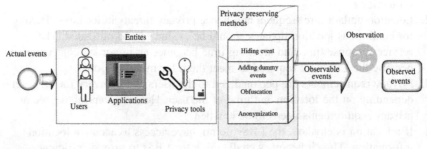

FIGURE 9.14

Location privacy preserving mechanisms.

An event is called the actual event of a particular user if id = user id, time stamp = Time T and location stamp = location L. Actual events thus represent the actual location/state of the users over time. The actual route of a user is the trace of all of that user's actual events.

Applications: A mobile device user can employ various applications that can be categorized into (1) manual or automatic (based on how the location context is communicated to authorized users/ecosystem agents) and (2) continuous or discrete (based on the how the user location context information is sent over time by the application). For example, an application using maps can be automatic and continuous, while online shopping application can be manual and discrete.

Methods: These are the basic functions of any location privacy preserving mechanisms that perform transformation of a hidden or unobservable event into set of observable events. There are four different such transformation functions discussed briefly here that can be deployed on the events. Hiding events (modify event set), adding dummy events (modify event set), obfuscation (modify time stamps and location stamps), and anonymization (modifies event identity). Event refers to the spatiotemporal state of the user in the real-world and in the eyes of an observer.

- *Hiding Events*: This is the basic function of user location privacy protection where the information of user's route is hidden by removing a subset of events in the transformation process, thereby making these removed events unobservable at the output of privacy mechanism. Mobile devices or service providers would become silent during certain time periods to implement a "hiding event" mechanism.

For example [16], in Fig. 9.15, two users U1 and U2 enter the silent period at the same time and while in this region their aliases are updated (A → Y and B → X). The anonymity of the users is now protected because an attacker cannot accurately link the new pseudonyms to the original users. The attacker cannot determine accurately if PATH1 corresponds to A or PATH2.

- *Adding Dummy Events:* In this mechanism the external observer is misled by addition of some dummy events using event injection method of the transformation function. The trace of events generated using this mechanism appears just like any normal user route (Fig. 9.16).
- *Obfuscation:* Using this mechanism the location stamp and/or time stamp of the actual events of the users are altered by adding noise to these time/location stamps, resulting in an inaccurate location or time for the event.
- *Anonymization:* Using this mechanism, the link between the user and user events is broken by changing the identity of the event. To achieve this, the transformation function can replace real identity of the user on each of the events with user's valid aliases. These aliases can be added or rescinded by the user over time, while the user is silent in some predetermined zones called

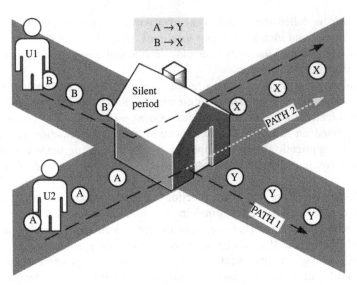

FIGURE 9.15

Hidden events or silent period.

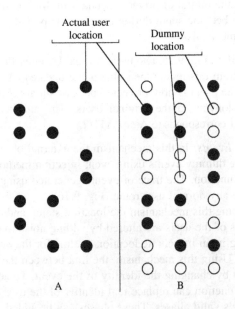

FIGURE 9.16

A = without dummy events/nodes; B = with dummy events/nodes.

mix zones and then changed when the user comes out of the mix zone (thus also using hiding event mechanism). In full anonymization, all of the event's identities are replaced and hence the event is left with no identity.

LOCATION PRIVACY PRESERVING METHODS

A location service providing LBSs requires the user's exact location but this subjects the user's location data to privacy threats. By using various location privacy preserving mechanisms for users of LBSs in mobile environments, the privacy threats can be reduced. This section describes the details of these methods that were briefly described in "Mechanisms to preserve location privacy" section.

k-Anonymity

k-Anonymity [17,18] refers to the concept in which the information about each person in the released or disclosed data is indistinguishable from the information of at least $k - 1$ individuals whose information is also contained in that disclosed data.

Anonymity refers to a state where a subject is not identifiable within a set of subjects, and location anonymity guarantees that any location information cannot be linked to a particular individual/group/institution through inference attacks, by controlling the information flow and by preventing disclosure of unnecessary information, such as individual identity and location.

In the k-anonymity approach, the user-specified parameter k controls the privacy level and has two operations that makes it difficult for the observer/consumer of the released data to identify the user, the sensor, or the device:

- Generalization: This operation hides the critical privacy-related user/sensor/device attributes by replacing it with more generic attributes.
- Suppression: This operation removes or suppresses the critical privacy-related user/sensor/device attributes.

Table 9.1 has eight records and five attributes. By using generalization, the critical attributes are replaced with more general attributes, such as exact age being replaced by a range of 10 years. By using suppression, the critical attributes are removed and replaced with null, such as name and sports. So after using the two operations, the resulting attribute table would look like Table 9.2.

If the process of k-anonymizing can ensure that at least k individuals are undetectable using the generalization and suppression operations, then the privacy of the users in the disclosed data can be ensured at the user-specified privacy level k.

Table 9.2 represents 2-anonymity because there are three attributes (age, gender, and state) such that any combination of them would result in finding at least two records that would have all the attributes same and hence indistinguishable from each other such that the identify of a real user cannot be inferred from it.

Table 9.1 User Attributes

Name	Age	Gender	State	Sports
John	21	Male	California	Tennis
Marry	34	Female	Oregon	Swimming
Mark	24	Male	Florida	Cycling
Smita	44	Female	California	Badminton
Rambha	33	Female	Oregon	Dancing
Julie	56	Female	California	Hiking
Sunil	27	Male	California	Tennis
John	21	Male	Florida	Tennis

Table 9.2 User Attributes After Generalization and Suppression Operations

Name	Age	Gender	State	Sports
Null	$20 < Age \le 30$	Male	California	Null
Null	$30 < Age \le 40$	Female	Oregon	Null
Null	$20 < Age \le 30$	Male	Florida	Null
Null	$40 < Age$	Female	California	Null
Null	$30 < Age \le 40$	Female	Oregon	Null
Null	$40 < Age$	Female	California	Null
Null	$20 < Age \le 30$	Male	California	Null
Null	$20 < Age \le 30$	Male	Florida	Null

The user specify at least following four parameters for protecting the location privacy:

- k: This parameter indicates the anonymity level in the location k-anonymity model. To achieve anonymity, each cloaked region needs to cover at least k different users, with larger values of k meant for higher protection of privacy.
- A_{min}: To ensure that the cloaked region is not too small for highly populated areas, this parameter specifies the minimum area needed for the cloaked region.
- A_{max}: This parameter specifies the maximum area of the cloaked region so as to ensure appropriate QoS (accuracy and size of query result).
- Maximum tolerable cloaking delay: Larger the value of this delay, lower will be the service quality. When the cloaking delay is higher, there is a higher chance that the user will move away from that location at which the query was issued.

The location of a mobile device user can be represented by 3-tuple ([x1, x2], [y1, y2], [t1, t2]). An n-tuple is a sequence (or ordered set) of n-elements. The intervals [x1, x2] and [y1, y2] describes the two-dimensional user location and

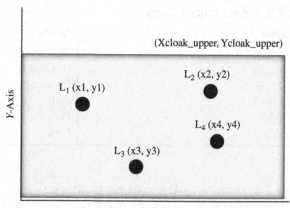

FIGURE 9.17

Location *k*-anonymity.

Table 9.3 Anonymity Region/Location

Users	Actual Location	Cloaked Location
L_1 (x1, y1)	(x1, y1)	([x_{ck_l}, xck_{ck_u}], [y_{ck_l}, y_{ck_u}])
L_1 (x2, y2)	(x2, y2)	([x_{ck_l}, xck_{ck_u}], [y_{ck_l}, y_{ck_u}])
L_1 (x3, y3)	(x3, y3)	([x_{ck_l}, xck_{ck_u}], [y_{ck_l}, y_{ck_u}])
L_1 (x4, y4)	(x4, y4)	([x_{ck_l}, xck_{ck_u}], [y_{ck_l}, y_{ck_u}])

[t1, t2] describes a time period during which the user was present in the area [x1, x2] and [y1, y2]. A user's location tuple is *k*-anonymous, if $(k-1)$ other subjects are also presented in the area and the time period as described by the tuple.

For example, Fig. 9.17 shows location L_1, L_2, L_3, and L_4 mapped to a rectangle, which represents the cloaked region denoted by (X_{CLOAK_LOWER}, X_{CLOAK_UPPER}, Y_{CLOAK_LOWER}, Y_{CLOAK_UPPER}) or in short ([x_{ck_l}, xck_{ck_u}], [y_{ck_l}, y_{ck_u}]). The corresponding table representation is shown in Table 9.3. When the locations are mapped into the cloaked region, the attackers/adversaries cannot determine the exact location of each of the mobile users. In this example there are four users in the cloaked region. These users form the cloaking set.

Extensions of k-anonymity

k-Anonymity prevents the association between the user and the query but does not prevent the association between the users and the sensitive query contents. The privacy provided by *k*-anonymity is not sufficient if all the user queries are to the same location and are grouped together in the same set (anonymized with

Table 9.4 Anonymized Query

Location	Query
[(2, 3);(5,7)]	Park
[(4, 6);(5,8)]	Bus station
[(3, 7);(5,9)]	Restaurant
[(2, 3);(5,7)]	Park
[(2, 3);(5,7)]	Park
[(2, 3);(5,7)]	Park

Table 9.5 Location for Users Visible to Attacker

Location	User ID
[(2, 3)]	U_1
[(5,8)]	U_2
[(3, 7)]	U_3
[(5,7)]	U_4
[(3, 5)]	U_5
[(4,10)]	U_6

each other). For example, if group of friends plan for a movie, then they could issue a location query referring to a particular movie theater. These queries being in same location proximity, it is likely that they are anonymized together. In such a case, even though a specific query cannot be linked to a specific user, an attacker can still know that all those users were looking for a particular movie theater.

Additionally, the sensitive location information is present in the query even if the queries are not to the same location. Hence k-anonymity protects location privacy to some extent but does not protect query privacy. This drawback can be serious for sensitive queries (such as a particular restaurant and hospital) versus common queries (such as traffic and weather).

It is possible that an attacker could obtain the information regarding the queries, locations, and users as indicated in Tables 9.4 and 9.5 and try to infer a relation between them.

Assume there are six users U_1–U_6. The anonymized table appears as in Table 9.4 where the location column represents the cloaked region. Table 9.5 represents the user IDs and their respective locations.

There are four queries to park in Table 9.4 and from Table 9.5 the attacker can infer that user U_1 could have made one of the four queries (with [(2,3)] in location column). The attacker cannot conclude which exact query was made by U_1 but since all those queries were to park, the attacker can conclude U_1 must have queried for the "park," thus violating location privacy of user U_1 and obtaining sensitive information about that user. Such an attack is referred to as a query homogeneity attack.

There are many extensions [13] to k-anonymity such as strong k-anonymity, l-diversity, t-closeness, p-sensitivity, and historical-k-anonymity.

In strong k-anonymity, the calculated cluster of k-users remains the same over several queries, essentially preventing attacks that works on several k-clusters of different queries from identifying the user.

In l-diversity, location of the user cannot be uniquely differentiated from a set of l different physical locations (such as restaurants, hospitals, parks, and so on). And the users in the k-cluster have locations that are distant from each other. If all the user positions are related to same location then the attacker can infer user's targeted location (may be with low accuracy).

In t-closeness, the distance between an attribute's distribution within k-users and the same distribution over all users should not be smaller than parameter t.

In p-sensitivity, within k-users each group of the confidential attributes has at least p distinct values for each of the confidential attribute within the same group. For example, in Table 9.4, too many members from the k-cluster have location as park, thus enabling an attacker to know that a particular user was querying for the park.

Some LBSs requires the mobile device to have continuous communication [19] of location to receive services. k-Anonymity may not be enough since the device/user maintains continuous session with the LBSs and successive cloaking regions can be correlated to associate a session back to the user/device. User/device trajectory can be revealed through such session association and hence any sensitive user/device information. Such session association can be prevented if there are k common objects/users in every cloaking region in a session.

Fig. 9.17 shows cloaking regions for mobile device L_1 along with other such devices. Device L_1 is not uniquely distinguishable from the other device in the anonymity set. The cloaking region is represented by a minimum bounding rectangle (just as in Table 9.3) that covers all devices in anonymity set. This cloaking region ensures that there is an acceptable level of balance between anonymity and the service quality. However, maintaining this balance in continuous LBSs is difficult.

Fig. 9.18 shows a minimum bounding rectangle at different times for device L_1 with three devices in the anonymity set. The different time instances T_1, T_2, and T_3 correspond to different exclusive location updates in case of continuous LBSs for the devices. In a continuous LBS, the same identifier is associated with all the minimum bounding rectangles. In such a scenario, the knowledge of location of the three devices at time instance T_1, T_2, and T_3 is sufficient for adversaries to infer that device L_1 is the only common device between the anonymity sets made by the three shown cloaking regions (indicated by *dotted boundaries*). Even if adversaries have location information only for two of the three instances, it will seriously compromise the privacy of devices in the anonymity set. Historical

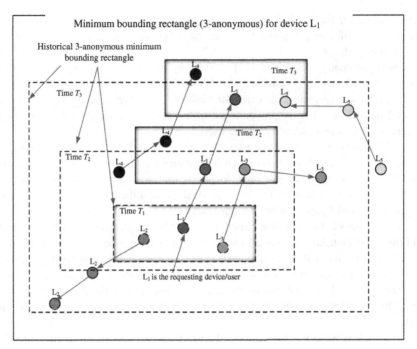

FIGURE 9.18

Conventional and historical *k*-anonymity.

k-anonymity resolves these risks by ensuring that the cloaking region changes over time in such a manner that all anonymity sets during a service session contain at least *k* common devices and hence devices have historical *k*-anonymity.

Obfuscation

There are various obfuscation techniques [20] that can be used to protect the location privacy of the users by altering, substituting, or generalizing locations and purposefully reducing the accuracy of user's position/location information. Some of the techniques used to achieve obfuscation are use of pseudonyms or aliases, spatial cloaking, invisible cloaking, adding noise, and so on.

Some of the obfuscation [21] techniques are described here. Following are some of the working assumptions:

- A location measurement of user U is a circular area with its center at (x_c, y_c) and a radius of r. The real position of the user U is represented by (x_u, y_u) and the mobile device sensors guarantee that the user's real position falls within that area (the probability of a user being in the circular area is one, which means the user is within that circular area).

- The probability of real user position to be in the neighborhood of a random point in the circular region is uniform over the entire location measurement area. A joint probability density function of the real user position (x_u, y_u) to be in the neighborhood of a random point (x, y) can be defined as

$$Pdf_r(x, y) = \left[\frac{1}{\pi r^2}\right] if \ (x, y) \ falls \ within \ circular \ area \ with \ radius \ r \ and \ center \ (x_c, y_c)$$

$$Pdf_r(x, y) = 0 \ if \ (x, y) \ falls \ outside \ the \ circular \ area \ with \ radius \ r \ and \ center \ (x_c, y_c)$$

- The accuracy of location measurement depends on the device sensors, and location privacy reduces with increase in accuracy of user's location.
- $r_{measured}$ is the radius of the location measurement area measured by the sensors and $r_{optimal}$ is the radius of the area that would be produced with best accuracy of sensors.
- The user can specify a minimum distance, which states that the user does not want location accuracy to be better than this minimum distance. This means that the location measurement circular area has a radius equal to this minimum distance. This is represented as $r_{minimum}$.
- Relative privacy preference is given by

$$\lambda = \frac{\max\left(r_{measured}, r_{minimum}\right)^2 - r_{measured}^2}{r_{measured}^2}$$

$$\lambda = \frac{\max\left(r_{measured}, r_{minimum}\right)^2}{r_{measured}^2} - 1$$

The term $\max(r_{measured}, r_{minimum})$ gives the maximum of either the $r_{measured}$ or the $r_{minimum}$.

If $r_{minimum}$ (the minimum distance) is lesser than the $r_{measured}$, then the privacy preference of the user is already satisfied by $r_{measured}$ and hence $\lambda = 0$. In such case there is no transformation required to the original measurement.

If $r_{minimum}$ (the minimum distance) is greater than the $r_{measured}$, then the privacy preference of the user is not satisfied by $r_{measured}$ and hence $\lambda > 0$. In such a case transformation is required to the original measurement depending on the value of λ, which refers to required percentage accuracy degradation.

The obfuscation techniques are used to produce an obfuscation area that degrades the original accuracy depending on the value of λ.

- The term relevance refers to the accuracy of the obfuscated area. A relevance $R = 1$ means the location has best accuracy while $R \rightarrow 0$ means the location information is not accurate enough for the location-based application to provide services. Any number in between refers to varying degrees of accuracy. The location privacy as provided by the obfuscated location $= 1 - R$.

R_{initial} refers to the accuracy of user location measurement as provided initially by the device sensors.

R_{final} refers to the accuracy of obfuscated area that is obtained depending on the value of relative privacy preference λ.

$$R_{\text{initial}} = \frac{r_{\text{optimal}}^2}{r_{\text{measured}}^2}$$

$$\lambda + 1 = \frac{\max\left(r_{\text{measured}}, r_{\text{minimum}}\right)^2}{r_{\text{measured}}^2} = \frac{r_{\text{minimum}}^2}{r_{\text{measured}}^2} \quad \text{where } r_{\text{minimum}} \text{ is greater than } r_{\text{measured}}$$

$$\lambda + 1 = \frac{\frac{r_{\text{minimum}}^2}{r_{\text{optimal}}^2}}{\frac{r_{\text{measured}}^2}{r_{\text{optimal}}^2}} = \frac{\frac{r_{\text{minimum}}^2}{r_{\text{optimal}}^2}}{\frac{1}{R_{\text{initial}}}} = \frac{\frac{1}{R_{\text{final}}}}{\frac{1}{R_{\text{initial}}}} = \frac{R_{\text{initial}}}{R_{\text{final}}}$$

$$R_{\text{final}} = \frac{R_{\text{initial}}}{\lambda + 1}$$

$$R_{\text{final}} = \frac{r_{\text{optimal}}^2}{r_{\text{minimum}}^2} \quad \text{where } r_{\text{minimum}} \text{ is greater than } r_{\text{measured}}$$

Obfuscation by enlarging radius

A location measurement area can be obfuscated by increasing the radius of the area because it reduces the joint probability density function (Fig. 9.19).

If original radius of circular location measurement area is r then

$$\text{Joint probability density function } Pdf_r(x, y) = \left[\frac{1}{\pi r^2}\right]$$

If the increased radius of circular location measurement area is $r_{\text{obfuscated}}$ then

$$\text{Joint probability density function } Pdf_{r-\text{obfuscated}}(x, y) = \left[\frac{1}{\pi r_{\text{obfuscated}}^2}\right]$$

$$\frac{R_{\text{final}}}{R_{\text{initial}}} = \frac{Pdf_{r-\text{obfuscated}}(x, y)}{Pdf_r(x, y)} = \left[\frac{r^2}{r_{\text{obfuscated}}^2}\right] \quad \text{where } r < r_{\text{obfuscated}}$$

$$\frac{R_{\text{final}}}{R_{\text{initial}}} = \left[\frac{r^2}{r_{\text{obfuscated}}^2}\right] = \frac{1}{\lambda + 1}$$

$$r_{\text{obfuscated}} = r \sqrt{\lambda + 1}$$

For example,
The user privacy preference $r_{\text{minimum}} = 1$ mile,
The location measurement area of the user $r_{\text{measured}} = 0.5$ mile,
The optimal measurement accuracy $r_{\text{optimal}} = 0.4$ mile

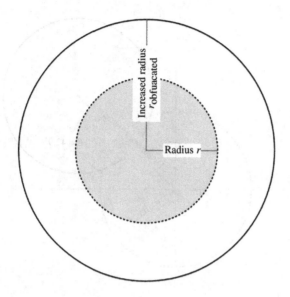

FIGURE 9.19

Obfuscation by enlarging radius.

Then

$$\lambda + 1 = \frac{\max\left(r_{\text{measured}}, r_{\text{minimum}}\right)^2}{r_{\text{measured}}^2} = \frac{1^2}{0.5^2} = \frac{1}{0.25} = 4$$

$$\lambda = 4 - 1 = 3$$

$$R_{\text{initial}} = \frac{r_{\text{optimal}}^2}{r_{\text{measured}}^2} = \frac{0.4^2}{0.5^2} = 0.64$$

$$R_{\text{final}} = \frac{r_{\text{optimal}}^2}{r_{\text{minimum}}^2} = \frac{0.4^2}{1^2} = 0.16$$

The obfuscated area with radius $r_{\text{obfuscated}} = r\sqrt{\lambda + 1} = 0.5\sqrt{4} = 0.5 \times 2 = 1$ mile

Obfuscation by shifting center

A location measurement area can be obfuscated by shifting the center [22] (Fig. 9.20) of the measurement area and then the new area calculated using the distance between the new and old center of the location area. There are two probabilities that are used in the calculations:

- Probability $P_{\text{user-intersection}}$ that the user position belongs to the intersection area $\text{Area}_{\text{intersection}}$ (between the Initial and final area).
- Probability $P_{\text{random-intersection}}$ that a random point selected from the whole obfuscated area belongs to the intersection (between Initial and final area).

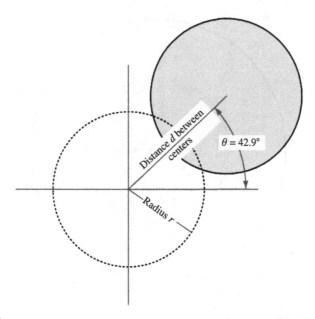

FIGURE 9.20

Obfuscation by shifting center.

The obfuscated $\text{Area}_{\text{obfuscated}}$ is with radius r but center shifted from

$x_c \rightarrow x_c + \Delta x$ and
$y_c \rightarrow y_c + \Delta y$

$$R_{\text{final}} = P_{\text{user-intersection}} \times P_{\text{random-intersection}} = \frac{\text{Area}_{\text{intersection}}}{\text{Area}_{\text{initial}}} \times \frac{\text{Area}_{\text{intersection}}}{\text{Area}_{\text{obfuscated}}}$$

$$= \frac{\text{Area}_{\text{intersection}}^2}{\text{Area}_{\text{initial}}^2} \times R_{\text{initial}}$$

$$\text{Also} \quad \frac{R_{\text{final}}}{R_{\text{initial}}} = \frac{1}{\lambda + 1}$$

$$\text{Hence} \quad \frac{R_{\text{final}}}{R_{\text{initial}}} = \frac{1}{\lambda + 1} = \frac{\text{Area}_{\text{intersection}}^2}{\text{Area}_{\text{initial}}^2} = \frac{\text{Area}_{\text{intersection}}^2}{\pi r^2}$$

$$\text{Area}_{\text{intersection}}^2 = \frac{\pi r^2}{\lambda + 1}$$

The distance between the two centers $= d$ and the circular area has radius $= r$. The angle θ can be selected randomly to generate obfuscated area.

If $d = 0$ then there is no privacy gain (as there is no center shift).
If $d = 2r$ then there is maximum privacy gain.
If $0 < d < 2r$ then there is a nonzero increase in the privacy.

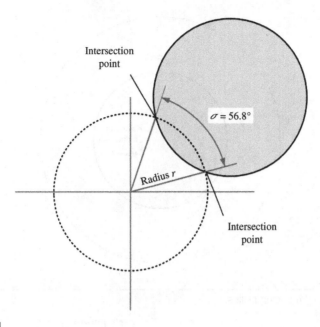

$\sigma = 56.8°$

FIGURE 9.21

Circular sector formed by two radii.

Variable σ is the central angle of the circular sector identified by the two radii connecting the center of the original area with the intersection points of the original and the obfuscated area (Fig. 9.21).

The derivation of the additional equations is beyond the scope of this chapter; however, the equation to calculate d is listed here:

$$d = 2r\cos\frac{\sigma}{2}$$

$$\sigma - \sin\sigma = \sqrt{\delta\pi}$$

$$\text{where} \quad \delta = \frac{\text{Area}_{\text{intersection}}}{\text{Area}_{\text{initial}}} x \frac{\text{Area}_{\text{intersection}}}{\text{Area}_{\text{obfuscated}}}$$

$$\text{Area}_{\text{obfuscated}} = \text{Area}(r, x + d\sin\theta, y + d\cos\theta)$$

Obfuscation by reducing radius

A location measurement area can be obfuscated by decreasing the radius of the area, because it reduces the probability to find the real user location within the returned area while the joint probability density function is fixed (Fig. 9.22).

If the real position of the user U is represented by (x_u, y_u), then the probability of user being in the circular area with radius r is 1, which means the user is

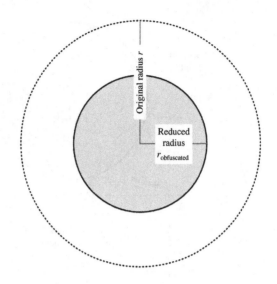

FIGURE 9.22

Obfuscation by reducing radius.

$$P(x_u, y_u) \in \text{Area}(r_{\text{obfuscated}}, x, y) = \int_0^{2\pi} \int_0^{r_{\text{obfuscated}}} \frac{1}{\pi r^2} \, s \, ds$$

$$= 2\pi \int_0^{r_{\text{obfuscated}}} \frac{s}{\pi r^2} \, ds = \frac{2}{r^2} \int_0^{r_{\text{obfuscated}}} s \, ds = \frac{r_{\text{obfuscated}}^2}{r^2}$$

within that circular area. Now if the radius of circular area is reduced then the probability of finding the user in the obfuscated area (reduced radius area) is less than 1.

The probability of having a user inside the location measurement area Area(r, x, y) is equal to 1:

$$P(x_u, y_u) \in \text{Area}(r, x, y) = 1$$

$$\frac{R_{\text{final}}}{R_{\text{initial}}} = \frac{P(x_u, y_u) \in \text{Area}(r_{\text{obfuscated}}, x, y)}{P(x_u, y_u) \in \text{Area}(r, x, y)} = \left[\frac{r_{\text{obfuscated}}^2}{r^2} \right] \quad \text{where } r > r_{\text{obfuscated}}$$

$$\frac{R_{\text{final}}}{R_{\text{initial}}} = \left[\frac{r_{\text{obfuscated}}^2}{r^2} \right] = \frac{1}{\lambda + 1}$$

$$r_{\text{obfuscated}} = \frac{r}{\sqrt{\lambda + 1}}$$

For example,
The user privacy preference $r_{\text{minimum}} = 1$ mile,
The location measurement area of the user $r_{\text{measured}} = 0.5$ mile,
The optimal measurement accuracy $r_{\text{optimal}} = 0.4$ mile

Then

$$\lambda + 1 = \frac{\max\left(r_{\text{measured}}, r_{\text{minimum}}\right)^2}{r_{\text{measured}}^2} = \frac{1^2}{0.5^2} = \frac{1}{0.25} = 4$$

$$\lambda = 4 - 1 = 3$$

$$R_{\text{initial}} = \frac{r_{\text{optimal}}^2}{r_{\text{measured}}^2} = \frac{0.4^2}{0.5^2} = 0.64$$

$$R_{\text{final}} = \frac{r_{\text{optimal}}^2}{r_{\text{minimum}}^2} = \frac{0.4^2}{1^2} = 0.16$$

The obfuscated area with radius $r_{\text{obfuscated}} = \dfrac{r}{\sqrt{\lambda + 1}} = \dfrac{0.5}{\sqrt{4}} = \dfrac{0.5}{2} = 0.5$ mile

Cloaking

Cloaking is used to reduce spatiotemporal resolution of the user location wherein an actual and precise user location is replaced with a cloaked region so as to prevent the attacker from getting information on the user's exact location (Fig. 9.23).

The cloaked region is a closed shape with predefined probability distribution of the user in the region, generally, in the shape of rectangle or circle with uniform probability distribution of the user in the region. Larger cloaked regions offer greater privacy but with reduced QoS.

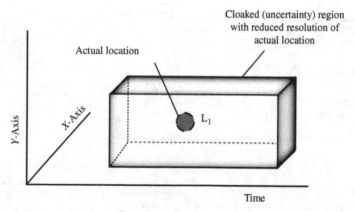

FIGURE 9.23

Cloaked region.

Cloaking architecture example

Fig. 9.24 shows an example of cloaking architecture [23] with the following components:

- Privacy model selector: The users are aware of their respective locations and provide information to this block about their privacy preference, such as that the users specify that they do not want location accuracy to be better than a certain minimum distance.
- Location cloaking block: This block has inputs about the user's sensitive areas/information, any prior available user background information, and the size of cloaking area that fulfils location accuracy requirements. This block generates the cloaking area.
- Message builder: This block replaces the user location with a cloaked region for the user and sends that information to a LBS server or servers.
- LBS server: This server processes the queries and provides back results (with probability indicating the confidence level on results/component of results). The server also evaluates QoS. Cloaking area impacts QoSs: the larger the cloaking area, the lower the QoS. If QoS does not meet user requirements, then the user can reduce the cloaking area (privacy level) and query the server again.
- Results interpreter: This block processes the result provided by the LBS server in a format that can be understood by the result.
- Fig. 9.25 shows possible modes of attack on a cloaking area. An attacker can attempt to infer a user's sensitive location information by linking a cloaking area with available user background information or can attempt to decipher user's cloaking preference through various observations.

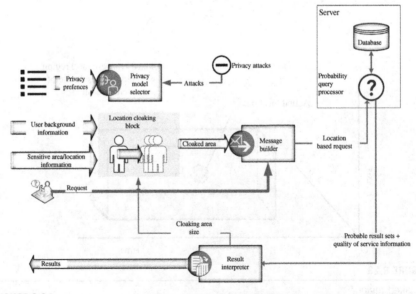

FIGURE 9.24

Example cloaking architecture.

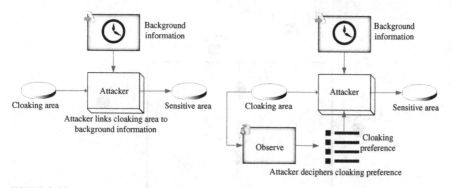

FIGURE 9.25

Possible attack modes on cloaking area.

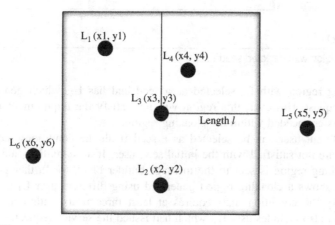

FIGURE 9.26

Simple example of cloaking region generation.

Cloaking region generation basics

Fig. 9.26 shows a simple explanation of the process of generating a cloaked region around the user who has issued a request to LBS applications. Assume that there are six users: L_1, L_2, L_3, L_4 L_5, and L_6. User L_3 has issued a service request.

A rectangular area around user L_3 is considered and a range query is generated to find out other users within that rectangle. Consider that there are three other users within the range l. From these three users, one user say L_2 is selected as a seed and rectangle is constructed around it with length of side equal to l. This could be a possible cloaking region candidate such that user L_3 lies within the cloaking region. For k-anonymity, it is important to ensure that the cloaking region has at least k-users with predetermined probability value. Fig. 9.27 shows

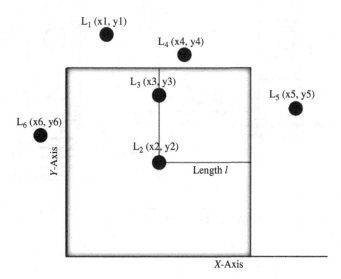

FIGURE 9.27

Cloaking region with selected seed user.

a cloaking region with L_2 selected as a seed and has L_3, which generated the service request. However, this region will not satisfy the requirement if at least three users are needed within the cloaking region.

A different user can be selected as a seed if all the conditions required for cloaking are not satisfied with the initial seed user. If all conditions are satisfied, then cloaking region is sent to the message builder block for further processing. Fig. 9.28 shows a cloaking region generated using different user L_1 as seed and can satisfy the condition that requires at least three users within the cloaking region and also includes user L_3, which had issued the service request.

Sample cloaking mechanisms

There are various cloaking mechanisms and their variations. Some the basic cloaking mechanisms [24] such as interval cloak, Casper cloak, and Hilbert cloak are briefly described here.

In the interval cloak technique, the anonymizer indexes the users with a quad-tree, which is a tree data structure used to partition two-dimensional space by repeatedly subdividing into four quadrants/regions. Interval cloak will use the quad-tree up to the topmost user/node to include at least k-users (including the user making the service request, say user L_1) to form an anonymizing spatial region (ASR) for the user L_1.

For example, in Fig. 9.29, if user L_1 issues a query with $k = 4$, the interval cloak will search till quadrant [(x0, y0), (x1, y1)] but since quadrant [(x0, y0), (x1, y1)] contains less than 4 users, it will backtrack for one level and return the parent quadrant [(x0, y0), (x2, y2)] as the ASR, which has 12 users. Since the

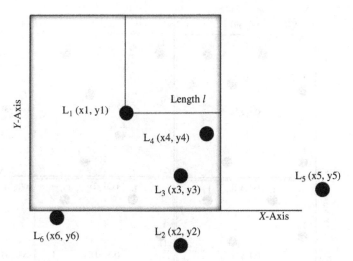

FIGURE 9.28

Cloaking region with three users.

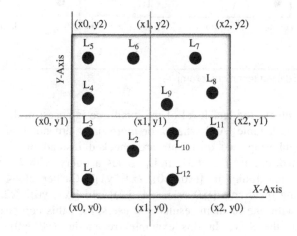

FIGURE 9.29

Interval cloak cloaking technique.

returned quadrant contains more than k-users, this technique can burden the LBS servers during query processing.

For the example in Fig. 9.30, if user L_1 issues a query with $k = 4$, the interval cloak will search till quadrant $[(x0, y0), (x1, y1)]$ but since quadrant $[(x0, y0), (x1, y1)]$ contains less than four users, it will backtrack for one level, and return the parent quadrant $[(x0, y0), (x2, y2)]$ as the ASR, which has six users. Since the returned quadrant contains more than k-users, this technique can burden the LBS servers during query processing.

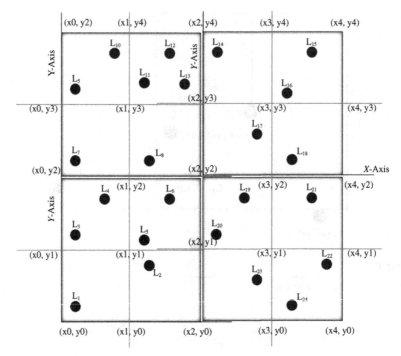

FIGURE 9.30

Interval cloak cloaking technique example.

In Casper cloak, the leaf level of the quad-tree is accessed directly through the use of a hash table. And when k or more users are not found in a quadrant, the neighboring two quadrants are checked instead of backtracking to the parent quadrant. In Fig. 9.31, if L_1 issues a query with $k = 4$, and when enough users not found in [(x0, y0), (x1, y1)], Casper cloak first checks the neighboring quadrants [(x0, y1), (x1, y2)] and [(x1, y0), (x2, y1)]. If the combination with one of them results in k-users, then this composite rectangle is returned as the ASR. In this example, rectangle [(x0, y0), (x1, y2)] is returned as the ASR.

In Hilbert cloak, the users are sorted according to the Hilbert space-filling curve. The sorted sequence is equally divided into buckets of k-consecutive users. An anonymizing set is formed by the bucket that contains the querying user L_1. The reported ASR is computed as the minimum bounding rectangle of the anonymizing set.

If L_1 issues a query with $k = 3$, then four Hilbert buckets can be created as shown in Fig. 9.32.

Bucket 1: L_1, L_2, L_5, L_6, L_4, and L_3
Bucket 2: L_7, L_9, L_{10}, L_{11}, L_{12}, and L_8

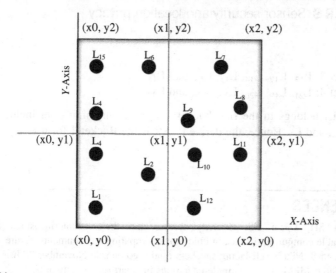

FIGURE 9.31

Casper cloak cloaking technique.

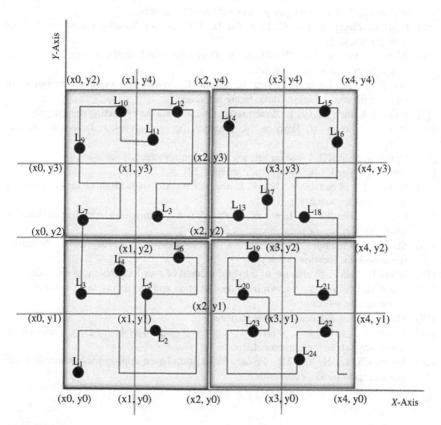

FIGURE 9.32

Hilbert cloak example.

Bucket 3: L_{13}, L_{17}, L_{14}, L_{15}, L_{16}, and L_{18}
Bucket 4: L_{21}, L_{19}, L_{20}, L_{23}, L_{24}, and L_{22}

User L_1 belongs to the first bucket, and its anonymizing set includes L_1, L_2, L_5, L_6, L_4, and L_3. Hence, the derived ASR is the Bucket 1 for user L_1.

REFERENCES

[1] Kim SH, Leem CS. Security threats and their countermeasures of mobile portable computing devices in ubiquitous computing environments, figure.
[2] Vincent J. Nike's self-lacing sneakers finally go on sale November 28th.
[3] Firdhous MFM. Security implementations in smart sensor networks.
[4] Al-Haiqi A, Ismail M, Nordin R. On the best sensor for keystrokes inference attack on Android.
[5] Mäntyjärvi J, Lindholm M, Vildjiounaite E, Mäkelä S-M, Ailisto H. Identifying users of portable devices from gait pattern with accelerometers.
[6] Li(B) B, Zhang Y, Lyu C, Li J, Gu D. SSG: Sensor Security Guard for Android smartphones, p. 223.
[7] Wang Q, Ren K, Lou W, Zhang Y. Dependable and secure sensor data storage with dynamic integrity assurance.
[8] Izu T, Ito K, Tsuda H, Abiru K, Ogura T. Privacy-protection technologies for secure utilization of sensor data, figure reference.
[9] Juma H, Kamel I, Kaya L. Watermarking sensor data for protecting the integrity.
[10] Henne B, Smith M, Harbach M. Location privacy revisited: factors of privacy decisions.
[11] Fawaz K, Shin KG. Location privacy protection for smartphone users.
[12] Meng X, Chen J. Location privacy [chapter 12], p. 173.
[13] Wernke M, Skvortsov P, Dürr F, Rothermel K. A classification of location privacy attacks and approaches. p. 13−17.
[14] Lee Y-H, Phadke V, Lee JW, Deshmukh A. Secure localization and location verification in sensor networks.
[15] Shokri R, Freudiger J, Hubaux J-P. EPFL-report-148708 July 2010, A unified framework for location privacy.
[16] Miura K, Sato F. Evaluation of a hybrid method of user location anonymization.
[17] Mano M, Ishikawa Y. Anonymizing user location and profile information for privacy-aware mobile services.
[18] Meng X, Chen J. Location privacy, p. 180.
[19] Dewri R, Ray I, Ray I, Whitley D. On the formation of historically k-anonymous anonymity sets in a continuous LBS.
[20] Jensen CS, Lu H, Yiu ML. Privacy in location-based applications: research issues and emerging trends, p. 38−40.

[21] Ardagna CA, Cremonini M, Damiani E, De Capitani di Vimercati S, Samarati P. Location privacy protection through obfuscation-based techniques.

[22] Yang LT. Mobile intelligence, p. 455.

[23] Yang L, Wei L, Shi H, Liu Q, Yang D. Location cloaking algorithms based on regional characteristics.

[24] Tan KW, Lin Y, Mouratidis K. Spatial cloaking revisited: distinguishing information leakage from anonymity.

Usability

10

INFORMATION IN THIS CHAPTER:

- Importance of Sensors in Mobile Computing
- Sensing Factors
- Human–Computer Interactions
- Customer Usages

NEED OF SENSORS IN MOBILE COMPUTING

Sensors are becoming key for mobile computing. Operating systems like Windows and Android have hardware requirements related to sensors to be met for any logo/certifications. An increasing number of sensors and applications are transforming mobile computing and use cases. Sensors are also used to increase efficiency and power response of the platforms. And of course sensors are used to mimic human responses of mobile computing devices. Fig. 10.1 shows some areas where sensors are becoming increasingly important.

Sensors with an ideal combination of functionality, versatility/performance, and ease of implementation can help achieve a user interface that is intuitive, dependable, and versatile [1]:

1. Intuitive: The user interface is considered intuitive when it respond to
   a. Predictable physical motion: For example, a swiping motion that is normally used to turn the page should be recognized by the user interface when reading an e-book.
   b. Operate in controlled field of view: The field of view and working distance together gives a fixed space within which the user interface controls are effective. Any action outside this fixed space is ignored by the sensor. Due to this fixed working space, all false triggers can be eliminated and the user can interact effectively and intuitively with the user interface of the device.
2. Versatility: When the sensor provides direction sense to the user motion, it enhances the user interface beyond the normal capability. For example, 2-mode direction (left-right or up-down) can be used for page turning or

Mobile Sensors and Context-Aware Computing. DOI: http://dx.doi.org/10.1016/B978-0-12-801660-2.00010-0

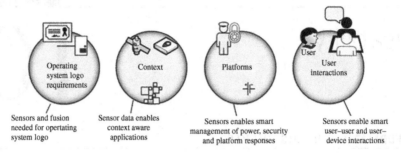

FIGURE 10.1

Sensors are becoming key.

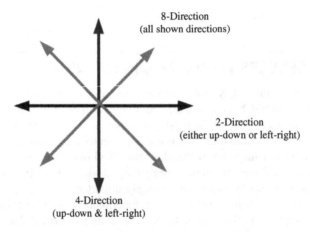

FIGURE 10.2

Direction possibilities of the user action.

volume control; 4-mode direction can be used for more complex functions like scanning radio stations or changing tracks on a music player; and 8-mode direction can be used to scroll a 2D or 3D image on the screen with gestures that the user would use to move similar objects by hand. Fig. 10.2 shows direction possibilities of the user action. Angular direction can also be supported by the system.

3. Ease of Implementation: Sensors that have a standard interface like I^{2}C do not require substantial processor or memory bandwidth, have simple digital/mechanical design, and appropriate polling/interrupt mechanisms can be easily implemented in the computing devices/system. Such multiple sensors can enhance the gesture recognition and support new applications for user interfaces.

OS LOGO REQUIREMENTS AND SENSOR SUPPORT

Both Windows and Android OS have provided requirements that the sensor vendors are trying to meet in their sensor releases, such as the Microsoft Windows Human Interface Device (HID) specification.

The HID specifications manage input peripherals such as mouse and keyboards, along with all the sensors. The sensors can represent human inputs. [2].

The Windows operating system [3] provides native support for sensor devices. As part of this support, the platform provides a standard way for device manufacturers to expose sensor devices to software developers and consumers. At the same time, the platform gives developers a standardized application programming interface (API) and device driver interface to work with sensors and sensor data.

Since sensors come in many configurations and include almost anything that provides data about physical phenomena either as a hardware device or in logical form, the sensor and location platform of the OS organizes sensors into *categories* (representing broad classes of sensor devices) and *types* (which represent specific kinds of sensors). For example, a sensor in a video game controller that detects the position and movement of a player's hand (perhaps for a video bowling game) would be categorized as an orientation sensor, but its type would be 3D accelerometer.

In code, Windows represents categories and types by using globally unique identifiers (GUIDs), many of which are predefined. Device manufacturers can create new categories and types by defining and publishing new GUIDs, when it is required.

Windows predefined GUID/category examples are given in Table 10.1 [4].

All of the above categories have data types that have to meet the minimum requirements for Windows logo certification (Tables 10.2 and 10.3).

Most Android-powered devices too have built-in sensors that measure motion, orientation, and various environmental conditions. These sensors are capable of providing raw data with high precision and accuracy, and are useful to monitor three-dimensional device movement or positioning, or to monitor changes in the ambient environment near a device.

The Android platform supports three broad categories of sensors:

- Motion sensors: These sensors measure acceleration forces and rotational forces along three axes. This category includes accelerometers, gravity sensors, gyroscopes, and rotational vector sensors.
- Environmental sensors: These sensors measure various environmental parameters, such as ambient air temperature and pressure, illumination, and humidity. This category includes barometers, photometers, and thermometers.
- Position sensors: These sensors measure the physical position of a device. This category includes orientation sensors and magnetometers.

Table 10.1 Windows GUID/Category

Category	Data Type	Meaning
SENSOR_CATEGORY_BIOMETRIC	SENSOR_TYPE_HUMAN_PRESENCE	Sensors that detect human presence
	SENSOR_TYPE_HUMAN_PROXIMITY	Sensors that detect human proximity
	SENSOR_TYPE_TOUCH	Touch sensors
SENSOR_CATEGORY_ELECTRICAL	SENSOR_TYPE_CAPACITANCE	Capacitance sensors
	SENSOR_TYPE_CURRENT	Current sensors
	SENSOR_TYPE_ELECTRICAL_POWER	Electrical power sensors
	SENSOR_TYPE_INDUCTANCE	Inductance sensors
	SENSOR_TYPE_POTENTIOMETER	Potentiometers
	SENSOR_TYPE_RESISTANCE	Resistance sensors
	SENSOR_TYPE_VOLTAGE	Voltage sensors
SENSOR_CATEGORY_ENVIRONMENTAL	SENSOR_TYPE_ENVIRONMENTAL_ATMOSPHERIC_PRESSURE	Barometers
	SENSOR_TYPE_ENVIRONMENTAL_HUMIDITY	Hygrometers
	SENSOR_TYPE_ENVIRONMENTAL_TEMPERATURE	Thermometers
	SENSOR_TYPE_ENVIRONMENTAL_WIND_DIRECTION	Weather vanes
	SENSOR_TYPE_ENVIRONMENTAL_WIND_SPEED	Anemometers
SENSOR_CATEGORY_LIGHT	SENSOR_TYPE_AMBIENT_LIGHT	Ambient light sensors
SENSOR_CATEGORY_LOCATION	SENSOR_TYPE_LOCATION_BROADCAST	Sensors that transmit location information by using transmissions such as television or radio frequencies
	SENSOR_TYPE_LOCATION_DEAD_RECKONING	Dead-reckoning sensors. These sensors first calculate the current location and then update the current location by using motion data
	SENSOR_TYPE_LOCATION_GPS	Global positioning system sensors
	SENSOR_TYPE_LOCATION_LOOKUP	Lookup sensors, such as those that provide information based on the user's IP address

	SENSOR_TYPE_LOCATION_OTHER	Other location sensors
	SENSOR_TYPE_LOCATION_STATIC	Fixed-location sensors, such as those that use preset, user-provided information
	SENSOR_TYPE_LOCATION_TRIANGULATION	Triangulation sensors, such as those that determine current location based on cellular phone tower proximities
SENSOR_CATEGORY_ MECHANICAL	SENSOR_TYPE_BOOLEAN_SWITCH	Two-state switches (off or on)
	SENSOR_TYPE_FORCE	Force sensors
	SENSOR_TYPE_MULTIVALUE_SWITCH	Multiple-position switches
	SENSOR_TYPE_PRESSURE	Pressure sensors
	SENSOR_TYPE_SCALE	Weight sensors
	SENSOR_TYPE_STRAIN	Strain sensors
SENSOR_CATEGORY_MOTION	SENSOR_TYPE_ACCELEROMETER_1D	One-axis accelerometers
	SENSOR_TYPE_ACCELEROMETER_2D	Two-axis accelerometers
	SENSOR_TYPE_ACCELEROMETER_3D	Three-axis accelerometers
	SENSOR_TYPE_GYROMETER_1D	One-axis gyrometer
	SENSOR_TYPE_GYROMETER_2D	Two-axis gyrometer
	SENSOR_TYPE_GYROMETER_3D	Three-axis gyrometer
	SENSOR_TYPE_MOTION_DETECTOR	Motion detectors, such as those used in security systems
	SENSOR_TYPE_SPEEDOMETER	Rate-of-motion sensors

(Continued)

Table 10.1 Windows GUID/Category *Continued*

Category	Data Type	Meaning
SENSOR_CATEGORY_ ORIENTATION	SENSOR_TYPE_AGGREGATED_DEVICE_ ORIENTATION	Specifies the current device orientation by returning a quaternion and, in some cases, a rotation matrix (the rotation matrix is optional)
	SENSOR_TYPE_AGGREGATED_QUADRANT_ ORIENTATION	Specifies the current device orientation in degrees
	SENSOR_TYPE_AGGREGATED_SIMPLE_DEVICE_ ORIENTATION	Specifies the device orientation as an enumeration. (This type specifies the device orientation using one of four general quadrants: 0 degrees, 90-degrees counterclockwise, 180-counterclockwise, and 270-degrees counterclockwise)
	SENSOR_TYPE_COMPASS_1D	One-axis compasses
	SENSOR_TYPE_COMPASS_2D	Two-axis compasses
	SENSOR_TYPE_COMPASS_3D	Three-axis compasses
	SENSOR_TYPE_DISTANCE_1D	One-axis distance sensors
	SENSOR_TYPE_DISTANCE_2D	Two-axis distance sensors
	SENSOR_TYPE_DISTANCE_3D	Three-axis distance sensors
	SENSOR_TYPE_INCLINOMETER_1D	One-axis inclinometers
	SENSOR_TYPE_INCLINOMETER_2D	Two-axis inclinometers
	SENSOR_TYPE_INCLINOMETER_3D	Three-axis inclinometers
SENSOR_CATEGORY_SCANNER	SENSOR_TYPE_BARCODE_SCANNER	Sensors that use optical scanning to read bar codes
	SENSOR_TYPE_RFID_SCANNER	Radiofrequency ID scanning sensors

Table 10.2 Windows Sensor Data Types Example 1

Feature/Property Type	Comments	Description
Target feature: Device.Input. Sensor.Accelerometer	Applies to • Windows 8 Client x86, x64, ARM (Windows RT) • Windows 8.1 Client x86, x64, ARM (Windows RT 8.1)	All accelerometer class sensors need to ensure that they accurately report the data at the required sampling rates to be efficient for gaming applications as well as power managed when not in full use
Sensor property type: SENSOR_PROPERTY_MIN_ REPORT_INTERVAL Device.Input.Sensor. Accelerometer. SensorReportInterval	Data type: VT_R8 Accelerometer function driver and firmware report data with minimum report interval of 16 ms (for a 60 Hz frequency for gaming)	The minimum elapsed time setting that the hardware supports for sensor data report generation in milliseconds

Table 10.3 Windows Sensor Data Types Example 2

Feature/Property Type	Comments	Description
Target feature: Device.Input. Sensor.compass	Applies to • Windows 8 Client x86, x64, ARM (Windows RT) • Windows 8.1 Client x86, x64, ARM (Windows RT 8.1)	A tilt compensated compass device driver shall accurately report the right data types for an inclinometer (leveraging the accelerometer and compass together)
Sensor data type: SENSOR_DATA_TYPE_TILT_ X_DEGREES (Pitch) SENSOR_DATA_TYPE_TILT_ Y_DEGREES (Roll) SENSOR_DATA_TYPE_TILT_ Z_DEGREES (Yaw)	Data type: VT_R8 To follow order of operation as yaw, then pitch, and then roll	Report pitch, roll, and yaw inclinations in degrees

Table 10.4 shows sensors supported by Android platforms [5].

CONTEXT- AND LOCATION-BASED SERVICES

Chapter 2, Context-Aware Computing, describes various aspect of context-aware computing along with various examples of context interactions. The use cases based on the context can be grouped mainly into four key experience categories as shown in Fig. 10.3:

• Know Me: The sensors in this case have information related to the user and can make decisions based on user preferences, location, and profile. In certain

Table 10.4 Sensors Types Supported by Android Platforms

Sensor	Type	Description	Common Uses
TYPE_ACCELEROMETER	Hardware	Measures the acceleration force in m/s² that is applied to a device on all three physical axes (x, y, and z), including the force of gravity	Motion detection (shake, tilt, etc.)
TYPE_AMBIENT_TEMPERATURE	Hardware	Measures the ambient room temperature in degrees Celsius. See note below	Monitoring air temperatures
TYPE_GRAVITY	Software or hardware	Measures the force of gravity in m/s² that is applied to a device on all three physical axes (x, y, and z)	Motion detection (shake, tilt, etc.)
TYPE_GYROSCOPE	Hardware	Measures a device's rate of rotation in rad/s around each of the three physical axes (x, y, and z)	Rotation detection (spin, turn, etc.)
TYPE_LIGHT	Hardware	Measures the ambient light level (illumination) in lux	Controlling screen brightness
TYPE_LINEAR_ACCELERATION	Software or hardware	Measures the acceleration force in m/s² that is applied to a device on all three physical axes (x, y, and z), excluding the force of gravity	Monitoring acceleration along a single axis
TYPE_MAGNETIC_FIELD	Hardware	Measures the ambient geomagnetic field for all three physical axes (x, y, and z) in µT	Creating a compass
TYPE_ORIENTATION	Software	Measures degrees of rotation that a device makes around all three physical axes (x, y, and z). As of API Level 3 you can obtain the inclination matrix and rotation matrix for a device by using the gravity sensor and the geomagnetic field sensor in conjunction with the getRotationMatrix() method	Determining device position
TYPE_PRESSURE	Hardware	Measures the ambient air pressure in hPa or mbar	Monitoring air pressure changes
TYPE_PROXIMITY	Hardware	Measures the proximity of an object in cm relative to the view screen of a device. This sensor is typically used to determine whether a handset is being held up to a person's ear	Phone position during a call
TYPE_RELATIVE_HUMIDITY	Hardware	Measures the relative ambient humidity in percent	Monitoring dew point, absolute, and relative humidity
TYPE_ROTATION_VECTOR	Software or hardware	Measures the orientation of a device by providing the three elements of the device's rotation vector	Motion detection and rotation detection
TYPE_TEMPERATURE	Hardware	Measures the temperature of the device in degrees Celsius. This sensor implementation varies across devices and this sensor was replaced with the TYPE_AMBIENT_TEMPERATURE sensor in API Level 14	Monitoring temperatures

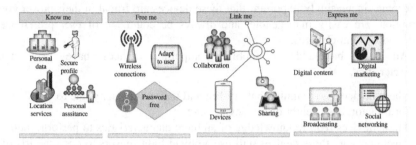

FIGURE 10.3

Context usages.

cases a history of previous decisions is maintained, which can be used along with current context to reach a decision, such as suggesting a dining space based on user, location, time, and preferences.

- Free Me: The sensors in this case help to recognize the user accurately and perform tasks on behalf of the user, such as eliminating the need for a password if the user is authorized or starting the device automatically as user proximity is sensed. When cooking or exercising, the user would want to use a smartphone without touching it. With gesture controls, the user can check or scroll notifications, identify a caller, answer the call with the speaker already enabled, ignore the call with no response, or ignore the call but send a predefined text message, send the caller to voicemail, or the like. If the phone has a proximity sensor, then it can provide touchless interaction using proximity detection.
- Link Me: With the help of user recognition, the device can connect with available networks and enable sharing among various devices, such as automatically connecting to social networks or applications to connect the user to external world.
- Express Me: The sensors help recognize the user, user gestures, and so forth, and help the users to express themselves without manual interaction with the mobile computing device. For example, the device can upload user status to a social networking site based on user expressions/time/location, reload or suggest videos/movies based on user mood/time/location, and so on. A four-direction single sensor can help enable gesture recognition for smart homes (which can be controlled through smartphones) and can turn on, off, or dim lights without touching the phone.

SENSOR-BASED POWER MANAGEMENT [6]

Handheld, mobile and small form factor devices are increasingly becoming integral part of user's life. Such devices are used in the home, offices, and on the road. As these devices become the key ingredient in the pervasive environments, it becomes increasingly important that these devices are frugal in their power consumption, are easily manageable, and always be cognizant of user preferences and environment changes.

All such handheld or mobile computing devices have two main characteristics:

- These devices have limited battery life and thermal capacity due to the size, form factor, and weight of the device; and
- These devices require knowledge of ambient characteristics to perform their functions, e.g., these devices will use ambient light sensors to open the iris of a camera, or will buffer the audio stream in a music player when it senses shock and vibration.

Since long battery life is a must for mobile devices, the system resource management becomes a priority for such devices. Power consumption in such devices should be minimized through dynamic and context-dependent optimal power distribution, and it should be continuously monitored to ensure that performance does not degrade to unacceptable levels.

Operating systems in the mobile devices or environments cannot maintain an optimal power consumption by using only the "idle time" detection mechanism. It has to use the concept of context to manage the subsystems and optimize the system power consumption. Since the mobile devices constantly gather or process information, the definition of "idle" may be less clear. If these operating systems are context-aware then it would be able to meet the user needs and also extend the battery life of the mobile systems in an always-connected world.

Mobile computing has seemingly contradictory requirements. For example:

- The applications demand higher capabilities, while users demand longer battery life.
- Users demand smaller form factors, while putting additional thermal constraints on the device.

These contradictory requirements become important design considerations for the manageability of mobile devices.

Sensor-based power management techniques are used to reduce average power consumption, increase battery life, and enable use of passive cooling (versus active cooling using fans). Several sensor-based applications such as GPS mapping, fingerprint-based authentication, and accelerometer-based hard disc protection are present in small handheld devices. Hence, such handheld devices may already have an accelerometer for use in various sensing applications. This accelerometer can be considered as a system resource and can be used for power management. This is the underlying concept of sensor-based power management. One such possible architecture of sensor-based power management is described below:

Basic Concept: The sensor-based power management system uses the knowledge of the context of the device to dynamically manage and adapt the system to the minimum active subsystems (and hence minimum power requirements) that is

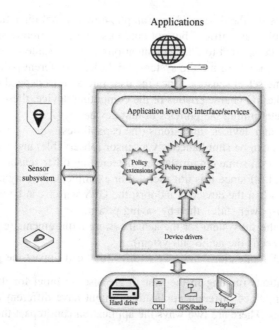

FIGURE 10.4

Application-OS-hardware-sensor subsystem architecture for power management.

required to meet the user's quality of service (QoS) expectations. The unused components are turned off and power consumption of used components is minimized to a level that is just sufficient to meet the QoS requirement. Hence the goal of sensor-based power management architecture is to control the system's devices, based on the information of the system context that is provided by the sensor data.

Model Framework: The overall mobile system can be split into two parts: *sensors* (the observable parts of the system) and *devices* (the controllable parts of the system). The data collected by sensors of the mobile computing system can be defined as *context*, while the rules applied to the sensors/device to make decisions to control the devices can be referred to as the *policies*. So policy can be expressed as an algorithm with state that can be updated with sensor inputs. Action can be performed by the algorithm if the state meets certain criteria or conditions. For example, if the sensors confirm that the device is in the pocket, an action like turning off the screen can be performed. The defined policies should be proactive and capable of anticipating user preferences/needs (or at least reactive) according to the actual context.

Architecture: Based on the above concept and framework, we can define the key architectural components as shown in Fig. 10.4:

1. The sensors-based policies.
2. Policies can be dependent on other policies and can behave differently based on state of other policies. The policies can be based on common usage models

and scenarios for the devices. For example, a policy that dims the backlight will be useful in an "office" but not outdoors. Hence, different subsets of policies can be applied to different situations with the same set of sensors. Also different kinds of mobile systems might have different policies, even with the same set of sensors. Since the user interactions depend on the form factor and the I/O characteristics of the computing device, these two are key factors in determining the policies of that device.

3. The sensors and devices subsystems (the capabilities).
4. A subsystem can be simultaneously a sensor (observable) and a device (controllable). In some circumstances (detected by other sensors), one sensor can be turned off since it is not useful. For example, GPS may not be needed indoors. So when the device is indoors, the GPS sensor can be turned off (or put in a low-power state), thereby saving power.
5. Monitoring the subsystem for the actual system requirements (e.g., an MP3 application needs the audio subsystem).
6. The external applications and user settings (that can impact the policies).

The applications running in the system are also an input for the power management system, since different applications might have different needs in terms of active devices. There are two ways the application can impact the policies:

- An application notifies which device it is using through the API provided by the infrastructure, or
- A monitoring system understands which processes are running in the system and which devices are being used. (In this case the application does not report devices being used directly.)

Fig. 10.5 shows sensor subsystem using sensor-based power management.

Sensor management [6]

Consider sensors as hardware/software subsystems that have a proprietary API for controlling the functionalities and gathering of data. In our example, the infrastructure can collect data from sensors from a multitude of applications, regardless of the actual type of sensor or data.

The main purpose of the sensor subsystem is to provide a unique API for all the sensors. Let us consider a subsystem where the request is available as a packet whose header mentions the type of data requested (request) and the body mentions input values of the request. Every request—response is two messages, one for the request (mentioning the input values needed) and one for the response (indicating success or failure plus requested values). For example, a GPS response will have a body composed of three fields: X, Y, and Z. Velocity response will be composed of two fields: speed and direction. Universally unique identifiers can be used to identify each sensor module and each request/response packet is needed.

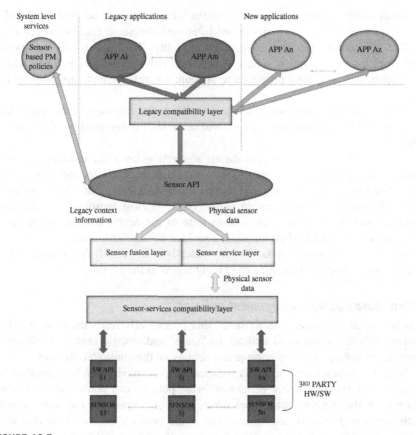

FIGURE 10.5

Sensor subsystem for sensor-based power management usage.

A compatibility layer can be used to respond to the original API of the sensors that are used for legacy applications.

Communication protocols

The architecture can use the following communication methods:

1. *Singly Synchronous*: The application sends a request once and waits until the data/event is available.
2. *Singly Asynchronous*: The application sends a request once and is notified when the data/event is available.
3. *Multisynchronous*: The application sends a request once and is notified every time the data or event is available.
4. *Selective Multisynchronous*: The application sends a request once in order to be informed on certain type of data and events. It is notified every time these data and events are available.

Additionally, caching of the most recent information can be used so that if a data is gathered from one request and afterward the same request comes from another application, the data is already available. This will avoid a response bottleneck for any request of data that is passed down to the sensor. The caching mechanism will also have provision to account for validity and expiration of the data.

The sensor subsystem needs to show to the entire mobile system "raw" data originating directly from the system and also logical information that can be inferred.

The Sensor Fusion Layer provide an abstraction layer for refining raw data provided by the physical sensors to most convenient logical information about the context of the system. This layer is composed of algorithms that need as inputs a subset of sensors and provides an output other "logical sensors" with different characteristics. For example, the motion state of the device (in motion, stopped, etc.) can be inferred based on measures provided by accelerometers.

The *Server Compatibility Layer* automatically discovers all the sensors. All of these sensors along with the data can be published to the system.

Sensor-based power management policies

A policy is an algorithm with a "state" that periodically reads the context information from the sensors and updates its "state" and when a certain condition is reached, the policy performs appropriate actions on the controlled devices.

Since the policies are not totally independent, one device can be controlled by different policies. And hence certain different policies can contradict each other in terms of the required action that needs to be performed on the same device. Such conflicting actions can be resolved if the policies are aware of the other policies that can produce conflicting action on the device in advance or with the use of external mediators.

Fig. 10.6 shows one such policy architecture where the device status, sensor data, and policy status information feeds into the policy architecture that resolves any conflicts and performs final power management action on the device.

Let us look at some examples of the policies that can be implemented to perform platform power management using sensor data.

1. *In pocket*: This policy understands if a mobile device is placed in the pocket by sensing the device orientation (if it is in an upright position) and if the view of integrated camera is blocked. When these two conditions occur, the policy achieves power management goals by turning off the display immediately. It then starts monitoring of WLAN and CPU usage/workload and can eventually turn off WLAN or put the device in standby mode. If the sensing subsystem notices a change in the state/context (either orientation or camera view) such that the device is no longer in the pocket, then it puts the device back in the normal use mode.

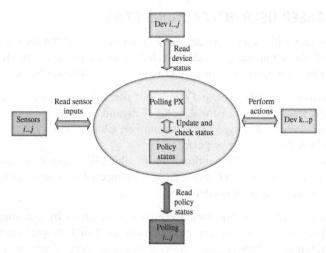

FIGURE 10.6

Policy architecture.

2. *User presence detection*: This policy can use the integrated camera of the device (one facing the user) for face detection or user-attention detection. When camera sensor senses that there is no face looking at it then it can turn off the display immediately to save platform power. When one or more user faces are detected to be looking at the device/camera then the policy brings the system comes back to the normal state.

3. *Ambient light detection*: The ambient light sensor is present in computing devices to detect illuminance level of the environment in which the device is present. Based on the illuminance level the backlight of the device gets adjusted. For example, the backlight intensity is adjusted to lower the power consumption depending on whether the device is outdoors with ample light or indoors or at night with limited light.

4. *Movement detection*: Power management policies can also control the sensor subsystem or individual sensors of the computing device. Location services are a key feature for mobile and pervasive computing but they also consume power and compute resources of the device. The location of a device can be obtained using integrated accelerometers, gyroscope, and compass. Based on the device location, various location-based services and/or sensors are enabled or disabled. For example, the policy can decide if the services/sensors like GPS, WLAN, and so on are needed or not based on whether the device is indoors or outdoors, stationary or in transit, climbing up or down (e.g., when the device is stationary and indoors then GPS may not be needed). The same policy also evaluates power-saving modes based on the sensor latencies (the time it takes to turn on and turn off the device vs power savings).

SENSOR-BASED USER INTERACTIONS [7,8]

Humans interact with computing devices in many ways and the interface between humans and the computing device is referred to as the user interface. When designing a user interface, it is important to consider following factors:

- *User environment*: The type and number of users. For example, experienced or novice, frequent or occasional, valid or invalid.
- *Task environment*: The type of tasks (number, latency, and so on), conditions under which they need to be performed.
- *Machine environment*: The environment in which the computing device is present or expected to work. For example, connected or remote, indoor or outdoor, always on or as needed.

Sensors and sensing techniques are highly determined by the uniqueness of the human—computer interaction environment as listed above, especially for mobile computing devices. These sensors help enable several new user interfaces that help improve and smoothen human—device interactions, such as recording memos when the device is held like a cell phone, switching between portrait and landscape display modes depending on device orientation, automatically powering up the device when picked up by the user, and so forth.

The computing devices should remain aware of various aspects of user context, otherwise they cannot adapt the interaction to suit the environments mentioned above (user, task, and machine). There are many gestures that users will demonstrate with the device, like picking it up, putting it down, walking to it, or walking around with it. These gesture recognition should become integrated into the device to enable the user interact with computing devices more easily and naturally.

By using various types of sensors a context-sensitive interface (one that recognizes gestures, locations, and so on) can be developed for the computing devices such that these interfaces help the device to respond to users and the environment more easily.

Sensors also provide support for background interaction using passively sensed gestures and activity, as opposed to the foreground interaction of traditional GUIs. An important part of enabling background interaction is to develop the sensors and software that can detect and infer information about the user's physical activity. For example, use pressure sensors to detect in which hand the user is holding a mobile device [9], a touch-sensitive mouse [10], integrated eye tracking with traditional manual pointing [11].

Sensors can also be used to augment or sense the environment itself. For example, a mobile device with a tag-reading sensor can determine the identity of nearby objects that have electronic tags and uniquely assigned IDs, a pick-and-drop technique using a unique identifier of each user's stylus to transfer information between devices, a light sensor for adjusting display quality, a phone that combines tilt, light, heat, and other sensors to sense contexts such as sitting on a table, in a briefcase, or being used outdoors, inferring attention and location via integration of sensed events (keyboard, mouse, and microphone), proximate selection using location awareness to emphasize nearby objects, making them easier for the user to select, and so on.

The above examples show the use of background sensing to support foreground activity (like modifying the behavior of the device, such as the tone and volume of the ring, powering on/off a device based on touch, or portrait vs landscape display mode selection).

Consider a system with following sensors:

- A large touch sensor covers the back surface and sides of the device, to detect if the user is holding the device.
- An accelerometer to detect the tilt of the device relative to the constant acceleration of gravity. This sensor also responds to linear accelerations, such as those resulting from shaking the device.
- A proximity sensor that can sense the reflected infrared light off of the user's hand or other object and the signal is proportional to the distance to the object.

An algorithm then takes the sensor data and converts raw data into logical form and derive additional information as indicated in Table 10.5.

Following are the various use cases that deploy gesture recognitions and sensors/sensor fusion to achieve enhanced user interactions.

Table 10.5 Context Information From Raw Sensor Data

Context Variable	Description
Holding and duration	If user is holding the device or not and for how long
Tilt angle	Left/right and forward/back tilt angles
Display orientation	If device is *flat, portrait, portrait upside-down, landscape left, and landscape right*
Looking at/duration	If user is looking at the device display
Moving/duration	If device is moving
Shaking	If device is being shaken
Walking/duration	If user is walking
Proximity	Distance to proximal object
Proximity state/ duration	Different proximity state like *close, InRange, OutofRange, and AmbientLight*
Scrolling	If user is scrolling
Voice memo gesture	If recording voice memo

Simplifying the user–device interface for voice memo recording

Activating voice recording through a physical record button or activating control through a screen requires significant visual attention from the user. Instead this feature interface can be simplified through the use of the above-listed sensors such that when the following conditions are met, the device recognizes the gesture and starts voice recording.

Conditions to start the recording:

1. The user holds the device (this condition prevents accidental activation when the device is in a purse or a briefcase).
2. The user holds the device in close proximity to speak into it (e.g., at 8 cm or closer to the face).
3. The device is tilted toward the user (a natural position the hand makes when an object is brought toward head).

When finished speaking, users naturally move the device away, which automatically stops the recording. So the conditions under which recording stops are

1. If the device enters the proximity OutOfRange state, or
2. If the device returns to a mostly flat orientation (± 25 degrees), or
3. If the user stops holding the device.

A sensed voice memo gesture requires less cognitive and visual attention.

Detecting orientation of device

A mobile computing device user can tilt or rotate the device to look at its display from any orientation. Using a tilt sensor, the device can detect this gesture and automatically reformat the display to adjust to the current device orientation for optimal viewing. For example, a user may change to landscape or portrait orientation depending on the content of an Excel spreadsheet.

The tilt angle is processed and the display window gets formatted to the nearest 90-degree rotation.

Other examples of sensor usage are a digital camera sensing the orientation at which the photograph is taken or a drawing application reformatting the screen to accommodate the desired dimensions or proportions of the sketch.

Fig. 10.7 shows how a tilt angle is converted to display orientation. There are two tilt angles being measured: forward-back and left-right. There are some dead zones defined (of around ± 5 degrees) to prevent jitters. In order for orientation to change, the tilt angles must overcome the dead zones and remain in new zone for time $t > t_{(\text{dead zone})}$.

If time is less than $t_{(\text{dead zone})}$ then there won't be any orientation change. Such a dead zone helps define stable position of the device before changing its orientation.

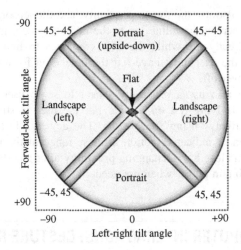

FIGURE 10.7

Device tilt and sensed orientation.

If both tilt angles fall within certain small percentage within the center region then the device is considered to be resting flat and there won't be any orientation change. Precaution should be taken to define this time and tilt dead zones otherwise it could result in annoying unintentional orientation changes (for instance, when device is put down by user, it can result in unintentional orientation change).

Power management

We can power on or power off the device using multiple sensors. For example, if the following conditions are met then the device is powered on:

1. The user is holding the device.
2. The user is looking at the display with a display orientation of Portrait (not Flat).
3. The device remains in above state for say 0.5 seconds.

The device cannot power up

1. When in the user's pocket or purse because the user is not holding it.
2. Or if the user simply touches it or pushes it out of the way, while it is resting on a desk because the user must be looking at the display in portrait orientation with preconfigured left-right tilt (e.g., ± 15 degrees) and forward-back tilt (> -5 degrees).
3. Or when the device is not in a stable orientation. The predefined timeout will prevent the device from waking up due to transient signals. Care should be taken that such a timeout is short enough and will not affect user experience negatively.

The device can also use the touch, proximity, and tilt sensors to prevent undesired power off or screen dimming due to the default system inactivity timeouts. If the device is already on, while the user continues to hold the device, then assumption is that the user must have left the device on for a reason and so the device does not power off.

The device can also use a proximity sensor to sense user activity, such as, e.g., if the device is lying flat on a table but the user is still referring to the display and not actively "using" the device. The device idle timer can be reset if the proximity sensor indicates motion in close range of the device. Care must be taken to ignore a close but unchanging proximity after a certain time otherwise the device will maintain power when not needed.

HUMAN–COMPUTER INTERACTIONS: GESTURE RECOGNITION

One of the mobile interface modes that enables interaction through certain body actions or movements and without stopping or impeding ongoing user activity/movement is known as gesture [12].

Since mobile computing devices like smartphones are an integral part of everyday life, the users often interact with their smartphones in mobile situations like walking on the street, driving a car, and jogging at a park. With a flexible, programmable gesture-based user interface, the need for the user to take the device, look at it, and then enter commands using conventional screen menu or touch keyboard is eliminated. The user can seamlessly and intuitively interact with various applications using gestures without halting his/her current actions. For example, using hand gestures while driving or jogging eliminates the need to stop driving/jogging to interact with mobile devices.

To support such a gesture-based user interface, an energy-efficient sensor device system would be needed.

A basic gesture processing system consists of components as shown in Fig. 10.8:

1. Sensors that collect data and send to the mobile device's detection circuitry.
2. A detection mechanism that detects and separates out the intended gestures, detecting hand movements, for instance, and categorizing them as scroll, zoom, or pan movement.
3. A classification mechanism that classifies the detected sensor data/gestures as predefined gestures or noise.

Such gesture processing system has the following challenges:

1. It requires continuous monitoring sensors that consume power and drain device batteries quickly.
2. The system needs to differentiate nongestural movement or mobility noise from intended gestures while the user is in motion. For example, a swinging

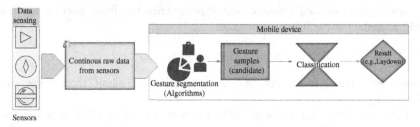

FIGURE 10.8

Gesture processing pipeline.

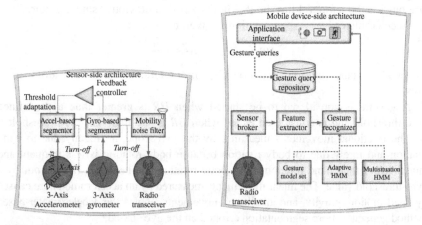

FIGURE 10.9

Sample gesture architecture.

hand motion would not be a gesture when the user is running. If the user moves around, then the same body movement would have different characteristics in a moving situation. In such a case, it becomes difficult to process a gesture and differentiate it from noise. The same hand gesture would have different sensor-data waveforms, e.g., when the user is moving versus stationary.

A sample gesture architecture is discussed below. The architecture could be logically broken down into sensor architecture and device architecture.

The sensor architecture performs motion sensing and gesture segmentation. A gyroscope in the sample architecture is added to an accelerometer to improve gesture classification accuracy as it can detect rotational movements. Fig. 10.9 shows:

- an accelerometer-based and gyroscope-based segmentor,
- a feedback controller, and
- a noise filter (removes false segmentation).

Accelerometer-based segmentation approximates the force exerted by hand (HF) according to the following formula:

$$HF = \sqrt{Ax^2 + Ay^2 + Az^2} - G$$

where HF = hand force; Ax, Ay, Az = acceleration along three axes; and G = gravity.

If HF is greater than some predefined threshold of say 0.15 G, then a gesture is triggered. If HF is less than the threshold, then the gesture is considered stopped. To avoid splitting a single gesture into multiple gestures, there is an additional threshold called temporal threshold. All gestures occurring within the temporal threshold are considered as one and merged into a single gesture. A gesture outside the temporal threshold is not a part of a previous "single gesture."

Accelerometer-based segmentation is given by:

$$HR = \sqrt{Gx^2 + Gy^2 + Gz^2}$$

where HR = hand rotation; and Gx, Gy, Gz = rotational movement along three axes.

A gesture is considered to be started when HR is greater than a predefined gyro-threshold and is considered ended when HR is less than that gyro-threshold.

The rotational movements measured by the gyroscope are mainly due to hand rotation and rarely due to body rotation because body rotation is less frequent and much slower than hand rotation. Such body rotation can be easily filtered out by a gyro-threshold value. The linear movements measured by an accelerometer are caused by hand motion, gravity, and also body movements. Hence the accelerometer-based method generates more segmentation errors than the gyro-based.

Equation for the feedback controller:

If (FP_{accel} (n) > MAX_FP) then
Increment (n) = α (FP_{accel} (n) − MAX_FP)
If (FP_{accel} (n) < MIN_FP) then
Increment (n) = β (FP_{accel} (n) − MIN_FP)
Threshold $(n + 1)$ = Threshold (n) + Increment $(n)$where Threshold (n) and FP_{accel} (n) is the current threshold and false-positive rate, respectively; α and β are empirically determined small constraints.

Fig. 10.10 demonstrates the operation of the segmentation architecture, which uses a gyro-based segmentor to validate the gesture segments detected by an accelerometer-based segmentor. The gyro-based segmentor is highly accurate but consumes more energy than the accelerometer-based segmentor. Since the accelerometer and the gyroscope-based segmentors are connected in series, the gyro-based segmentor is activated only when the accel-segmentor detects gesture segments. This reduces the power-on time of the high-energy gyroscope. The gyro-based segmentor adaptively reconfigures the accel-based segmentor under dynamically changing mobility situations, thereby reducing false segmentation by the accel-based segmentor.

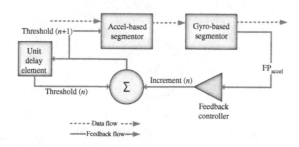

FIGURE 10.10

Processing flow of segmentation architecture.

The gyro-based segmentor monitors FP_{accel}, (the ratio of false-positive rate segmented by accel-based segmentor but invalidated by the gyro-based segmentor). It then regulates FP_{accel} by adaptively controlling the threshold of the accel-based segmentor. The threshold is raised if the FP_{accel} exceeds the maximum tolerable limit (MAX_FP). The threshold is lowered if FP_{accel} is below the minimum tolerable limit (MIN_FP).

While the accel-gyro segmentor removes most false gesture segments caused by dynamic mobility changes, some false gesture segments may still occur (like in on-the-go situations). For example, a "hand swing" gesture would end up as false gesture since humans swing their hands while walking or running. A filter that discard gestures that occur for longer than few seconds can reduce such false gestures—hand swings while walking occur for a much longer time than valid gestures.

The device architecture performs:

- Sensor brokering → receives sensor data and then interprets the data.
- Feature extraction → generates the gesture pattern that needs to be classified (analyzed).
- Gesture classification → identifies the gesture using adoptive or multisituation HMMs.
- Provides application interface → manages interactions with various applications.

Before understanding details of gesture classification, let us briefly discuss HMM (hidden Markov model). HMM is a statistical Markov model in which the modeled system is considered to be a Markov process with unobserved (hidden) states. In HMM, the state is not directly visible, but output that is dependent on the state is visible. Each state has a probability distribution over the possible output tokens. Therefore the sequence of tokens generated by an HMM gives some information about the sequence of states.

Consider an example as shown in Fig. 10.11 where a user is in a room is not visible to an observer. The room contains three containers X1, X2, X3 ... each of

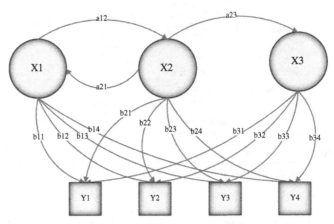

FIGURE 10.11

Hidden Markov model.

which contains balls labeled as y1, y2, y3.... The user chooses a container and randomly picks a ball from that container. The user then puts the ball in line, which can be observed by the observer. The observer can observe the sequence of the balls but cannot identify the sequence of container from which the balls were picked. The user uses Markov process to choose the container and the choice of the container for the nth ball depends only upon a random number and the choice of the container for the $(n-1)$th ball. The choice of container does not directly depend on the containers chosen before this single previous container.

Since the Markov process cannot be observed, and only the sequence of labeled balls can be observed, this arrangement is called a "hidden Markov process."

Gesture classification accuracy is impacted considerably but the noise caused due to body movements because such noise changes sensor data characteristic. To take care of this problem, an adaptive and multisituation HMM can be used. How do these HMMs accurately classify gestures under dynamic mobility situations? Some example approaches are discussed below.

In a *Basic gesture classification architecture*

- An HMM model is built for each gesture and trained based on some collected gesture samples/algorithms (e.g., use the Baum−Welch [13] reestimation algorithm, which is an algorithm to find the unknown parameters of a HMM).
- A separate garbage HMM model is also built to filter out nongestural movements or undefined gestures that frequently occur, such as swinging hands while walking.

A potential gesture when segmented by the sensor device is classified as one of the defined gestures or a garbage gesture/movement.

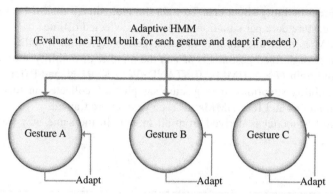

FIGURE 10.12

Adaptive hidden Markov model (HMM).

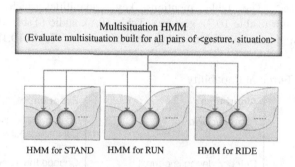

FIGURE 10.13

Multisituation hidden Markov model (HMM).

While garbage gestures are rejected, the following steps are performed to identify classified gestures:

1. A feature vector series is calculated based on data from the accelerometer and gyroscope (e.g., raw data, delta data, and integral data for each axis: 3 data types $\times$ 3 axes $\times$ 2 sensors = 18 elements).
2. The Viterbi algorithm [14] is used to select a likelihood of gesture model. (The Viterbi algorithm is a dynamic programming algorithm for finding the most likely sequence of hidden states—called the Viterbi path for HMMs).
3. A gesture model with highest likelihood is selected as a classified gesture.

In *Adaptive HMM architecture* as shown in Fig. 10.12, the HMM models are updated continuously to better fit the models to the current mobility situation. A few algorithms (like Maximum Likelihood Linear Regression (MLLR)) can be used to compute a set of linear transformations that reduce the mismatch between an initial model set (including a garbage model) and the adaptation data.

In *Multisituation HMM architecture as shown in* Fig. 10.13, HMMs are built for each mobility situation. Multisituation HMMs capture gestures performed under different mobility situations. To train the multisituation HMMs, a sufficient amount of gesture data per situation needs to be collected offline.

An HMM is built and trained for each pair of ⟨gesture, mobility situation⟩. If the number of defined gestures is M and the number of mobility situations is N, we build and train $M \times N$ HMMs. If STAND, WALK, RUN, and RIDE are representative mobility situations, then gesture samples are collected in four different mobility situations and four HMMs for each gesture are trained.

The garbage model is derived from all models in the same way as the basic model.

SENSOR USAGES

Let us now look at various use cases that are possible with the help of sensors in mobile devices. The table mentions key capabilities such as terminal (Table 10.6), user (Table 10.7), gestures (Table 10.8), audio (Table 10.9), location (Table 10.10), biosensors (Table 10.11), and soft sensors (Table 10.12).

Table 10.6 Terminal Capability

Capability	Algorithms	Experience
Terminal	Face up/down	The device is facedown so put into standby or mute a call
	Detect if device is portrait up/down	Change the screen orientation smoothly based on the position in which the device is being held
	Detect if device is landscape left/right	Change the screen orientation smoothly based on the position in which the device is being held
	Detect if device is still/active	Can be used for power management as a trigger to power up if active
	Detect if device is in hand, pocket, purse, bag, or bag pack	The device can change security settings dependent on if it's in the user's hands or close proximity or if it not on the user
	Detect if device is on desk	The device can alert the user if they have forgotten it on the desk

Table 10.7 User Capability

Capability	Algorithms	Experience
User	Determine user in a moving car	The device is updated to aid the user with a map, is GPS enabled, and is in hands-free mode
	Determine if user is stationary	The user is sitting at a restaurant, so GPS can be powered down or put in a lower power state until the user starts walking (power management)
	Determine if user is cycling	If the user is cycling the device can preemptively track user activity and calories burned. The low latency motion can be used for interactive games
	Determine if user is walking	See the user's transition from stationary to walking for power savings. In addition, can be used to track activity as a pedometer
	Determine if user is running	If the user is running, the device can preemptively track your activity and calories burned. Can be used as a transition
	Low latency: running, walking, jumping, and stationary	The user can interactively play first-person games, the avatar would mimic the user's motions. Put the user in the game
	Determine if user is on an airplane	When the user is on the airplane, the device will shut off radios
	Determine if user on a train, bus, or on a boat	When the user is on a train, bus, or on a boat, the device will automatically switch between the best connection (Wi-Fi, 3G, etc.) and update with information such as route, and time to the next stop
	Determine if the user is the driver	If the driver of the car can be detected, then the device can automatically go into hands-free mode and update with driving UI (maps, GPS, directions, etc.)

Table 10.8 Gesture Capability

Capability	Algorithms	Experience
Gestures	Single, double, and directional flick	Can be used as UI input for gaming or productivity. Turn the page while reading on a device with flick gesture as opposed to with two-hand finger swipe
	Shake detection	The user can shake the device to wake or to update
	Pan gesture	The user takes a 360-degree panoramic image of their surroundings
	Zoom gesture	The user can zoom in/out of an image, by just tilting the device forward/back

(Continued)

Table 10.8 Gesture Capability *Continued*

Capability	Algorithms	Experience
	Single, double, and tap	The user can tap anywhere on the device as input and is not limited to only the glass on the screen
	Lift and look	The user can log in to their device by simply picking up the device and looking at it. It can tailor the experience to a specific user
	Directional tap	The user is playing a first-person shooter game and when they tap the right side a shot occurs; when tapped on the left, weapons are changed. UI enhancement
	Detect if user has removed the device from ear and placed device on table (phone only)	Automatically hang up the call
	Lift the device to vertical for camera	The device will automatically enable the camera application and prompt the user to take the picture
	User programmable gestures	At an OEM level the OEM can make a motion signature to enable the OEM app store. At an ISV level, a game can be enhanced with advanced UI. At a user level, the user can make a specific motion signature their login mechanism

Table 10.9 Audio Capability

Capability	Algorithms	Experience
Audio classification	Detect loud (crowd) environment	Modify the device settings to adjust for ambient acoustic environment (volume, notifications, alerts)
	Detect loud (mechanical noise) environment	
	Detect scuffing sound	
	Detect quiet environment	
	Detect speech and/or detect keyword (a special word or phrase that triggers the device on when heard). Can be used for user identification	Voice-enabled personal assistant performs user interaction
		Enable user to "actively" authenticate themselves to the device
		Enable user to "actively" authenticate another user to use device (child or family member, e.g., who may *not* have access to every application on the device)
	Volume control on side (capacitive sensor)	Slider on side for volume control

Table 10.10 Location Capability

Capability	Algorithms	Experience
Location	Determine if user is in the proximity of a known Wi-Fi hotspot	The user can identify and label (home, work, school, etc.) and therefore can tailor the device to those locations
	Continuous location: determine absolute location, no matter if the user is indoors/outdoors	The user can continuously track their locations, and the device can prompt the user if the location is often used to add as important (e.g., grandparents)
	Calculate indoor location using dead-reckoning accuracy. Be able to differentiate between store level accuracy and aisle level accuracy, with assist for indoor/outdoor switching and GNSS buffering	Once the user has entered a mall, the device can assist the user in getting to the store. The device can alert the user of coupons to the stores they often frequent
	Determine if the user is within 5 m from the phone through multifactor triangulation (voice, location, communications (Bluetooth, etc.))	In safe areas (home), the authentication requirements can be reduced, and therefore read aloud an incoming e-mail or text

Table 10.11 Biosensors Capability

Capability	Algorithms	Experience
Biosensors	Fitness with connectivity to wireless biosensors	The device can accurately do estimation of calories burned with the aid of oximeters and heartrate monitors
	Health by gait	The device can do analysis of the gait of a user who is susceptible to seizure, such as Parkinson patients
	Weight loss by image tracking	The device tracks pictures of the user overtime and shows the user how much weight has been lost to give motivation
	Hydration of user alerts	The device can use the temperature and humidity sensors to provide information of proper hydration levels
	Air quality alerts	The device can, e.g., alert the user on smog or allergens and recommend the user to take their allergy or asthma medication or take precautions against smog
	Voice quality	The device can automatically detect if the user has a hoarseness in the voice
	Skin analysis	The device can do analysis of the user appearance through the camera (jaundice)
	Eat right wherever you go	The device provides menu selection advice as you enter restaurants for diabetics or just for the folks who need to lose the love handles

Table 10.12 Soft Sensors Capability

Capability	Algorithms	Experience
Soft sensor data	Know what is on my calendar, who I'm meeting with and where my meetings are	Prior to a meeting, the device can provide the user notification with minutes to appointment and route information
	Know my contacts Know my friends (and in which circle they exist)	Create serendipitous moment based on location: the user's best friend is at the grocery store at the same time, create an alert
	What applications are installed on my phone Know how long I use each application on my phone Know the "kind" of application each application I use is (entertainment, productivity, finance, travel, gaming, etc.)	The home screen of the device is automatically tailored to the user with preferred applications, time of day, location, context, etc.
	URLs that I have visited in the past 3 months Know my cookies Know what I have purchased in the past x months	The device can make recommendations based on the user shopping history and alert of any sales

A FEW SENSOR EXAMPLES

This section discusses few sensor examples and their usage.

1. Lid Closure Sensor—Capella

   The CM36262 [15] has an optical lid sensor that can help power down touch screen devices, an ambient light sensor that controls screen brightness to improve battery life, and a proximity sensor that senses that the device/smartphone is held close to ears to listen and it turns off the dialing feature.

   The chip uses cheaper and more reliable optical method to sense the presence of a lid or fabric cover on touch screen devices instead of using magnets or mechanical switches. The chip can initiate power down mode in the device when it senses a device cover closing on the device or the device in a facedown position. This chip eliminates the need to align an embedded magnet over a pickup sensor to initiate power down mode in the device.

   The optical method can distinguish the shadow of a user's hand from the shadow of a closed lid (or fabric cover). This allows the touch screen to stay powered up when the user's hand is holding the screen or making touch screen selections and will power down only when a lid is closed. The chip works along with infrared LED and proximity sensor to recognize the user hand over the touch screen. The infrared LED emits beam from the touch screen of the device. When a user hand is over the screen, the photodiode within the proximity sensor detects darkness but will also sense the infrared beam which propagates through the user hand. In case of lid or a cover over the touch screen, the proximity sensor does not detect infrared beam and hence initiates power down of the touch screen.

2. Pico Projector—STM

The STPP0100 and STPP0101 [16] chips are integrated video processor and application controllers that can be used for laser pico-projection systems and HD laser Pico projection systems. It can be integrated into mobile devices such as phones, tablets, digital still camera, video camera, gaming consoles, and MP3 players. These chips take a video input stream, render it to modulate the lasers with the correct color/timing, output the results on a laser diode driver interface, and generate the ST MEMS mirror driver commands.

3. Haptics—AMI, Immersion

With Immersion's haptic technology, users feel the vibrating force or resistance as they push a virtual button, scroll through a list, or encounter the end of a menu. In a video or mobile game with haptics, users can feel the gun recoil, the engine rev, or the crack of the bat meeting the ball. When simulating the placement of cardiac pacing leads, a user can feel the forces that would be encountered when navigating the leads through a beating heart, providing a more realistic experience of performing this procedure.

Haptics can enhance the user experience through:

- Improved Usability: By restoring the sense of touch to otherwise flat, cold surfaces, haptics creates fulfilling multimodal experiences that improve usability by engaging touch, sight, and sound. From the confidence a user receives through touch confirmation when selecting a virtual button to the contextual awareness they receive through haptics in a first-person shooter game, haptics improves usability by more fully engaging the user's senses.

- Enhanced Realism: Haptics injects a sense of realism into user experiences by exciting the senses and allowing the user to feel the action and nuance of the application. This is particularly relevant in applications like games or simulation that rely on only visual and audio inputs. The inclusion of tactile feedback provides additional context that translates into a sense of realism for the user.

- Restoration of Mechanical Feel: Today's touch screen-driven devices lack the physical feedback that humans frequently need to fully understand the context of their interactions. By providing users with intuitive and unmistakable tactile confirmation, haptics can create a more confident user experience and can also improve safety by overcoming distractions. This is especially important when audio or visual confirmation is insufficient, such as industrial applications, or applications that involve distractions, such as automotive navigation.

Haptics is used in mobile phones, automotive, consumer, and commercial electronics, gaming and medical appliances. For example:

- Automotive: Lexus's Remote Touch Interface (RTI) touchpad: the touchpad will gently thump and pulse as the driver navigates menus and vehicle systems, which helps the driver move through options intuitively.
- Consumer/Phones: The touch screen has vibration feedback for the various menu options.
- Commercial: Samsung Smart MultiXpress series MFPs are also considered the industry's first application of haptic technology that recreates the sense of touch with vibrations for a more tactile user experience.
- Gaming: Thrustmaster TX Racing Wheel Ferrari 458 Italia Edition can make user really feel the virtual road. The way a car fights to go straight when driver is going to fast into a turn is very realistically modeled. The use experience is as if the user is actually sitting behind the wheel of a sports car in video game form. The force feedback felt on the game steering is strong, detailed, and fast.

4. Grip Detection

A user's hand posture used to manipulate a mobile device is very important contextual factors affecting mobile device. The hand postures (grip, one or two hands, hand pose, the number of fingers used, and so on) significantly affect performance and usage of mobile devices. For example, for pointing to something on mobile device screen using index fingers is better than using a thumb or using two hands is better than using one hand. Similarly, using a user's dominant hand is better than using the nondominant hand. Today most mobile devices do not know how they are being held or manipulated, and therefore cannot respond appropriately with adapted user interfaces better suited to different hand postures.

GripSense [17] is an example of a system that can infer hand postures and pressure with help of the touch screen, the built-in inertial sensors (gyroscope, accelerometer), and built-in actuators (vibration motors). GripSense detects hand postures over the course of a small number of interaction steps (e.g., tapping, swiping the screen). It infers postures like the use of an index finger, left thumb, right thumb, which hand is holding the device, or whether the phone is lying on a flat surface. GripSense performs this sensing by measuring a device's rotation, tap sizes, and the arc of swiping motions. It additionally leverages the built-in vibration motors to help infer the amount of pressure being applied to the screen of the mobile device. For example, users can use GripSense to zoom in and zoom out of maps using pressure input and can also detect when the phone is being squeezed (and quickly silence a phone while in a pocket).

Design of GripSense: GripSense uses touch screen interaction and device rotation information to infer whether the phone is

- in a user's left hand and operated with left thumb,
- in a user's right hand and operated with right thumb,
- in either hand and operated with the index finger of the other hand,

- on a flat surface, or
- being only grasped by the user and not operated.

GripSense use a combination of three features to detect hand postures:

1. Relative variance in rotation
2. Change in touch size
3. Direction of arc for finger swipes.

Rotation of the Device: The first feature is the rotational movement of the device as the user touches the screen. When the user has one-handed interaction with the device, the phone rotates in response to touches at the top of the screen more than it does to touches at the bottom of the screen. When thumb is used to reach the top of the device screen, the fingers move the device to compensate for the limited range of the thumb. When the user touches at the bottom of the screen, the angular motion is less because the thumb can reach the bottom area of the device easily. When the user uses index finger to touch the device screen, the angular motion from touches at the top is same as when the user touches the bottom of the screen. When the device is on a table, there is no change in any of these parameters before the touch event is sensed. To utilize these understandings, the angular velocities around the x-axis from the gyroscope is stored in a buffer. The low-frequency angular velocities are then isolated from the stored data using a low-pass filter. The last two angular velocities observed for touches in the top third of the screen and the bottom third of the screen are recorded. If the difference in variance of angular velocities for touches in the top is five times greater than for touches in the bottom of the screen; it is assumed to be a thumb-based interaction. If the difference in the variances is less than the threshold for three consecutive touches, then it is assumed to be index-finger–based interaction.

When a user holds the phone in the left hand and interacts with the left thumb, the range of motion of the thumb is limited. This causes the angular velocity due to touches on the right of the screen is more than the angular velocity due to touches that occurs nearer to the palm. If the phone in the right hand and interaction with device screen is done with the right thumb, the angular velocity due to touches on the left of the screen is more than the angular velocity due to touches that occurs nearer to the palm.

When a thumb-based interaction is inferred, the variance in the y-axis (instead of x-axis) of the gyroscope for touches on the left third of the screen and the right third of the screen is used to determine if the phone is in the right hand or left hand of the user. The phone is assumed to be in the right hand of the user if the variance in angular velocity of the last two touches on the left side is greater than that on the right side. If the variance in angular velocity of the last two touches on the right side is greater than that on the left side then the phone is assumed to be in the left hand of the user. If the difference in angular velocities is more than 10 times greater in consecutive touches, then a "high confidence flag" is set to indicate that "rotation of device" feature is more likely to be used in final decision.

Touch Size: This feature refers to the change of size of touch in different regions of the touch screen. In one-handed interaction, the shape of the thumb and rotation of the device in the hand of a user influences the touch size across the left and right side of the device screen. The touch size on the same side of the thumb would be smaller than the touch size on the side farther from the thumb.

The device screen can be divided into six parts (three on left side and another three on right side) and last two touch sizes are stored to infer if the interaction was thumb-based or finger-based. For a thumb-based interaction, the difference in the mean of the touch sizes between the left third and the right third for the same third of the screen height is more than 25%. If the difference is less than 25%, then it is considered index-finger−based interaction. A right thumb interaction will have larger tap size on the left side of the screen, while a left thumb interaction will have larger tap size on the right side of the screen. If the difference in touch sizes is more than 40% for consecutive touches, the heuristic sets a "high confidence flag" for "touch size" feature to be used in final decision.

Shape of the Swipe Arc: This feature uses the arc of the swipe that user makes while swiping on the screen to determine user's hand posture. The swipe arc is not consistent when index finger is used. However, when thumb is used, the user draws an exaggerated arc on the screen instead of a relatively straight line. If right thumb is used to interact with the device screen then the exaggerated arc is formed on the left side of the screen and vice versa. If the difference in coordinates of the start and end position of a vertical swipe are more than 5% of the screen resolution, GripSense biases itself toward one of the two thumb postures (right thumb or left thumb).

Sometimes a thumb swipe will result in the angular motion of the phone in hand instead of an arc. A right-handed swipe from bottom to top can cause a counterclockwise rotation and vice versa. The swipe arc and angular motion of the phone can together help to determine the handling posture. As with the other two heuristics, the final intraheuristic decision is made when the system biases toward the same posture twice in a row.

Making the Final Decision: If swipes are present, a majority voting on the output of each heuristic is used to decide the posture.

- If all three votes disagree, the posture is marked as "unknown."
- In the absence of swipe,
    - A final decision is made only if both touch size and rotation heuristics agree or if the "high confidence flag" in one of the heuristics is set.
    - If both heuristics come up with different decisions, then the system chooses the heuristic with a "high confidence flag."
    - If both confidence flags are set or no confidence flags are set with disagreement, the posture is set to "unknown."

Detecting Pressure Applied to the Touch Screen: The pressure applied by the user on the device touch screen can be categorized as light, medium, or heavy. GripSense uses the gyroscope and vibration motor to help in this classification (Fig. 10.14).

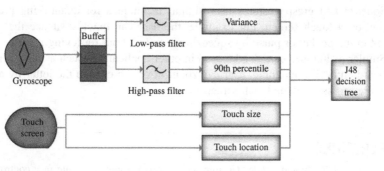

FIGURE 10.14

GripSense pressure detection components.

Following are the few assumptions

- Damped motor-induced vibrations: When a user touches the screen, the built-in vibration motor triggers. The user's hand will absorb a portion of these vibrations in proportion to the amount of pressure applied on the screen. The on-device gyroscope can measure the resulting damping effect.
- Touch-induced vibrations: When the user exerts a force on the touch screen, there is an oscillating motion between the user's thumb and the fingers that support the back of the device. This oscillating motion occurs because the user's thumb and fingers try to compensate continually for pressure exerted on the touch screen. This oscillation is of much lower frequency compared to that induced by the vibration motor and is independent from the vibration motor.

The damped motor-induced vibration and the touch-induced vibration together can help determine the user's touch pressure and intensity.

A touch can trigger the phone's built-in vibration motor and the angular velocities around the three axes through the built-in gyroscope can then be stored in the buffer as shown in Fig. 10.14. The low-frequency touch-induced vibrations are obtained by passing the signal through a low-pass filter, while the motor-induced vibrations are obtained by passing the original signal through a high-pass filter. If the user presses the screen harder, the damping effect caused by the user's hand is higher and such damping is qualified using the 90th percentile of the high-frequency component of the observed signal. For the low-frequency signal, the movement of the phone is quantified using the signal variance.

In Fig. 10.14 screen touch is used along with vibration analysis and touch-zone information to determine pressure exerted by the user. Touch-zone information is added in the calculation because the motor-induced vibrations absorbed by the hand and thumb or finger is also dependent on the location of touch on the screen. The gyroscope data, along with touch screen features (zone and size), can then be used by machine learning tools (e.g., Weka [18]) to classify to pressure level.

Squeeze and grasp gestures uses similar techniques for quantifying pressure exerted on a touch screen. For example, the user can quickly silence the phone placed in the pocket or purse by squeezing it and without retrieving it fully.

Similar techniques can also be used in other applications such as navigation or keyboard entry. For example, user can zoom in or can change the letter by applying more pressure on the touch screen.

REFERENCES

[1] Jacobs D. Technical article "Gesture sensors revolutionize user interface control".
[2] Moyer B. Sensors in Windows: Microsoft Lays Down the Law. Electronic Engineering journal article.
[3] Sensor and Location Platform. <https://msdn.microsoft.com/en-us/library/windows/hardware/dn614612(v=vs.85).aspx>.
[4] Sensor Categories, Types, and Data Fields. <https://msdn.microsoft.com/en-us/library/windows/hardware/ff545718(v=vs.85).aspx>.
[5] Sensors Overview. <http://developer.android.com/guide/topics/sensors/sensors_overview.html>.
[6] Chary R, Nagaraj R, Raffa G, Cinotti TS, Sebastian P. Sensor-based power management for small form-factor IA devices.
[7] Hinckley K, Pierce J, Sinclair M. Sensing techniques for mobile interaction, <ftp://ftp.research.microsoft.com/pub/ejh/PPC-Sensing_color.pdf>.
[8] Pulli P, Hyry J, Pouke M, Yamamoto G. User interaction in smart ambient environment targeted for senior citizen. Med Biol Eng Comput 2012;50:1119−26 doi:10.1007/s11517-012-0906-8 Received: May 1, 2011/Accepted: April 10, 2012/ Published online: April 26, 2012 International Federation for Medical and Biological Engineering 2012.
[9] Harrison B, et al. Squeeze me, hold me, tilt me! An exploration of manipulative user interfaces, CHI'98.
[10] Hinckley K, Sinclair M. Touch-sensing input devices, CHI'99. p. 223−230.
[11] Zhai S, Morimoto C, Ihde S. Manual and Gaze Input Cascaded (MAGIC) pointing, CHI'99. p. 246−253.
[12] Park T, Lee J, Hwang I, Yoo C, Nachman L, Song J. e-Gesture: a collaborative architecture for energy-efficient gesture recognition with hand-worn sensor and mobile devices, e-Gesture.
[13] Baum−Welch algorithm. <https://en.wikipedia.org/wiki/Baum%E2%80%93Welch_algorithm>.
[14] Viterbi algorithm. <https://en.wikipedia.org/wiki/Viterbi_algorithm>.
[15] Industry's First Optical Lid Sensor Chip for Tablet Computers and Notebooks. News item at the CAPELLA MICROSYSTEMS website.
[16] STPP0100, STPP0101 Laser pico projection specific image-processor datasheet (STMICROELECTRONICS).
[17] Goel M, Wobbrock JO, Patel SN. GripSense: using built-in sensors to detect hand posture and pressure on commodity mobile phones.
[18] Drazin S, Montag M. Decision tree analysis using Weka machine learning— Project II.

Sensor application areas

11

INFORMATION IN THIS CHAPTER:

- Augmented Reality
- Sensors in Automotive Industry
- Sensors in Energy Harvesting
- Sensors in Health Industry

INTRODUCTION TO SENSOR APPLICATIONS

There are many applications for sensors and sensor hubs. With innovation and technological advances in previously unrelated fields such as biology and micro-electronics, many new applications are emerging and will continue to expand beyond that which is currently identified or known [1].

Some of the key domains for sensor applications are listed in Table 11.1.

AUGMENTED REALITY

Augmented reality [2,3] represents a view or content where a computer-generated view or content is superimposed or added over the real physical view or content in real time. The resulting view or content is thus augmented with additional information from devices and sensors such as imaging devices (camera) global positioning system (GPS) data or audio devices (microphones). The real and virtual view or content is aligned in such a way that a user perceives the entire content as real. Augmented reality differs from virtual reality because in virtual reality the entire real-world environment is replaced by a virtual environment.

When context information gathered by the sensors is aligned or superimposed on the real environment such that it enhances the user's perception of reality or enables the user to interact or manipulate the information about the real world surrounding the user, then it is known as context-aware augmented reality. Fig. 11.1 shows the basic components that constitute augmented reality.

Table 11.1 Sensor Application Domains

Domains	Example Applications
Automotive	Airbag systems, vehicle security systems, headlight leveling, rollover detection, automatic door locks, active suspension
Consumer	Appliances, sports training devices, computer peripherals, car and personal navigation devices, active subwoofers
Industrial	Earthquake detection and gas shutoff, machine health, shock and tilt sensing
Military	Tanks, planes, equipment for soldiers
Biotechnology	DNA amplification and identification, microscopes, hazardous chemical detection, drug screening, biosensor and chemosensor

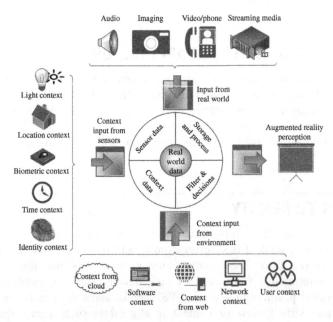

FIGURE 11.1

Components of context-aware augmented reality.

With the increase in computational capability, availability of advanced context-aware sensors, and imaging devices along with widespread adaption of mobile computing, the context-aware augmented reality applications provide innovative opportunities in fields such as interactive gaming, advertisements, military equipment, navigation, commerce, and education.

HARDWARE COMPONENTS OF AUGMENTED REALITY

As shown in Fig. 11.1, the basic hardware components of augmented reality are:

1. The devices that provide real-world data such as live streaming audio–video.
2. The sensors that provide the context information regarding user environment such as location sensors, biosensors, and environmental sensors.
3. The sources such as cloud, web, network, or stored user preferences that provide additional context data [4].
4. The central processor hardware that merges or superimposes the hardware generated data onto real environments.
5. The final hardware component to project/display/present augmented reality to the user such as the interactive screen of the mobile device.

AUGMENTED REALITY ARCHITECTURE

Fig. 11.2 shows a high-level model without augmented reality [3,5] where the real-world data from the input devices is directly fed to the display/user interface. Each of the input devices can simultaneously send data to the display/user interface such as in a video conference among team members located in different geographical areas.

Fig. 11.3 shows an architectural model with augmented reality. In this architecture the real-world data from the input devices is input to an augmented reality overlay. The overlay also receives real-time context related to various environmental parameters around the user from the device sensors, while the user preferences or passive context, including historical user decisions, is provided by various sources such as cloud, web servers, network, and software components.

The overlay merges the real data with context data from sensors and passive context from other sources to obtain augmented data. For example, the input data can be a video or a picture of the user near a landmark. The overlay can have pattern matcher, which will use pattern-matching techniques to match the received input (in this case video or picture) with a set of predefined or stored application-specific patterns. These patterns could be landmarks around the world or famous car models or museum artefacts and even audio samples related to music or songs. If the matcher finds a match between input data and one of its

FIGURE 11.2

Model without augmented reality.

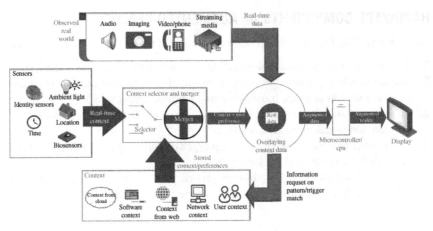

FIGURE 11.3

Model with augmented reality.

predefined patterns (such as landmarks, vehicle models, and audio samples) then it will inform the overlay function about the match. The overlay will then obtain information of pattern (such as landmark, car model, or museum artefact) from passive context sources such as web or cloud and it will overlap this information over the received input data (such as picture, audio, or video stream). The augmented data will now have user data (such as video or picture) marked with the information from the context sources (such as location, time, and specific information on the known landmark, car model, or artefact).

The augmented data then goes through final processing in the device's microcontroller or CPU before it is presented to the user on device's user interface such as device display or device speakers.

APPLICATIONS OF AUGMENTED REALITY

There are many possible applications of augmented reality; however, for simplicity they can be grouped into the following categories [6]:

- Commercial: Advertising campaigns can use augmented reality to promote products online. For example, when a user shows a printed advertisement on webcam while at the product website, then the website presents the user with detailed information or a model of the product in the advertisement.
  Augmented reality can also be used to demonstrate prototypes of the products to the users. For example, instead of building costly prototypes, an augmented image can be shown to the user where the body of real car is enhanced per the requirements of the new model. Virtual dressing rooms with augmented reality and a webcam on a smartphone or tablets can enable the user to virtually wear any selected apparel. Such a virtual dressing system automatically detects

appropriate points on the user body and accordingly aligns items such as clothes, shoes, jewelry, or watches to produce a 3D view on the device screen for the user to check how the product would fit or look.

- Entertainment/Gaming [7]: Augmented reality is really changing the gaming industry with amazing user experiences. Even the small form factor devices like smartphones can support advanced games due to the availability of sensors, GPS data, and advanced computing environments along with high-resolution displays. For example, in the shooting games on mobile phones, the target characters can be superimposed on the display with a real-world background.
- Education: During training where it is important to demonstrate the use of expensive equipment under different operating conditions, augmented reality provides solutions where the students can explore such equipment through augmented real-world simulations without any negative consequences from mistakes, as in, e.g., air force flight simulators and military training exercises.
- Medical [7]: Advanced augmented reality capabilities can be used by medical students and physicians to practice surgery in a controlled environment and explain complex medical conditions to patients using augmented images. Augmented reality can also help reduce the risk of surgery by providing an augmented or enhanced view and perception to the surgeon by combining or superimposing radiological data from different sources such as MRI or X-rays over the real-world view of an ailing organ or body part. For example, in neurosurgery augmented reality provides the ability to superimpose 3D brain images obtained from radiological data over the patient's actual anatomy. This can help the neurosurgeon in numerous ways, such as deciding the exact location of the required surgery, depth of required incision, and so on.
- Location-based services: Augmented reality is very helpful in providing enhanced location-based services. For example, a smartphone user can point a camera at an artefact in a museum and the augmented reality infrastructure can match that artefact with its stored information and superimpose the camera image with appropriate information about the artefact (and maybe in 3D view). Similarly, a user location can be identified with a "pin" generated by augmented reality.

SENSOR FUSION FOR AUGMENTED REALITY

While aligning virtual image/object over a real-world image/object or scene, it is important that the virtual or computer-generated image/object is aligned correctly over the real-world image/object. To achieve this, the position of input devices like cameras needs to be tracked accurately and fast enough with respect to the changing real-world image, object, or scene. A single sensor cannot effectively track the position of an input device and hence sensor fusion [8] may be required.

Fig. 11.4 shows a sample augmented reality fusion system used in an unmanned aerial vehicle (UAV) [9,10].

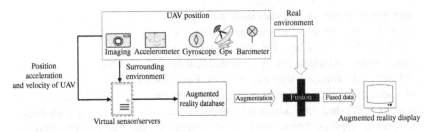

FIGURE 11.4

Sensor fusion example in unmanned aerial vehicle (UAV).

The system involves four basic steps:

1. Obtain information of a real scene using sensors: The UAV will have navigation sensors such as an inertial navigation system (INS), a GPS, and a barometric pressure sensor. UAVs can also have sensors such as monochrome, color, and infrared vision sensors, a secondary imaging system (which is a vision system improved with a laser range finder), and radar.

2. Analyze and process real-scene information: The navigation component of the UAV fuses the INS/GPS and barometric sensor data to generate a navigation solution/scene that is used by the UAV. The imaging sensors on the UAV will observe static scenes and capture target positions. The imaging sensor data will be fused to plot the image positions of targets known in real-world coordinates.

3. Generate a virtual scene: Simulated or virtual sensors interact with the virtual entities in the augmented world. The augmented world for virtual entities has items created in the synthetic environment, such as, the 3D terrain of the operational space, simulated vehicles, stationary and/or moving targets, and the live-virtual copy of the real UAVs. In this synthetic environment, the data from ground control stations of the real UAVs (such as the position, velocity, and acceleration data) is linked to the simulated UAV models. The movement of simulated UAVs in the virtual/synthetic 3D world corresponds to the movement of real UAVs (of which the simulated UAV is a virtual copy) in the real 3D world.

4. Fusion of real-virtual data and display of the real scene with fusion information: Data fusion refers to estimation of the states of the augmented world through a mixture of information obtained from real and virtual sensors. The augmented reality for the UAV means the real world observed by its sensors is enhanced by the virtual observation from the AR system. The observations made by virtual sensors and synthetic environment are processed to perform feature extraction and transformed into a common reference frame (Earth frame). Given the relative position and attitude of the UAV and the location of the sensor payloads relative to the vehicle and the sensor model characteristics, the position of the target in an observation can be calculated in the Earth frame.

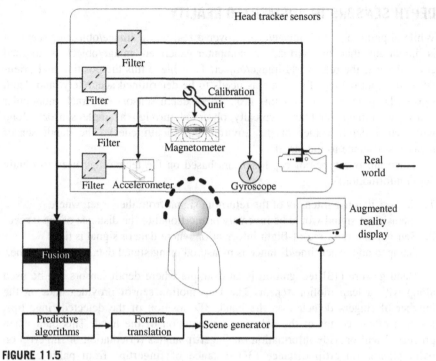

FIGURE 11.5

Head tracker system.

Fig. 11.5 shows components of a possible ground control unit with a head tracker for a UAV. The head movement is tracked in terms of yaw (side-to-side movement caused by looking left or right), pitch (caused by up-and-down movement of the head), and roll (caused by tilting the head side to side).

The head tracker [11] uses an accelerometer to measure linear acceleration along three axes, a gyroscope to measure angular velocity, and a magnetometer to measure strength and direction of Earth's magnetic field. The accelerometer also measures the Earth's gravitational force and hence can provide magnitude and direction of the acceleration. When all three sensors are used, with measured sensor data in three directions, the resulting head tracker is called a *9-axis* or *9-sensor* module.

The sensor fusion involves combining the data from the various sensors into output that is more accurate than each of the sensors. In the ground control unit with head tracker for a UAV, the fusion algorithm also helps in fusing the real video scene captured from imaging sensors/camera/video along with sensor data from the head tracking sensors. The fused data then goes through a predictive algorithm that tries to predict the orientation of head into a short time in the future to reduce the response time of the head tracker. The format translator then processes the data into a format that can be used to generate an augmented scene for display on the augmented reality monitor.

DEPTH SENSORS IN AUGMENTED REALITY

While aligning a virtual image/object over a real-world image/object or scene, it is important that the virtual or computer-generated image/object is aligned correctly over the real-world image/object. To achieve this the position and orientation of input devices like cameras needs to be determined accurately, and depth sensors [12] can be used for this task. These depth sensors can track monocular clues (two-dimensional and typically observed through a single sensor) along with actual depth values of the environment (depth cues). The depth sensor measures distance to the target.

There are two types of depth sensors based on the technology used to obtain depth information:

1. Sensors that use intensity of the returning signal from the target, where intensity of signal would be inversely proportional to the distance of the target.
2. Sensors that use time-of-flight information where data or signal is time stamped and exact time/distance is measured using signal data and return time.

Hand gesture [13] recognition is an example where depth sensors can be used along with a leap motion sensor. The leap motion sensor provides data on the number of fingers detected on the hand, 3D position of the detected fingertips, location of the center of the palm, and orientation of the hand. This data when processed will provide information on fingertip angles (orientation of fingertip on palm plane), fingertip distance (3D distance of fingertips from palm center), fingertip elevation (distance of fingertip from palm plane), and fingertip position (coordinates of fingertip in 3D space).

The depth sensor/camera data provides information on the curvature of the hand, shape of the hand through distance of each point on the hand contour from the center of palm, and the size and number of connected components of the hand in the gesture.

Hand gestures can be recognized from the combined information of leap motion and depth sensor using a gesture recognition system [14]. The main steps of such a gesture recognition system are:

1. Hand samples are segmented from background using the color and depth data:
   a. Colors of a sample are compared with the user's reference skin color (which was obtained previously), the difference between each sample color and the reference skin color is evaluated and the samples whose color difference are below a predefined threshold are discarded. So samples that match user skin color are retained. These samples could be of a user's hand, face, or other body parts.
   b. A sample with the minimum depth value on the depth map is searched and selected as a starting point for the hand detection procedure. A sufficient number of samples need to be present with a similar minimum depth value to avoid selection of an isolated object.

c. The hand samples are then further divided into palm, fingers, and wrist or arm samples. The wrist/arm samples are ignored, because they do not have useful information on gestures.

2. From the segmented samples, information related to features of fingertips and palm is obtained, such as distance of fingertips from the center of palm, elevation of fingertips with respect to the palm, curvature of the contour of palm and finger regions, shape of the palm region, whether the finger is raised or bent, and so on.

3. All extracted features are collected into a feature vector that represents a gesture.

Gesture Feature vector $F = [F_{Distance}, F_{Elevation}, F_{Curvature}, F_{Palm\ Area}]$ is a concatenation of four feature vectors. This gesture feature vector is fed into a multiclass support vector machine classifier, which matches it with various gestures in the database and recognizes the user's gesture.

The depth sensors play a crucial role in recognizing hand gestures without the need of special physical devices like gloves or other such wearable devices. Thus they enable a more natural interaction with mobile and wearable devices like smartphones or tablets and in 3D virtual/augmented environments.

SENSOR APPLICATIONS IN THE AUTOMOTIVE INDUSTRY

Sensor technologies are installed and used in the automotive [15] industry to ensure a safer and more comfortable user experience. These sensors take physical readings such as barometric air pressure, car tire pressure, or various magnetic fields, and convert them into electronic signals for additional processing that can be used to derive information that the user can understand and act upon as required. This sensor information can also alert or inform the user about any safety issues.

Table 11.2 lists some of the sensors that can be installed in vehicles to perform functions and measurements related to the automotive status update, safety, and comfort.

The following section discusses details related to application of some of the sensors in automotive applications.

Electronic power steering (EPS): Power steering adds controlled energy to the steering mechanism so that the driver has to spend less effort to turn the wheels of the vehicle. Magnetic, optical, or induction-based sensors are used in the various components of the EPS. These sensors also contribute in the electronic stability control system that automatically controls the brakes and engine output if the vehicle starts to skid during turns, or controls adaptive headlights, or assists in lane keeping. For example, when the driver steers the vehicle, the steering angle sensor sends signals to the antilock braking system

Table 11.2 Sensor Examples in Automotive Applications

Sensor	Usage	Placement	Comments
Pressure sensor	Passenger- and driver-side airbags	Doors	Detects spike in pressure caused by side impact
	Pedestrian protection system	Front bumper	Detects collision (pressure change) with pedestrian and releases hood to reduce impact
	Tire pressure monitoring	Tires	Alerts driver of tire pressure loss
RF transmitter and receiver	Automotive cruise control	Various	Allows/manages cruise control
	Blind-spot detection		Detects object presence in blind spot
	Autoemergency braking		Brakes automatically in emergency/collision
Barometric air pressure sensor	Car seat comfort system	Car seat	Enables different pressure zones in car seat for comfort
Wheel speed sensor	Wheel system	Wheel	Measures speed of each wheel
			Detects if wheel is blocked when automatic braking system is active
Magnetic angle sensor/ linear hall sensor	Body action/ information systems	Steering wheel wipers, power seat, engine, transmission	Measures steering angle and torque
	Safety system		
	Automotive power train system		

(ABS). On a curved path, the inside wheels of an automobile rotate at slower speed compared to the ones on the outside. If the driver understeers the vehicle, there is loss of traction on the front wheels causing the vehicle to make a wider turn and the speed difference between the right and left front wheels decreases. If the driver oversteers the vehicle, there is loss of traction on the rear wheels, causing the vehicle to spin and the speed difference between the right and left wheels increases. The sensors send data to the ABS module, which then applies brakes to the appropriate wheels and also reduces the engine power to regain stability [16].

Some of the sensors used are steering torque sensors, steering angle sensors, and EPS motor position sensors.

STEERING TORQUE SENSOR

The steering torque sensor [17] measures and records the steering force/torque applied by the driver on a rotating steering shaft. The amount of steering assistance provided by the power steering depends on this measured torque. As shown in Fig. 11.6, the steering shaft is split into an input and output shaft separated by a torsion bar on which a torque sensor is placed. The input shaft is from the steering wheel to the torque sensor and the output shaft is from the torque sensor to the steering shaft coupler.

A contact-type torque sensor can use strain gauges bonded to the steering wheel shaft or the torsion bar [18]. Four strain gauges placed in Wheatstone bridge configuration as shown in Fig. 11.7 (at say 45 degrees to the torque axis) provide temperature-compensated measure of the shear stresses that are induced when the driver applies the torque to the steering wheel.

A contactless-type torque sensors use the principle of magnetic measurement. An example is the Infineon torque sensor as shown in Fig. 11.10.

Such a torque sensor consists of rotor (rotating) and stators (stationary). The rotor as shown in Fig. 11.8 is made of multiple magnets fixed on top of soft ferromagnetic yoke and is fixed on the rotating input steering shaft.

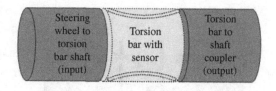

FIGURE 11.6

Torque sensor placement on steering wheel shaft.

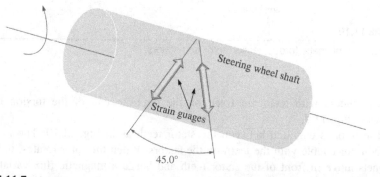

FIGURE 11.7

Steering torque sensing using strain gauges.

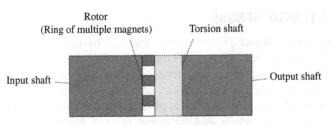

FIGURE 11.8

Contactless magnetic torque sensor: rotor placement.

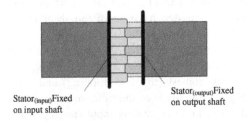

FIGURE 11.9

Contactless magnetic torque sensor: stator placement.

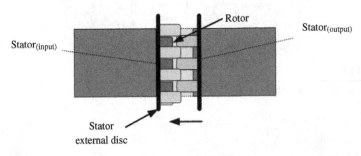

FIGURE 11.10

Contactless magnetic torque sensor: rotor and stators.

The stators with teeth are fixed on the opposite end of the torsion bar as shown in Fig. 11.9.

The rotor is engulfed between the stator teeth as in Fig. 11.10. The magnets on the rotor couple with the teeth on the stators. When the rotor rotates, the rotor magnets move in front of the stator teeth and hence a magnetic flux variation is generated in the stator teeth. The external disc of the stator integrates the magnetic flux generated by each magnet-teeth coupling.

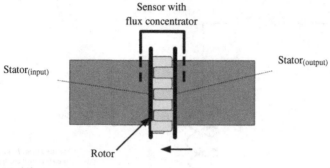

FIGURE 11.11

Contactless magnetic torque sensor: complete assembly.

The angular position of the magnet (and hence of the steering), which is a linear function of the magnetic flux variation in the stator teeth, is measured by a sensor placed over the rotor—stator assembly as shown in Fig. 11.11.

STEERING ANGLE SENSOR

The steering angle sensor measures the steering wheel position angle and rate of turn. It is placed in the steering column of the vehicle. More than one angle sensor can be used to provide redundancy and data validation. The steering control program would generally require two signals from two angle sensors to confirm the steering wheel position. These sensors are mainly based on optical, magnetic, or inductive working principles.

Fig. 11.12 shows the concept used in an inductive steering angle sensor [19]. The conductor plate is attached onto the rotating rotor. The rotor rotates proportionately to the steering wheel rotation. The area of conductor changes as the steering wheel rotates. This causes a proportional change in induction of the coil. Thus the change in induction of the coil corresponds to the steering wheel rotation angle.where L = total inductance, L_{COIL} = intrinsic inductance of the coil, and M = mutual inductance, which depends on the area, magnetic permeability, and thickness of the conductor plate.

Fig. 11.13 shows a digital steering angle sensor [20,21] using a guided light transmitter and a disc with apertures of different sizes attached to the rotating steering shaft/wheel. Each aperture size on the disc can correspond to an angle within 360 degrees. The optic sensor or array of sensors is located on the other side of the disc. This sensor/sensor array measures interruption in the light of varying degrees corresponding to the aperture size on the rotating disc. The sensor output is a digital square wave signal with the frequency depending on the speed of the turning wheel. Thus the sensor can help determine actual angle of rotation α with a certain resolution from the reference position zero (reference marker)

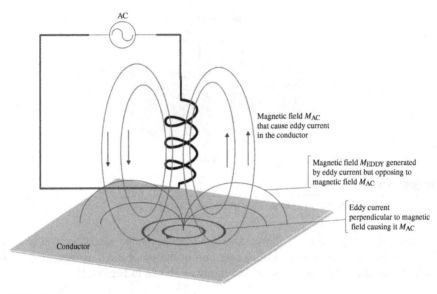

FIGURE 11.12

Concept of inductive steering angle sensor.

$$\text{The total inductance } L = L_{\text{COIL}} - M_{\text{Mutual inductance}}$$

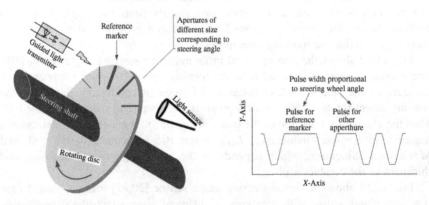

FIGURE 11.13

Optical steering wheel angle sensor.

depending on the pulse width. Detection of multiturns can be handled through software that can keep a count of the number of times the reference marker is detected in the same direction of rotation. Such a digital sensor is also known as a "contactless sensor."

A steering angle sensor [22] can also be implemented using gear wheels with different gears. The angular position of gear wheels with different gears is measured by two angle sensors. The Vernier principle can then be used to calculate absolute steering wheel position.

POWER STEERING MOTOR POSITION SENSORS

In EPS, a brushless direct current (DC) motor [23] is used to drive a gear that is connected to the steering shaft or the steering rack. The process of converting the alternating current in the winding of the DC motor/generator into DC is called commutation. A brushless DC motor uses electronic commutation of winding, using position sensors and electronic switching.

As shown in Fig. 11.14, permanent magnets are mounted on the steering shaft. The sensors sense the position of the rotating magnet. When the rotating magnet moves across the face of sensor, the sensor changes its state and communicates the angular position of the shaft to a sensor data processing circuit. The processing circuit analyzes the sensor data and produces the appropriate amount of assist excitation/current and polarity of the windings. The windings will alternate in

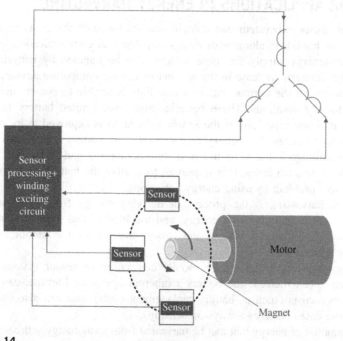

FIGURE 11.14

Electronic power steering motor positioning sensor.

Table 11.3 Industrial Applications of Sensors

Sensor	Usage	Example Placement
Current sensor	Solar panel systems	Solar panels
	Motor current sensing	
Pressure sensor	Barometric pressure sensing	Windmills
	Pneumatic sensing	Factory machines
Speed sensor	Wind speed sensing system	Windmills
	Gear wheel speed sensing system	Trains
		Factory conveyors
Magnetic sensor	Smart metering, proximity sensing	Factory valve controls
		Factory/home meters

polarity, thus they have the effect of rotating with respect to the shaft position. The windings react with the field of the rotor's permanent magnets to develop the required torque.

Some of the other industrial applications of sensors are listed in Table 11.3.

SENSOR APPLICATIONS IN ENERGY HARVESTING

A typical sensor subsystem can contain sensors for such things as temperature, pressure, or humidity, along with microcontroller and communication interfaces. The power/energy supply for these systems can be handled by batteries. There has been a dramatic increase in the number of mobile computing devices (such as smartphones) but the current battery technology is unable to power such devices for satisfactory durations. These batteries also have limited battery life, which becomes an issue especially if the sensor subsystem is deployed at locations that are difficult to access for battery replacement. The battery weight and size can also be a limiting factor of its use in mobile computing and in Internet of things applications. In such cases, it is important to resolve the battery replacement and management problem by using energy harvesting.

Energy harvesting is the process of deriving energy from external sources (such as solar radiations, wind energy, and mechanical and thermal sources) and storing it for autonomous devices and sensors that are used in mobile computing or sensor subsystems.

Energy harvesting can reduce mobile computing or sensor system's weight and volume, can increase the battery's inherent operating lifetime, can decrease maintenance costs (such as battery replacement costs), and can also enable new sensing use cases (such as always-on sensing).

The amount of energy that can be harvested from such energy sources is limited and variable. Hence an energy harvesting system needs to be accompanied by an efficient power management system that can scale up or down depending on the user power requirements and available energy. The main objective of such a power management system would be to optimize energy efficiency between harvested energy and energy supplied to the sensor subsystem or mobile computing device.

COMPONENTS OF ENERGY HARVESTING

As shown in Fig. 11.15 the main components of an energy harvesting system are energy sources/harvesters, energy converters, and a power management system [24]. The main purpose of energy harvesters is to capture small amounts of energy from the available energy sources and provide it to energy converters, which can then output energy/power useful to the mobile devices or sensor subsystems.

Some of the energy harvesting materials [25,26] types are:

- Piezoelectric materials: These materials/crystals are capable of converting the charge that accumulates in the materials/crystals (such as quartz and lead titanate) due to mechanical strain, constraints, or deformation, into electricity. Some of the sources of mechanical strain/pressure could be vibrations, acoustic noise, or motion.
- Thermoelectric materials: These materials/crystals are capable of converting the temperature gradient within the materials/crystals (such as bismuth telluride (Bi_2Te_3) and lead telluride) into voltage. A constant voltage can be generated if there is a constant temperature gradient across the material/crystal.
- Pyroelectric materials: These materials/crystals are capable of converting the changes in temperature of the materials/crystals (such as tourmaline or gallium nitride (GaN)) into electrical charge. No electrical charge is generated if there is a constant temperature within the material/crystal.
- Photovoltaic materials: These materials are capable of converting light or radiation into an electrical charge. Silicon, copper indium diselenide (CIS), and cadmium telluride (CdTe) are some of the materials used in manufacturing of photovoltaic components.

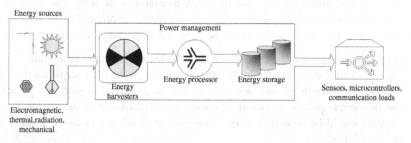

FIGURE 11.15

Components of an energy harvesting system.

- Electrostatic materials: These materials are capable of charge build-up on the surface when they are brought in contact with other certain surfaces and then separated (triboelectric effect or electrostatic induction). The built-up charges can be drained and used as electrical energy.

The energy sources from which energy can be harvested can be categorized into mechanical, radiant, and thermal sources. Mechanical energy can be harvested by piezoelectric, electromagnetic, and electrostatic harvesters. Radiation energy can be harvested by a photovoltaic harvester. Thermal energy can be harvested by thermoelectric and pyroelectric harvesters.

The power generated from energy harvesting sources can have a wide range, where sometimes it can generate zero power or an unusable amount power, while at other times it can generate such a large amount of power that it can damage the electronic parts or circuitry. Thus a power management system is needed to mitigate the problem of unpredictable flow of electricity through appropriate energy processing, saving, and storage.

NET-ZERO ENERGY SYSTEMS

Net-zero energy systems (NZSs) [27] are the electronic devices/systems that autonomously perform sensing or monitoring of context(s), collect and process that context data, and/or send it to the cloud. These systems do not need external batteries, external power, or recharge, but instead operate exclusively and autonomously from harvested ambient energy.

As shown in Fig. 11.16, the NZS [28] can have the same building components as discussed in Fig. 11.15. It has energy harvesters, a trigger subsystem, a power management subsystem along with sensors, a microcontroller, and/or communication device to send data to the cloud if needed. These components are described briefly.

Trigger: The NZS's functionality of data sensing, processing, and communication can be activated by a trigger depending on application needs. The trigger may be activated when there is an external change on the monitored parameter (such as change in ambient light, pressure, temperature, motion, and so on) or when the power management unit indicates availability of sufficient energy for the operation of the NZS. Depending on the application and type of energy harvest source, the triggers [28] could be periodic, opportunistic, or event based.

- A periodic trigger can be used if sensor samples are required at regular intervals and if there is predictable energy harvest from the energy sources. If the power management unit does not have enough energy in store to operate one or more required sensors at a periodic rate, then some of the sensor samples would be missed (if it is in intermittent or no-power range as shown in Fig. 11.17).
- An opportunistic trigger is used when the power management unit does not have enough power storage and can supply power to the sensor subsystem

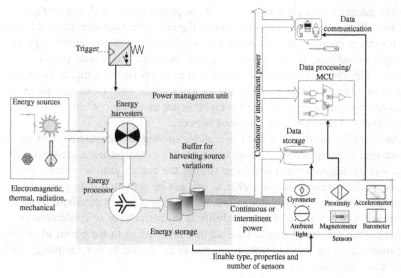

FIGURE 11.16

Net-zero energy system.

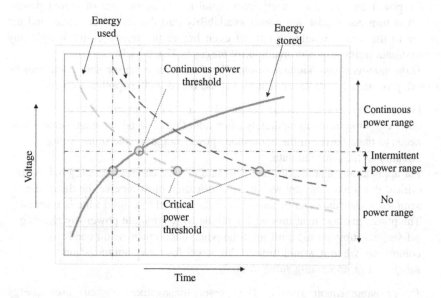

FIGURE 11.17

Power availability in net-zero energy systems.

only intermittently (if it is in intermittent power range as shown in Fig. 11.17). Once the power storage reaches above the critical power threshold, the sensor subsystem operates at a sampling rate as allowed by the intermittent power supply condition. If the power storage is above the continuous power threshold, then the sensor subsystem can even operate at a higher sampling rate as allowed by the power management unit. In such cases the sensor subsystem sampling rate could even be faster than in a conventional nonenergy harvest/battery operated system.

• An event-based trigger is used to activate the sensor subsystem when an external event of interest occurs (such as user context change/motion). The power management unit will keep storing the energy until an event trigger occurs. The sensor subsystem/MCU will not be activated if an event trigger occurs when power available is below the critical power threshold. If an event trigger occurs when power availability is in intermittent or continuous power range then the sampling rates are adjusted according to the power availability (lower sampling rate in intermittent power range and higher sampling rate in continuous power range).

Sensor and monitoring subsystem: The selection of sensors for the NZS should be made after careful consideration of a sensor's power, sampling rates, and latency requirements. A sensor with a higher wake-up latency between receiving power and being ready to take samples may not function properly in the intermittent power range because if the latency is higher, the sensor would need to remain in the power-on state for longer times, resulting in higher use of stored power, which in turn could push the power availability into the no-power range, and the power to the sensor would be cut off even before the sensor could sample any context/data (refer to power availability ranges in Fig. 11.17).

Data management/communication: The data from a sensor subsystem can be stored, processed by MCU, or sent to a cloud based on the application need.

• For real-time applications the sensor data would be transmitted to a cloud or other output systems immediately after sampling. The power management unit needs to have power in the continuous power range for the transmitting circuitry to transmit the data.

• For applications that are not real time and require certain data only before its critical threshold time (by which the application must receive the data), the sampled sensor data can be stored until the critical threshold time is reached. The power management unit will continue to accumulate power (by shutting off various subsystems) until the time when data transmission needs to commence, when it would turn on the power for the communication subsystem or processing subsystem.

Power management system: The power management system uses energy harvester devices/circuitry to harvest energy from various sources (such as mechanical, radiation, electromagnetic, or temperature), processes the harvested energy into AC–DC as per system requirement, and stores processed power in a power storage device (such as solid-state batteries with longer life). Depending on the characteristics of the energy harvest source, the power management unit can provide continuous power (power always available) or intermittent power to the sensor, trigger, communication, processing, and storage subsystems of the net-zero system. The power management unit will enable the number and type of sensors, and it adjusts their sampling rate based on the available power. For example, when in intermittent mode, it will enable only a limited number of sensors and will not enable those sensors that require continuous sampling and/or consumes high power.

Fig. 11.16 shows a basic power management architecture [24] with three components: energy harvesters, energy processor, and energy storage.

Fig. 11.18 shows a slightly modified multipath power management architecture that adjusts according to the characteristics of the energy harvest sources. In the case where the energy source is continuous and of sufficient magnitude (such as solar energy during the day), the power management unit will harvest the energy and directly provide it (or provide it through a simple small storage device such as a capacitor) to the various subsystems of the NZS. If the energy source is intermittent and/or of smaller magnitude, then the power management unit will

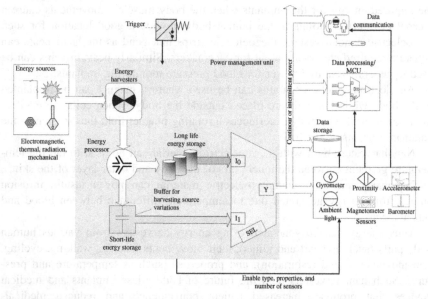

FIGURE 11.18

Net-zero system multipath power architecture.

store it in larger/long-life storage such as solid-state batteries and provide power to the needy subsystem from this storage. Other cases when the energy would be stored in long-life storage devices irrespective of energy source characteristics (continuous or intermittent, smaller or sufficient) are when the subsystems do not need power and there is surplus power or when the small storage gets full while power is being supplied to the subsystems through small storages (such as the case when a capacitor gets fully charged and cannot accept any more charge).

MEDICAL APPLICATIONS OF ENERGY HARVESTING [29]

Pacemakers, infusion pumps, and other implantable devices with lithium batteries will require battery replacement every few years. Such battery replacements would require surgeries that result in increased maintenance costs and patient inconvenience. If an energy harvesting mechanism can be used for such implants, then it would greatly benefit the patients.

Small form factor energy harvesting devices used for implants, also referred to as nanoharvesters (NHs), are built with nontoxic material. These nanoharvesters can use mechanical energy (generated from human body motion, muscle movements, or through blood flow) to generate the required energy by using piezoelectric, thermoelectric, or electromagnetic effect.

Nanoharvesters built with piezoelectric or pyroelectric materials can generate the required energy for the implants when the body muscles' movements cause a piezoelectric effect. Joints in the human body provide a good location for such piezoelectric nanoharvesters. Piezoelectric strips that bend as the heart beats can generate required electrical output for pacemakers. Similarly beats in veins can be used to generate required power for blood pressure monitoring implants.

An electromagnetic apparatus can be used where a magnet can be implanted in the body while the coils are placed outside the body. When coils are excited, the magnet inside the body experiences a rotating magnet field thus triggering the nanoharvester inside the body.

Nanoharvesters built with thermoelectric material can be used to tap the temperature gradient between the inner parts of the body and outer layer of the skin.

Nanoharvesters built with pyroelectric material can power insulin infusion pumps from energy generated due to temperature difference between blood and subcutaneous tissue.

Thus energy can be generated using energy harvesters from various human body parts (such as heart and joints), their movements (such as walking, cycling, arm movements, and respiration), and properties (such as temperature and pressure). Such nanoharvesters hold the future of battery-less implants and medical devices that promises increased patient convenience and reduced medical-maintenance costs. Hence this field represents a promising area for development and use of energy harvesting technology.

SENSOR APPLICATIONS IN THE HEALTH INDUSTRY

Users are increasingly using mobile devices, smartphones, and associated health-related applications to monitor their health. New health monitoring applications are more accessible with the spread of mobile devices and smartphones. Some of the example usages are described here.

HEART RATE MONITORING

The heart rate monitoring applications in smartphones use the process of photoplethysmography [30], which is an optical technique to obtain a plethysmograph. The plethysmograph is a measure of the blood volume changes in the microvascular bed of tissue. To measure heart rate using photoplethysmography, the user places a finger on the smartphone camera [31] (covering both the LED and camera, as shown in Fig. 11.19). When the heart beats, it sends a pulse of blood through the body, which causes the tiny capillary vessels in the skin to expand. The light from the smartphone's powerful LED flash passes through the finger and the illumination/color changes caused by the change in the blood volume due to heartbeat is detected by the camera, which acts as an optical sensor. The finger pressure and color saturation of the video are considered while calculating the heart rate using this technique. Thus the heart rate fluctuations are captured through smartphone at the fingertip.

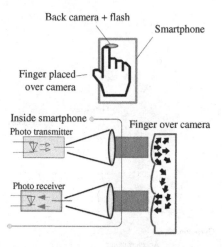

FIGURE 11.19

Heart rate monitoring using smartphone camera.

HEALTH EVENT DETECTION

The mobile device/smartphone has built-in sensors that can be used to detect a fall and immobility of the user and send alerts to emergency contacts, hospital, or even call an emergency hotline. To detect a fall [32,33], the acceleration data sampled by an accelerometer can be processed by the mobile device processor. However, certain other daily living activities like sitting down quickly or jumping can also result in substantial vertical acceleration, which can trigger a false alarm of a fall. Hence along with accelerometer, the body orientation information is also used to detect a fall. A tilt sensor can be used to monitor body orientation or two accelerometers can be used to monitor inclination and inclination speed or gyroscope (e.g., a gyroscope placed at sternum) can be used to measure angular velocity, angular acceleration, and change in chest angle to detect falls.

Fig. 11.20 shows the placement of a three-axis accelerometer and three-axis gyroscope on the human body. One set of sensors can be attached to chest and another to thigh.

The fall detection steps consist of activity intensity analysis, posture analysis, and transition analysis.

Fig. 11.21 shows the fall detection flow.

The first phase involves identifying the user posture at the current time. Sensor readings are taken at the nodes attached to the user to determine if the

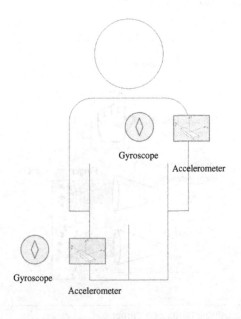

FIGURE 11.20

Sensor placement on human body for fall detection.

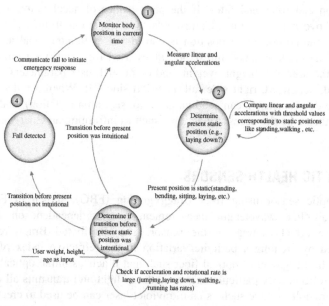

FIGURE 11.21

Fall detection flow.

user has a static or a dynamic posture at the current time. If the nodes shown in Fig. 11.20 can measure linear acceleration and rotational rate at chest and thigh, it would be represented by equations:

Linear acceleration at chest is $\alpha_A \quad = \sqrt{\alpha_{Ax}^2 + \alpha_{Ay}^2 + \alpha_{Az}^2}$

Linear acceleration at thigh is $\alpha_B \quad = \sqrt{\alpha_{Bx}^2 + \alpha_{By}^2 + \alpha_{Bz}^2}$

Rotational rate at chest is $\omega_A \quad = \sqrt{\omega_{Ax}^2 + \omega_{Ay}^2 + \omega_{Az}^2}$

Rotational rate at thigh is $\omega_B \quad = \sqrt{\omega_{Bx}^2 + \omega_{By}^2 + \omega_{Bz}^2}$

If the linear acceleration and rotational rates obtained from sensors readings and corresponding equations fall below certain threshold values then the user can be classified as in static posture (amplitude of these parameters in static positions are small) and if above threshold range, it is classified as dynamic posture.

In static posture, the linear acceleration at chest and trunk would be near the gravitational constant $1.0g$. Based on the inclination angles of the chest and thigh, the static posture can be categorized as standing, bending, sitting, and lying. The second phase of the flow identifies the user to be in one of these static posture.

Intentional or unintentional transition to the above-mentioned static posture is identified in the third phase. A fall is defined as an unintentional transition from any other user position to a lying position. Falls and other high-intensity activities (jumping, running, quickly climbing up or down the stairs, and so on) have higher acceleration and rotational rates. If the peak values of acceleration and angular rate are above a predetermined thresholds then transition from a previous user position to the current lying position is considered as unintentional and a fall is detected. The predetermined threshold values used for identifying fall are influenced by the user age, height, weight, and other such user parameters. A fall can be forward, backward, right side fall, or a left side fall. When a fall is detected, the mobile device/sensors can send an alert (to, say, a base station), and the computer can then take the necessary actions, such as informing an emergency center.

FIBER OPTIC HEALTH SENSORS

A fiber optic sensor using fiber Bragg grating (FBG), shown in Fig. 11.22, provides absolute wavelength measurement that is dependent on strain and temperature effects acting on the sensor. The distributed Bragg reflector is constructed by creating a periodic variation in the refractive index of the fiber core in a short segment of optical fiber such that it acts as inline optical filter that blocks or reflects only particular wavelengths of light and transmits all others. An intense ultraviolet source such as an ultraviolet laser can be used to create the variation in the refractive index into the fiber core.

The sensors using FBG are unaffected by the overall system light levels. Such sensors can be used to monitor pressure at foot sole of diabetic patients [34]. The foot supports the human body while helping in running, walking, and standing. Several bones that form the arc of the foot absorb shocks during various activities and provide flexibility while adapting to uneven surfaces. Along with bones there are several layers of muscles, nerves, and blood vessels. Patients with diabetes experience various foot problems due to nerve damage and circulatory issues related to diabetes. Diabetic patients can experience inflammation and damaged heels, as such patients are unaware of excessive pressure that can get exerted on one particular area of the feet during normal daily activities. An incorrect standing posture can cause severe ulcerations at the sole that can require amputation if not resolved in time.

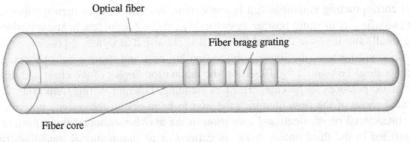

FIGURE 11.22

Optical fiber with fiber Bragg grating.

A foot pressure sensor based on FBG can help measure pressure distribution over the patient's foot and determine force exerted at crucial points of the feed. With this information the medical experts can help correct patients' walking, running, or standing posture so that pressure at the crucial points and across the feet does not result in any inflammation. The collected sensor information can also help design orthopedic shoes for individual patients or can help in sports medicine for athletes.

REFERENCES

[1] EE Herald online article, Design guide.
[2] Azuma R. Augmented reality systems.
[3] Singh M, Singh MP. Augmented reality interfaces, Natural web interfaces.
[4] Ramdas CV, Parimal N, Utkarsh M, Sumit S, Ramya K, Smitha BP. Application of sensors in augmented reality based interactive learning environments.
[5] Fukayama A, Takamiya S, Nakagawa J, Arakawa N, Kanamaru N, Uchida N. Architecture and prototype of augmented reality videophone service.
[6] Total Imersion, Top 10 Augmented Reality Use cases.
[7] Perdue T. Applications of augmented reality, Augmented reality is evolving as computing power increases, updated June 9, 2014.
[8] Hol JD, Schön TB, Gustafsson F, Slycke PJ. Sensor fusion for augmented reality.
[9] Cai Z, Chen M, Yang L. Multi-source information fusion augmented reality, Benefited decision-making for unmanned aerial, Vehicles, A effective way for accurate operation.
[10] Göktoğan AH, Sukkarieh S. An augmented reality system for multi-UAV missions.
[11] Boger Y. What you should know about Head Trackers, The VRguy's Blog.
[12] Taskinen M, Lahdenoja O, Säntti T, Jokela S, Lehtonen T. Depth sensors in augmented reality solutions.
[13] Marin G, Dominio F, Zanuttigh P. Hand gesture recognition with jointly calibrated leap motion and depth sensor.
[14] Dominio F, Donadeo M, Zanuttigh P. Combining multiple depth-based descriptors for hand gesture recognition.
[15] Infineon. Sensing the world Sensor solutions for automotive, industrial and consumer applications.
[16] Chess T. Understanding 'Yaw Rate' and the 'Steering Angle Sensor.'
[17] Bosch Mobility Solutions. Torque sensor steering, Steering systems—Sensors.
[18] Applied Measurements Ltd. Torque transducers & torque sensors explained.
[19] Furukawa Review, No. 30 2006. High-resolution steering angle sensor.
[20] Hamamatsu website. Steering angle sensor.
[21] Methode Electornics. Inc. Optical.
[22] Application note. Electric power steering (EPS) with GMR-based angular and linear hall sensor, October 2008.
[23] Honeywell. Application Note: Magnetic position sensing in brushless DC electric motors.
[24] Christmann JF, Beigné E, Condemine C, Willemin J, Piguet C. Energy harvesting and power management for autonomous sensor nodes.

[25] IOP Institute of Physics. Types of energy harvesting materials.

[26] Yildiz F. Potential ambient energy-harvesting sources and techniques.

[27] Grady S, Zero Power Wireless Sensors Energy. Harvesting-based power solutions.

[28] Campbell B, Dutta P. An energy-harvesting sensor architecture and toolkit for building monitoring and event detection.

[29] Paulo J, Gaspar PD. Review and future trend of energy harvesting methods for portable medical devices. In: Proceedings of the world congress on engineering 2010 Vol II WCE 2010, June 30–July 2, 2010, London, UK.

[30] Pappas S. The best heart rate monitor apps, January 30, 2015.

[31] Parra L, Sendra S, Jiménez JM, Lloret J. Multimedia sensors embedded in smartphones for ambient assisted living and e-health.

[32] Chen J, Kwong K, Chang D, Luk J, Bajcsy R. Wearable sensors for reliable fall detection.

[33] Li Q, Stankovic JA, Hanson M, Barth A, Lach J, Zhou G. Accurate, fast fall detection using gyroscopes and accelerometer-derived posture information.

[34] Soh C-S, Yang Y, Bhalla S, Suresh R, Tjin SC, Hao J. Smart materials in structural applications of fiber Bragg grating sensors health monitoring, control and biomechanics, Chapter 11.

Index

Note: Page numbers followed by "*f*" and "*t*" refer to figures and tables, respectively.

Printed in the United States
By Bookmasters